KT-447-580

Louise Willder has been a copywriter at Penguin Books for twenty-five years. During this time, she estimates she has produced about 5,000 blurbs. She doesn't follow people round bookshops, willing them to buy the books she's written copy for. Really, she doesn't.

Blurb
Your
Enthusiasm

An A–Z of
Literary Persuasion

Leabharlanna Chathair Bhaile Átha Cliath
Dublin City Libraries

LOUISE WILLDER

ONEWORLD

A Oneworld Book

First published by Oneworld Publications in 2022

Copyright © Louise Willder 2022

ISBN 978-0-86154-217-8
eISBN 978-0-86154-249-9

'The Outing' from *The Collected Stories of Lydia Davis* by Lydia Davis published
by Penguin Books. Copyright © Lydia Davis, 2009, first published in the USA
by Farrar, Straus and Giroux 2009, in Great Britain by Hamish Hamilton 2010,
Penguin Books 2011, 2013. Reprinted by permission of Penguin Books Limited.

Typeset by Tetragon, London
Printed and bound in Great Britain by Clays Ltd, Elcograf S.p.A.

Oneworld Publications
10 Bloomsbury Street
London WC1B 3SR
England

Stay up to date with the latest books,
special offers, and exclusive content from
Oneworld with our newsletter

Sign up on our website
oneworld-publications.com

For my parents

Contents

CONTENTS

Question any thinking person as to why he 'never reads novels', and you will usually find that, at bottom, it is because of the disgusting tripe that is written by the blurb-reviewers.

GEORGE ORWELL,
'In Defence of the Novel'

Everyone engaged in publishing knows what a difficult art blurb-writing is.

T. S. ELIOT

It's just the blurb. You can have fun with it.

NANCY MCAVOY,
my niece, aged seven

$\mathbb{I}$ntroduction
'Wonderful Imaginative Lying'

> Bloody hell. I'm sweating here. Roasting. Boiling. Baking.
> Sweltering. It's like a sauna. A furnace. You could fry an
> egg on my stomach. It's ridiculous. Tremendous. Fantastic.
> Fan-dabby-dozy-tastic.

I could fry an egg on that script, too.

Many books about books begin with beloved memories of
childhood reading, or an evocative description of an ancient
library. I decided this one should start with Ray Winstone in
yellow speedos. The words above open the film *Sexy Beast*, as
our hero lies, basted and basking, by a pool in the blazing heat
of the Costa del Sol. They build and build like an incantation;
a prayer offered up to the Spanish sun gods. I'm hooked, suck-
ered, skewered.

What about the effect of these words, from Shirley Jackson's
The Haunting of Hill House?

> No live organism can continue for long to exist sanely under
> conditions of absolute reality. Hill House, not sane, stood by
> itself against its hills, holding darkness within.

Or these, from John Donne's poem 'The Sun Rising' describing
his annoyance at the dawn disturbing him and his lover:

Busy old fool, unruly sun,
Why dost thou thus,
Through windows, and through curtains call on us?

Can a house be insane, or the sun unruly? How many ways can you describe being hot? There's just *something* about the way the specific, well-chosen combinations of words in these examples make me feel: intrigued, unsettled, surprised, drawn into a world that I want more of. This book is all about that 'something': the power of words. How they persuade, shock, seduce, cajole, manipulate, affect and operate; how they create and capture desire.

I've worked in publishing for twenty-five years as a copywriter, and during this time (in fact perhaps ever since encountering the word 'soporific' in Beatrix Potter) I've been fascinated by how words work, and how they work on us. I spend my days writing, rewriting, honing, shaping, trimming, polishing and tweaking words – like a linguistic beauty therapist – ostensibly to try and persuade people to buy books, but also to try and capture the essence of a book in a way that is instantly appealing; to dig out its unique qualities and make them sing. Put plainly, I write the blurb.

If you've ever been into a bookshop, chances are you will have seen something I've written, although my name will never appear.* Most of us will read – or at least glance at or skim – more blurbs than books in our lifetimes, even if we do treat them with caution, as something not *quite* to be trusted.

There is, naturally, an element of deceit in what copywriters do. Writing 'blurbs', or the copy that appears on the back of a

* I tried to work out how many blurbs I've worked on in my career, and it's something like five thousand and counting.

book, involves distorting the truth in some way. As the Italian writer and editor Roberto Calasso describes it in *The Art of the Publisher*, blurbing is like introducing someone at a party: 'you must overcome the slight embarrassment that always exists in every introduction … respecting the rules of good manners that prevent you from emphasising the defects of the friend being introduced.'

So, just as I wouldn't present an esteemed colleague as someone who rambles on incessantly, sags in the middle and could do with slimming down, neither would I tell a potential reader this about a book, true as it might be. We concentrate on the good bits. There's always something to love in a book, just as there's (usually) something to like in a person.

A decent blurb writer cannot just recite the plot or the contents of a book; there has to be some kind of sugar coating and, yes, lying. If we literally told people what happened, we could end up with something like this deliberately inappropriate TV listing for *The Wizard of Oz*: 'Transported to a surreal landscape, a young girl kills the first person she meets and then teams up with three strangers to kill again.'*

As Oscar Wilde put it, 'All Art is lying, wonderful imaginative lying. Lying, the telling of beautiful untrue things, is the proper aim of Art.' I wouldn't dare to say that writing blurbs is an art; it's a craft that can be learned and honed over time, like any other. But that element of 'wonderful imaginative lying' has to be at the heart of it.

The manipulation of words can be far more nefarious and dangerous, of course. Take your pick from any recent

---

* It was created by writer Rick Polito in 1998 and went viral years later. He joked, 'That line is going to follow me to the grave.'

political slogan or government communication – Care in the Community, collateral damage, world-beating test-and-trace – and you have instant proof of Orwell's maxim that political language 'is designed to make lies sound truthful and murder respectable, and to give an appearance of solidity to pure wind'.*

I hope that what we do in publishing is more of a fib than a lie. I also think that, as readers, sometimes a small part of us wants to be seduced and sucked in. I once bought a book because the quote on the front said, 'If George Clooney had walked into the room I would have told him to come back later when I'd finished,' and I was glad I did.†

Take the comforts of genre fiction. My husband reads everything from historical tomes to political diaries, but on holiday he wants wartime thrillers and only wartime thrillers. If he sees some copy beginning 'Berlin, 1944' – or 'East Germany, 1963' if he's in a Cold War state of mind – it's likely he'll buy the book. Sometimes copy can be a clear, familiar signal that cuts through the noise.

There are now more books published than ever, and more words and messaging vying for our attention, but there's also nothing new under the sun. I don't think we ever existed in some prelapsarian age of innocence. Writers have been eliciting words of praise from other writers for hundreds of years, markets have always been 'crowded' and the oldest known printed advert in English is from the fifteenth century – and is for a book.

Almost as long as there have been books, they have been promoted by their authors and their publishers. The word 'blurb'

* I still love the surprise of 'wind' at the end of this sentence every time I read it; it shows how clever and cunning Orwell's own artistry is.

† *A Gathering Light* by Jennifer Donnelly.

made its appearance relatively late in literary history,* coined in a 1907 advert by the American author Frank Gelett Burgess. It proudly states: 'Yes, this is a BLURB! All the other Publishers commit them. Why Shouldn't We?' and features an image of an enthusiastic-looking lady, 'Miss Belinda Blurb in the act of blurbing'. Blurbing she certainly is, describing Burgess's book, *Are You a Bromide?*, as making you 'want to crawl through thirty miles of dense tropical jungle and bite somebody in the neck'. Have I missed a trick all this time by not describing the physical feats a book will compel readers to undergo? Dancing across hot knives, or subjecting themselves to a controlled explosion?

It's easy and fun to deride cliché and mock the hyperbolic language that is often used to describe books, whether it's Bridget Jones launching *Kafka's Motorbike* with the tagline 'the greatest book of our time' or Edmund Blackadder's magnum opus *Edmund: A Butler's Tale*: 'a giant rollercoaster of a novel in four hundred sizzling chapters. A searing indictment of domestic servitude.' I wonder too, though, if most of the time we're all in on the joke, and that's okay?

As someone who spends most of my days working with and worrying about words, and sometimes hammering them into submission (which the otherwise slightly naff moniker 'wordsmith' accurately conveys), I think copywriting is, well, fun. Ultimately we want to tell a story to the reader. D. J. Taylor says that 'Of all the minor literary arts, none is quite so delicate as the production of jacket copy.' A great deal of thought, care and attention goes into the making of a book, how it looks and

* I generally use 'blurb' to mean a paragraph of copy describing a book, rather than a promotional quote from another writer, its more common usage in the US.

how we describe it. Perhaps, sometimes, we really can judge a book by its cover.

I'm intrigued by this tension between content and packaging, between the object and the description of the object, between serious purpose and frivolity. I read blurbs obsessively, not only on books, but also the copy on tube ads, posters, DVDs, catalogues, even sandwich packets, trying to calculate what is going on and whether it works: Who writes them? How do they decide what to say? Why do the film descriptions on Netflix never bear any resemblance to the film you've just seen?

On one level a blurb is just a folderol; a frippery. It's such a silly word, after all. When I told a class of five-year-olds what a blurb was, they thought it was the funniest thing they'd ever heard and fell about laughing on their little 'bug spots' on the carpet. But blurbs also tell us much about language. They require concision and concentration. Words have to work extra hard. According to Cecil Day-Lewis, the sonnet, the detective story and the blurb are all the most perfect crystallisation of literary form.

I have become obsessed with certain questions while writing blurbs, and this book is my attempt to answer them, drawing on the lessons I've learned as a writer of blurbs, a blurber, a blurbologist,* a blurbiste, or a Belinda. I have structured it as an A to Z for a pick'n'mix feel so that you can start where you wish, and it is divided into five parts.

....

* As far as I can tell, 'blurbologist' is first used in the 1999 romantic comedy *Forces of Nature*, starring Ben Affleck and Sandra Bullock. It is a terrible film (*TIME* called it a 'reprehensible fiasco') but redeemed in my eyes by its hero being a blurb writer, whose copy for the thriller *Me and My Pharaoh* describes it as 'A scintillating tale of erotic mummification.'

Part One is concerned with our initial impressions of a book. How do the things we first see – title, strapline, quotes, opening line, cover design – work together to make us want to pick it up? The second section stays with the bigger picture to consider the blurb's literary history. Has the way we use words to sell books changed over time – when did the earliest blurb appear? What can great writers from Austen to Salinger, and a few lesser-known figures, tell us? Which authors *really* hated blurbs?

Then we narrow our focus and home in on the rules of good copy. What is the best way to capture something in as few words as possible, while still making those words feel fresh and original? How do shape, structure, pace and style work together? Is it *ever* okay to swear, or give away the ending? (Spoiler: yes.) We stay focused in the fourth section, examining copy in different genres, from children's books to bonkbusters.

The final part of the book widens out again, encompassing what blurbs say about us, and how their lessons play out in our world. What's happening in our brains when we read a piece of persuasive copy? Can blurbs be sexist? How does copywriting relate to language, culture, screenwriting, fairy tales, advertising and, yes, even musicals?

This is the outside story of books. It's all here, everything you ever wanted to know about blurbs and the art of words, plus some titbits on the eccentric, gossipy, brilliantly creative publishing world that has been my home for over two decades. I never thought I was capable of writing anything longer than 100 words after all these years blurbing, but it turns out that playing with many words is even more enjoyable than a few. I hope you enjoy them too.

1.

COVER STORIES

First Impressions

Alone in Berlin

The Life-Changing Magic of a Title

Have you ever heard of a novel called *The High Bouncing Lover*, a boast of gymnastic proportions? The patriotic-sounding *Under the Red White and Blue*? Or the extremely niche *Trimalchio in West Egg*? The last one is perhaps a clue.

These are all 'the ones that got away': just some of the alternative titles that F. Scott Fitzgerald considered before his editor talked him out of it and he decided to call his novel *The Great Gatsby*. Thank goodness he did – although he was still lamenting his choice even after publication, writing to his editor Max Perkins, 'I feel Trimalchio might have been best after all.' Would his novel still occupy the hallowed place it does in literature today without its emphatic, and ultimately ironic, title? On one level it works because it plays with the idea of the Great American Novel and the country's view of itself: according to Gary Dexter in *Why Not Catch-21?*, 'the dreams of greatness, wealth and success that form the nation's myth are brutally dispelled … Fitzgerald was gunning for America.' But on another, more basic level, it just feels *right*.

How else to open a book about literary persuasion than with the title: the piece of copy on the cover that grabs the reader before any other. If the blurb on the back of a book tells a story of sorts, then the title is the 'once upon a time', offering, as

Raymond Chandler said, 'a particular magic which impresses itself on the memory'. It asks a question, and the rest of the copy helps to provide the answer. Like all aspects of a cover, the title is one component of a harmonious whole, working together to persuade us that we need this book in our lives.

Lost titles give us a tantalising glimpse of a parallel literary universe where now-famous works could have sunk into obscurity without that ineffable magic. The examples of what might have been are legion. William Thackeray was toying with the idea of calling his saga of Becky Sharp *Pen and Pencil Sketches of English Society* or *A Novel Without a Hero*, before *Vanity Fair*, taken from John Bunyan's *Pilgrim's Progress*, came to him 'unawares in the middle of the night'. He then got up and ran around his room, Archimedes-style, saying, 'Vanity Fair, Vanity Fair, Vanity Fair' (although it's not on record if he was naked like his Greek counterpart).

Jane Austen's *Pride and Prejudice* was originally called *First Impressions* when she began working on it in 1796, before settling on the brilliant alliterative smack of the title we know and love today. *Dracula* was *The Un-Dead*. *Lord of the Flies* was *Strangers from Within*. *Moonraker* was the unglamorous *Mondays Are Hell*. *Nineteen Eighty-Four* had the working title *The Last Man in Europe*, which Orwell was still hesitating over with his publisher Fredric Warburg right up to publication. They're just, how can I put it… not as good, are they? In more recent years, Ian McEwan's *Atonement* was intended to be *An Atonement* almost until printing, until a fellow writer begged him to drop the indefinite article because it was 'clumsy on the tongue'.

What about *Every Man Dies Alone*? It's a sobering sentiment, whether you take it literally or metaphysically. It was also the original title of a novel by the German writer Hans Fallada, which had been all but forgotten outside his native land until its first English translation was published in 2010 with the new title *Alone in Berlin*. This obscure, grim story of an unheroic act of resistance by an unassuming couple in Nazi Germany became, against all expectations, a genuine worldwide publishing sensation, selling over three hundred thousand copies in the UK alone. This is extraordinary for most novels in English, let alone a work in translation.

Why did the book work? Well, the words 'Nazi Germany' are a clue. It is also a visceral, gripping novel with a cat-and-mouse chase plot, set in a city under terror. It had a fascinating backstory, based on a real-life German couple who deposited anti-Nazi postcards all over Berlin before the Gestapo caught up with them. It had a tragic author, Rudolf Ditzen,* who spent his life battling addiction and wrote the novel in just twenty-four days at the end of the war, dying a few months later. It was given a noirish cover by acclaimed designer Jon Gray, boasting endorsements from writers such as Primo Levi and Alan Furst. Yet these things alone are not enough to create a bestseller.

While it's true that, as Hollywood screenwriter William Goldman said, the first rule is 'nobody knows anything', I'm convinced that a large part of the reason for *Alone in Berlin*'s success was its title change.

Every Man Dies Alone is, in itself, intriguing (the literal translation from the German would actually be 'Everyone dies for himself alone'), but its mood is downbeat and bleak. *Alone in Berlin* conjures up something rather different. It is smoother

* He based his *nom de plume* Hans Fallada on two Brothers Grimm tales, one of which involved a talking horse.

and less verbally cluttered; open rather than final. It has a sense of place: one that conveys an atmosphere of danger or intrigue for many readers. Yet at the same time as being more specific and rooted, it also feels more universal – it could be any of us alone in that city (and not just men). If *Every Man Dies Alone* is the plaintive string of an arthouse movie soundtrack, *Alone in Berlin* is the ominous opening of a thriller score. It makes a promise, and that is what a good title should do.

According to the book's UK editor, Adam Freudenheim, who made the title decision, it came from some serendipitous borrowing:

> Including Berlin in the title seemed a good idea to signal to readers right away where the action takes place – and of course it signals much more besides. However, I can't take all the credit for this title – much as I'd like to! It was actually inspired by the French translation, which was published a couple years before the English, and used the title *Seul dans Berlin*; it had worked for them and so we borrowed it for our edition. The hugely successful Penguin edition sold at least twice as many copies as the American edition … and I think the title undoubtedly had something to do with it.

Many novels, and not just those in translation, have been published with different titles for international audiences. The original Swedish title of Stieg Larsson's novel was *Men Who Hate Women*, until it was changed to *The Girl with the Dragon Tattoo* for the UK, becoming a smash hit and spawning countless 'Girl with/on/in' titles in the process. The first volume of Philip Pullman's *His Dark Materials* trilogy, *Northern Lights*, became *The Golden Compass* for the US, and *Harry Potter and the*

Philosopher's Stone became *Harry Potter and the Sorcerer's Stone* after, it's rumoured, the UK version was considered too arcane. This is now less likely to happen in our age of online book-buying, when it can cause confusion on Amazon, but it shows how a publisher's eye is always on a specific market when it comes to a book's title.

My own experience of trying to come up with titles as part of the creative process around a book means that there are plenty of 'ones that got away'. I remember trawling through tabloid headlines seeking inspiration for the perfect pun to sum up the MP Tom Watson's exposé of the newspaper hacking scandal. *Dial M for Murdoch* was the winner. The losers were *Wapping Lies*, *Hacks Against the Wall*, *Up Yours News Corp* and *News of the Screwed* (more on puns later). Incredible scenes. My list of alternative titles for *this* book was as long as Mr Tickle's arms before I took a punt on a pun, and I know that, like many authors, I will still be worrying about it at the time of – and probably after – publication.*

Titles matter, both to those who make books and those who read them. After all, you can't have a word-of-mouth hit if you can't remember its name. Ever since the boom in publishing in the nineteenth century, publishers have increasingly used intriguing, come-hither titles to try to stand out: think *Can You Forgive Her?*, *The Strange Case of Dr Jekyll and Mr Hyde* or *Lady Audley's Secret*.

Titles can be a clear signifier of what's to come: *Murder on the Orient Express* or *The Rats* need no explanation. They can make

----

* It included *Cover Stories*, *Everything is Copy*, *Blurb Perfect*, *Finding the Words*, *Playing with Words*, *Magic Words*, *My Words Are Just Wrapping*, *100 Words* and lots of other things with 'words' in them. And *Unputdownable!*

an obvious promise and tie it up with a ribbon – Marie Kondo's *The Life-Changing Magic of Tidying* being a recent example. Or, as is often the case with literary fiction, they can be more elusive, withholding their full meaning from the reader and instead teasing us with a sideways look or an evocative phrase, such as *The Hare with Amber Eyes*, *One Hundred Years of Solitude* or *The Quickening Maze*. They can be ironic: *Normal People*, say no more. And sometimes they've just got rhythm, or as Douglas Adams said of P. G. Wodehouse, 'word music': *Extremely Loud & Incredibly Close*; *Pearls, Girls and Monty Bodkin*; *Wide Sargasso Sea*. Titles are a mystery, and a game. They signify what kind of book we are going to get, and they help us to figure out what kind of reader we want to be through our choice of book.

As Professor John Sutherland puts it in *How to Read a Novel*, 'Once browsers have homed in on a particular section of the bookshop, titles play an important role – particularly if would-be readers are in the familiar situation of not knowing what they want but knowing they want *something* … In bookshops there is also the self-dignifying feeling that by your purchase you are, in a sense, making a statement about yourself.'

What's in a name, then? Everything.

'It's never safe to go back in the water...'

In June 2020, when bookshops had just started reopening after the first lockdown of the Covid-19 pandemic, a strange phenomenon was reported in the media. Branches of Waterstones were displaying books with their back covers facing outwards, so that they could be read without customers having to touch them. The Piccadilly branch tweeted 'apologies to all book designers', but on the whole the reaction was positive, with the artist and designer Jon Gray saying stoically, 'Our job is really to grab the reader's attention and get them to turn over and read the amazing blurb, so Waterstones have saved us a job.'

As for me, well, I was ecstatic. This was my moment! I envisaged my fellow blurb writers and I emerging, blinking and blushing, into the limelight, the unsung heroes of publishing finally getting their day in the sun. There would be applause, ticker tape. Possibly sequins.

Then I started having doubts. Is it really the same experience to read the back cover of a book without having looked at the front first? Does it put too much pressure on the blurb to stand alone? I felt... exposed. It made me realise how much fronts and backs of books are part of a whole, speaking to each other as well as the reader. And sometimes there's something so important that you have to shout about it before the reader has even turned the book over. It could be an amazing review quote, a Booker Prize win, the fact that millions of copies have been sold, or sometimes you just want to make some noise. This is where shoutlines, straplines, copy lines, taglines – whatever you want to call them – come in. They all appear on the front of a book and they all supplement or enhance the title in some way, and aim to get us excited.

Genre fiction is where shoutlines really come into their own. It's a way of making your book stand out in a crowded field and giving it that extra boost, like the pushy parent of a child actor.

Thrillers often feature neatly balanced taglines, such as 'Somebody's getting married. Somebody's getting murdered' on the front of Ruth Ware's *In a Dark Dark Wood*. (I imagine this line being narrated in the voice of Max from the 1980s TV series *Hart to Hart*: 'when they met, it was moider'.)

And of course there's the wellspring of all great copy lines, *Jaws*. The movie poster of the sequel, *Jaws 2* (a far inferior film, as it doesn't feature Robert Shaw chewing the scenery before the shark chews him), featured the immortal line: 'Just when you thought it was safe to go back in the water'. As homage and nod-wink to the audience, a recent Pan edition of Peter Benchley's original novel echoes this with 'It's never safe to go back in the water' on its front cover. How pleasing. For the record, my favourite film tagline is *Alien*'s 'In Space No One Can Hear You Scream', which instantly gets across that it's both science fiction and horror without ever having to use those words.

Numbers are a big thing in many thriller taglines. Just a few random examples include: 'One house. Two families. Three bodies.' (*The Family Upstairs* by Lisa Jewell.) 'Five went out. Four came back.' (*Force of Nature* by Jane Harper.) 'Seven days. Three families. One killer.' (*The Holiday* by T. M. Logan.)

You could say this formulation is clichéd; of course it is. But clichés can be reassuring, and enjoyable. I only have to think of my favourite movie clichés – the family 'breakfast bar' scene before something terrible happens; someone sliding down a wall with their head in their hands upon hearing bad news (has a real person ever done this?) or alternatively sitting in the shower, crying, with all their clothes on; everyone standing up and clapping at the end, ideally in a courtroom; annoyed spouse pointedly scraping uneaten food into the sink/bin after a row – and I smile. Clichés on books work in the same way; they say, you know what you're going to get, and everything's going to be all right. As Cyril Connolly remarked, clichés 'are not fatal' as 'the eye rests lightly upon them'.

Young Adult books are fertile ground for nicely rhythmical taglines, such as *The Hunger Games* ('Winning will make you famous. Losing means certain death.') or *Percy Jackson and the Lightning Thief* ('Half boy. Half god. All hero.'), while comedy books also mine a rich seam: Frankie Boyle's *Scotland's Jesus* boasts surreally that he is 'The only officially non-racist comedian', while Charlie Brooker's *I Can Make You Hate* says, 'The Potential All-Time No. 1 Bestseller'. Reader, I chuckled.

Perhaps these examples aren't essential to the overall package of a book, but they certainly add that something extra: a tease, or a promise, a joke, or words that fizz. They're a nice accessory, a bit of book bling. And, whatever else happens, they can't actively hurt, can they? Witness the endless variations on the quick/easy/simple/50 recipes formulations that adorn the front of cookbooks. We know these dishes can't all be foolproof, and probably don't care how many recipes there are, but the words soothe all the same: 'In Mary We Trust', or 'Reassuring Advice' on the front of *Nigella Christmas*. They're a far cry from the headmistress-like tone of the copy on my ancient *St Michael Casserole Cooking*: 'Economy-minded cooks appreciate the usefulness of the casserole…' (In fact, ancient cookbooks are a treasure trove of questionable copy: 'A man's first choice for dessert? Pie!')

Sometimes covers go even further, and have a kind of mini-blurb on the front, or a contents list of the treats to come inside, in the way that magazines do. I noticed the front cover of cleaning queen Mrs Hinch's book *The Little Book of Lists* follows this magazine formula, proudly boasting that it includes:

· Hinch Lists
· Tadaa Lists
· Fresh'n Up Fridays

I don't know what any of these are, but they sound great. I wonder, however, if Mrs Hinch knows that her cover is harking back to a fine tradition of classic book jackets laying out their wares, as it were, right on the front. I present the 1942 Pelican guide *Explosives*, which is brimming with information: 'Tells of Explosives, their Magical Creation, their Fierce Energy, their Sudden Disruption, their History and Romance, and their Uses in Peace and War.'* Ah, the romance of nitroglycerine! But this beauty is nothing compared to the copy that adorns the front of *New Biology* from 1946:

....

* Founded in 1936 by publisher Allen Lane, and revived in 2014, Pelican books are accessible and authoritative introductions to topics ranging from ecology to economics, with the occasional byway into subjects like *Space in the Sixties* and *The Strange Case of Pot*.

CONTAINS

The Potato – Master or Servant?
The Measurement of Human Survival
Wireworms and War-time Agriculture
Malaria, Mosquitoes and Man
Photogravure Illustrations

Haven't we all wondered that about potatoes?

I can't help thinking that copywriters had a bit more fun in ye olden days. The taglines on books from times of yore are so often more outré and outlandish than today's formulae, making them look rather arid in comparison. A rummage through tattered old paperbacks from a few decades ago (bookshelves in holiday cottages are particularly fertile ground for this, I find) reveals a juicy embarrassment of riches. M. M. Kaye's 1978 blockbuster *The Far Pavilions*: 'The great bestseller! A story of love and war as towering as the Himalayas.' Georgette Heyer's *False Colours*: 'It's double trouble for a beautiful heiress forced to choose between dashing twin brothers.' The front cover of one edition of *Flowers in the Attic*, Virginia Andrews's multi-million-selling 1979 novel of sibling imprisonment and incest (reviewed as 'deranged swill' by the *Washington Post*), even advertises the next volume: 'The horror begins with *Flowers in the Attic*. The shocking fury continues with *Petals on the Wind*…'

Going further back in time, the publisher Victor Gollancz was a pioneer of using book covers as advertising space, with their trademark bright yellow and red graphic designs. This was branding before branding. The Gollancz 1963 first edition of John le Carré's *The Spy Who Came in From the Cold* proudly states, in a neat box on the front of its jacket: 'This is, in our view, a novel of the first order – a terrible novel, of great actuality and political import. It is also immensely thrilling.' The grand, flowery language makes me strangely happy, and it also really makes me wish that I had been a copywriter in the 1960s (minus casual office sexism).

This more enthusiastic, somehow less knowing and more innocent way of writing was honoured to perfection by some recent retro cover designs for le Carré's Smiley novels, created by David Pearson with words by the copywriter Nick Asbury. As Asbury told me, 'The le Carré covers were a conscious attempt to revive the copy style of the type-only Gollancz covers from the early 1960s, when book covers were used as marketing vehicles, often written directly in the voice of the publisher. The language is high-flown but has an appealing authenticity to it – you feel the enthusiasm of the publisher for the work.'

What about the subtitle, that slightly poor, dowdy relation amid all these snazzy shoutlines? It is certainly a different beast: less showy and more functional, generally imparting information on a non-fiction book (How, Why, What, When, 'Essays', 'A Memoir', etc.). Necessary, perhaps, but not that exciting. According to author Mary Laura Philpott,

> Naming a book is a bit like naming a child. The title is the book's given name, what it goes by. The author's byline is the book's surname, which it has in common with every other book by that writer. And the subtitle? It's the book's middle name. That is, it's not what anyone calls the thing, but you're stuck with it forever, so you might as well pick something good … Once a book becomes popular, the subtitle typically disappears from our consciousness.

Ben Yagoda in the *New York Times* agrees that the subtitle is the wallflower at the party. 'Nobody really notices subtitles. They are a sort of lottery ticket in the economics of nonfiction book marketing. Publishers throw all kinds of elements in them – vogue words and phrases, features of the book the title didn't get around to mentioning, talismanic locutions like "An American Life" – in the (almost always) vain hope that something will pay off.'*

The literary critic Robert McCrum goes as far as saying that publishers should scrap subtitles, that 'fig leaf of authorial shame', altogether, following his apoplexy at seeing that a biography of William Golding featured the subtitle 'The Man Who Wrote *Lord of the Flies*' – I feel his rage on that one.

It's true that today, a lot of non-fiction subtitles can feel formulaic. They often start with a preposition (From, Beyond, Inside) or an introductory preamble such as 'Tales from', 'Notes on'. And many will almost certainly try to convince you that their book's subject shook the earth to its core, whether it is something that actually did, such as Spanish flu or the Wall Street Crash, or something more spurious, such as *Cod: A Biography of the Fish That Changed the World*. Did it? *Really?* It can all feel a little too pat – as one wag on Twitter remarked, if Adam Smith's *The Wealth of Nations* had been published today, it would probably have been called something like *Invisible Hand: The Incredible Story of How Markets Changed Our Lives Forever*.

There's also a fashion, particularly in the United States, for extremely long, flamboyant subtitles, such as that on Silvana

––

* I've checked my notes, and I came up with thirty-nine, yes, thirty-nine, different subtitles for my book (if I was working for me, I would have fired me), before realising that I needed to follow my own advice and keep it simple.

Paternostro's biography of Gabriel García Márquez, *Solitude & Company: The Life of Gabriel García Márquez Told with Help from His Friends, Family, Fans, Arguers, Fellow Pranksters, Drunks, and a Few Respectable Souls*. It reflects a trend for an enigmatic, almost coy title, followed by a word salad of explanation. Why make the subtitle, which is almost certain to be forgotten, do all the heavy lifting?

A *Washington Post* article from 2019 titled 'Book subtitles are getting ridiculously long. What is going on?' blames it on the internet: subtitles are larded with 'selling' keywords that will be picked up online. That's certainly true, but I wonder if sometimes publishers just get scared to tell the world what their book is about?

In the past a work of non-fiction would often have a straightforward, sensible kind of title – you certainly know what you're getting with Engels's *The Condition of the Working Class in England* – which did exactly what it said on the tin and required no subtitle, whereas it was more common for novels to feature some extra flourish, explanation, moral commentary or expression of irony. *Frankenstein: The Modern Prometheus*, *Vanity Fair: A Novel Without a Hero* or *Tess of the d'Urbervilles: A Pure Woman* are some of the most famous examples, but the fact that we would never use them when talking about these novels now supports the theory that subtitles are somewhat superfluous.

I'm not sure we should write subtitles off completely, though. They *can* be great. A good, well thought-out subtitle can seal a deal or make a promise – the jab to follow up the punch of the book's title. It can support, or contradict, or extend the title, such as *Stupid White Men… and Other Sorry Excuses for the State of the Nation!*, or *The Establishment: And how they get away with it*.

It can reflect the tone of the book, such as the delightful sub-title on *Very British Problems: Making Life Awkward for Ourselves, One Rainy Day at a Time*, or the deliberately school teacher-ish *Dreyer's English: An Utterly Correct Guide to Clarity and Style*. Feel the slap of that ruler. Susan Cain's book *Quiet* was subtitled 'The Power of Introverts in a World That Can't Stop Talking', which both amplified the title and flattered its bookish audience. By bringing the voice of a book alive, these subtitles give us a taste of what's to come and reassure us that we are in good literary company.

Subtitles might be forgotten in the end, but in the moment they can spark joy. Get them right, and, like all words on the front of a book, they will give it an extra lift and make us, the reader, feel something, whether it's intrigued, comforted, amused or just a bit clever.

A very wise person once told me that if it's too hard to come up with a good subtitle for a book, the title probably isn't right. And if it's too hard to come up with a good title, the book's probably a dud and the jig is up. Gulp.

King of First Lines

Many people will tell you that the best first lines in literature are from *Anna Karenina* ('All happy families are alike; each unhappy family is unhappy in its own way') or *Moby-Dick* ('Call me Ishmael'). But I wonder if that's because they didn't read much Stephen King as teenagers. I would like to make a case for King as the master of the opener.

Exhibit A: the beginning of *Needful Things*. Just one line, printed alone on a single page: 'You've been here before.' I've been where, when? Tell me more.

Exhibit B: the entire first paragraph of *It*: 'The terror, which would not end for another twenty-eight years – if it ever did end – began, so far as I know or can tell, with a boat made from a sheet of newspaper floating down a gutter swollen with rain.' Don't you want to know what 'the terror' is?

Exhibit C: *Carrie*, of course. The novel prefaces with a fictional newspaper article about a freak shower of stones in the town of Westover, but the first line of Chapter One is: 'Nobody was really surprised when it happened, not really, not at the subconscious level where savage things grow.' In the words of Maximus Decimus Meridius, are you not entertained?

These lines give us a tantalising hint of what's to come, and they also make us *feel* something – unsettled and curious at the same time.

I would also like to propose Gillian Flynn, domestic noir doyenne, as Queen. Witness this, from *Dark Places*: 'I have a meanness inside me, real as an organ.'

Or the classic *Gone Girl* opener: 'When I think of my wife, I always think of the back of her head.'

They are quintessential 'hooks', or what author Richard Cohen calls 'grabbers', plunging the reader into a moment, and throwing up questions that demand answers: Her *head*, really? Every copywriter needs to know about hooks.

But I think there's more to it than that. It's the atmosphere too: creepy, off-colour, *wrong* somehow. Stephen King sums it up brilliantly himself in an *Atlantic* article that has important things to say about connecting with a reader through words:

> I think readers come for the *voice*. A novel's voice is some-thing like a singer's – think of singers like Mick Jagger and Bob Dylan, who have no musical training but are instantly recognisable. An appealing voice achieves an intimate con-nection – a bond much stronger than the kind forged, intel-lectually, through crafted writing … With really good books, a powerful sense of voice is established in the first line … that's irresistible.

There's probably no better example of this than the start of *The Catcher in the Rye*: 'If you really want to hear about it, the first thing you'll probably want to know is where I was born, and what my lousy childhood was like, and how my parents were occupied and all before they had me, and all that David Copperfield kind of crap, but I don't feel like going into it, if you want to know the truth.' Right from the off you hear Holden Caulfield speaking in your head, whether you think he's a troubled outsider (as a teenager) or an irritating little turd (as a middle-aged reader).*

Different openings work in distinct ways at drawing the reader in through their author's voice. Sometimes, a line works simply because it is funny, such as the confessional beginning of Erica Jong's *Fear of Flying*: 'There were 117 psychoanalysts on the Pan Am flight to Vienna and I'd been treated by at least six of them.' (The next line is 'And married a seventh'!)

Often, they create an immediate mood of mystery, such as the beginning of Daphne du Maurier's *Rebecca*: 'Last night I dreamt I went to Manderley again.' It's the 'again' that nails it here: the narrator is looking back, and we are going to find out why. You can almost hear the fire crackling.

A great first line can also be confusing or surprising: '124 was spiteful' from Toni Morrison's *Beloved*; 'I write this sitting in the kitchen sink' from Dodie Smith's *I Capture the Castle*; and of course Gregor Samsa waking up one morning having been turned into a cockroach in *Metamorphosis* – although some translations of this notoriously ambiguous first line range from 'vermin' to a 'monstrous insect'.

With an opener by Graham Greene ('One never knows when the blow may fall' – *The Third Man*) or Robert Harris ('The moment I heard how McAra died I should have walked away' – *The Ghost*) there is reassurance that we are going to enjoy clear, smooth, swift writing – it's no coincidence that both these writers were journalists before they became novelists.

So first lines give us a clue as to what kind of book we are going to get, whether it's comic, surreal or nostalgic, and how we are

* The same principle applies to rewatching *Ferris Bueller's Day Off* as an adult. I am now firmly on Team Ed Rooney.

going to feel when we read it. In the words of William Goldman, beginnings 'set up a world'. But they are also a way in for a writer. Robert Harris has said that 'fifty per cent of the whole effort of a novel is the first paragraph', while Stephen King describes how he composes the opening lines of a new novel in his head before he goes to sleep, reworking them for months, even years, before he is happy and knows that, finally, he can write the book. Iris Murdoch noted that 'A novel is a long job, and if you get it wrong at the start you're going to be very unhappy later on.'

Opening lines have a huge amount of power, probably more than any other part of a text, and they are instructive for starting any piece of copy. But with the first line of a blurb, the stakes are even higher. If you're reading the first line of a novel then the chances are you're up for continuing – when you're reading the blurb, you haven't even bought the darned book yet. If those first few words don't hook a potential reader in, you've blown it. They must convey important details – person, place, idea or set-up – as well as creating a mood readers want more of. As the writer Sam Leith says of good prose, 'You are not only making a case or imparting information; you are cultivating a relationship.' The aim is to connect.

Over the years I have collected several books with excellent blurb openers. My crumbling paperback edition of Patricia Highsmith's Ripley omnibus is a case in point. Its front cover has now completely detached itself from the rest of the book and is only held on by several years' worth of Sellotape accretions, which have now formed a sort of lump of yellowing matter.*

* According to the essayist Anne Fadiman, a book reader is either a 'courtly lover', revering every pristine page of the untarnished physical object, or a lustful spoiler, a breaker of spines, a (gasp) folder-down of page corners. I am the latter.

But I will never throw it out. The reason is the copy on the back.

It begins with a line consisting of three words: 'Liar, psycho-path, killer…' And below that, in a strange red rectangle popping out from the left-hand edge, it says, 'This is Tom Ripley.'

It's so simple, and so bold, and I love it. It's something to do with the strong descriptors, and then the almost banal 'This is'. It could have been 'Meet Tom Ripley', but 'This is' is so much more matter of fact, just like Highsmith's deceptively simple writing. It also makes clear that the hero of our book is a very bad person. The blurb goes on to say he's an 'anti-hero', but let's face it, anyone who's read the Ripley novels knows he is the hero. He only bumps off people who *really* deserve it.

The first line on the back of my well-loved (for that, read virtually destroyed) Virago edition of *The Handmaid's Tale* is 'The Republic of Gilead allows Offred only one function: to breed.' So much is packed into eleven words, with a gut-wrenching twist at the end of the sentence. My *Virago Book of Fairy Tales* begins: 'Fairy tales are not for children, and neither is this book.' It's an excellent line, surprising and slightly chiding, true to the spirit of Angela Carter's writing. The blurb opener for Craig Brown's biography of Princess Margaret, *Ma'am Darling*, is: 'She made John Lennon blush and Marlon Brando clam up.' (This is followed by 'She cold-shouldered Princess Diana and humiliated Elizabeth Taylor. Jack Nicholson offered her cocaine and Pablo Picasso lusted over her.' Delicious.)* Each of these examples uses short sentences, and they defy our expectations in some way, with a twist or a tremor or something that makes us start.

* *Ma'am Darling* also tells Princess Margaret's story as a brilliantly entertaining 'blurb', on page 137.

Great blurb openings can, and in fact probably should, break the rules of grammar, such as this perky little number on the back of Jonathan Meades's *Pidgin Snaps*: 'What? It's a box. A boxed set. A boxette.' The first line of copy on Dawn French's *Because of You* is just 'Tick-tock, tick-tock, tick-tock … midnight.' Nice. The blurb on Hallie Rubenhold's superb *The Five: The Untold Lives of the Women Killed by Jack the Ripper* begins just with five names, in large, bold capital letters at the top of the back cover:

POLLY, ANNIE, ELIZABETH, CATHERINE AND MARY-JANE

are famous for the same thing, though they never met. They came from Fleet Street, Knightsbridge, Wolverhampton, Sweden and Wales. They wrote ballads, ran coffee houses, lived on country estates, they breathed ink-dust from printing presses and escaped people-traffickers.
What they had in common was the year of their murders: 1888.

This copy is, like the book, a bit of a masterpiece. It makes these women human. Jack the Ripper is not named once on the back cover. It is an act of reclamation and a shout of life, rather than a ghoulish revelling in death.

Questions are a useful way into a subject, but I think they should be treated like copywriting ammunition and only used when strictly necessary. If I don't care what the answer to the question is, why should a reader? For example, the first line of copy for Jared Diamond's epic history of humanity, *Guns, Germs and Steel*, asks: 'Why has human history unfolded so differently across the globe?' It's an incredible book, but I don't think this question – too big, too vague – does it justice.

43

But what about this? 'When you see your nation's flag flut-tering in the breeze, what do you feel?' It's at the start of the copy for Tim Marshall's *Worth Dying For: The Power and Politics of Flags*, and it immediately makes me think about the answer. The question a copywriter should always ask themselves is: 'Why should anyone care?'

There are two formulations to be avoided at all costs. The first crime is to start a blurb with the words 'In this book'. It's already clear that this is a book, and that there are things in it. Other variations include formulations such as 'In this necessary intervention', or 'In this ground-breaking study' or 'In this sen-sational debut', which I've seen far too many times. A slightly less heinous sin (venial rather than mortal) is starting a blurb with 'When'. I'm not always against clichés, but this feels too well worn; a slightly lazy way of trying to plunge readers into the action, but one that becomes redundant by overuse, much in the way the gravelly voiced 'In a world…' trope of cinema trailers does. It also means that a very long sentence with lots of clauses is on its way.

With openers, it's useful to think like a journalist and get to the point,* but also to think like a novelist and say, *come in and find out more.*

* *

* To quote Leith again, 'You will never get more people reading the second half of your article than read the first.'

Quotes, Puffs, Praise, Reviews

P. G. Wodehouse once said a critic should be eaten by bears, which seems a little harsh. As long as there have been literary critics, there have been critics of literary critics, calling their words 'preposterous' (Kurt Vonnegut) or 'a tissue of flatteries' (Edgar Allan Poe). John Updike said they were 'pigs at the pastry cart'. Book reviews are often a byword for lazy clichés – so much that the sadly short-lived Hatchet Job of the Year Award was set up by the Omnivore review website to reward those who punctured the puffery.

Of course, reviews are written by human beings and are therefore bound to be subjective or flawed. The examples of snark given to now-classic books are legion: 'Indifferent' – Henry James on *Middlemarch*. 'A book of the season only' – *New York Herald Tribune* on *The Great Gatsby*.

Yet despite these misgivings, and despite – or maybe because of – the anarchic world of 'non-professional' reviewers on Amazon, Goodreads, blogs and social media, publishers still set great store by book reviews in broadsheet newspapers, poring over them every week and picking out the best bits. And for good reason, as book sales will often spike after a positive piece has appeared. But I also think we like to be reassured that someone who has some kind of authority and legitimacy tells us something is worth reading.*

This is why one of our first encounters with the copy on a book cover is in the form of fulsome review quotes. Sometimes it can be hard for them to sound meaningful. A brief glance at the latest literary hits reveals a proliferation of adjectives such as 'breathtaking', 'spellbinding', 'dazzling', 'powerful' and 'beautiful', which perhaps reflects the tics of the book reviewer as much as the taste of the person picking them out. I can safely say that many reviewers do not seem to have read the *Times Literary Supplement*'s list of twenty words and phrases that should be cut from book reviews, which includes 'mordant wit', 'rich tapestry', 'consummate', 'writes like an angel', 'peppered with', 'couldn't put it down' and (ha ha) 'reminds one of Martin Amis'. In an article about the familiar clichés of 'reviewese' in the *Telegraph*, the book critic Tom Payne also suggests avoiding culinary comparisons such as 'Take Tobias Smollett, stew him in his own juices, reduce, mix in some finely chopped Poe, season with Patti Smith and serve with late Henry James.'

Not every book has an embarrassment of review riches, and sometimes the reviews will just be stinkers, which makes our job very difficult – though nothing could be as scathing as a Philip Hensher critique that ended 'on the evidence of *The Book of Kings*, he could not write "Bum" on a wall', which still makes me laugh every time I read it.†

....

* There is also what is known in psychology as 'The Third-Person Effect,' where most of us believe that other people are influenced by advertising and hype, but we aren't. As if.

† W. H. Auden observed that 'One cannot review a bad book without showing off.' But when showing off is this funny, who cares?

Sometimes book covers make a virtue of bad reviews, such as the glorious copy on the Picador paperback of Alasdair Gray's *Something Leather*. Not only does it boast a pretty perfect blurb – sample line: 'This is the first British fiction since *The Canterbury Tales* to show such a wide social range in such embarrassing sexual detail' – but also two columns of newspaper reviews, divided up into 'VERY FOR' and 'NOT VERY FOR'. The latter includes 'A book that shouldn't have happened' from the *Sunday Times*. It's inspired.

If I'm filleting reviews I try to home in on something 'noice, different, unusual', as Aussie TV heroines Kath and Kim would say.* I avoid the word 'readable' wherever possible – it's a book! The same rule applies to such ubiquitous adjectives as 'magisterial' – doesn't it just mean 'really long'? Comparisons can be fun, but I try not to get readers' hopes up. I've lost count of the number of times a serious work of history will be described as 'reads just like a thriller', when it really doesn't. I can only assume those reviewers don't read many thrillers.

Breaking up and reordering the words from a review is common practice, but pretending a bad review is good is beyond the pale. Witness Ben Macintyre's anecdote in *The Times* about a quote being nefariously taken out of context:

> Some months ago in this column I made a mildly disobliging remark about a forthcoming novel by Lance Price, Tony Blair's former spin doctor. Politicians and their acolytes seldom make good novelists, and I was not confident that Mr Price's effort

....

* My other televisual rule is to avoid the excruciatingly faint praise of the advance quote Shakin' Stevens provides for Alan Partridge's autobiography *Bouncing Back*: 'Lovely stuff!'

would be any better. I wrote, 'Perhaps *Time and Fate* will be the corking political novel that Blair's Britain so badly needs, but somehow I am doubtful.' Mr Price's book came out this month, and on the cover appears this ringing endorsement: 'The corking political novel that Blair's Britain so badly needs' – *The Times*.

I almost admire the shamelessness of whoever picked that out, but I like to think most publishers are above that sort of thing. Or maybe we're just scared of the comeback.

QUOTES PART 2: BLURBS (THE OTHER KIND)

As well as favourable reviews in the books pages, publishers also love it when a well-known figure provides an endorsement for a book ahead of its publication. This is the other meaning of the word 'blurb', more commonly used in the US: an advance piece of praise that appears on the jacket.

The practice of 'blurbing' has a fairly ignoble reputation, seeming to many like an endless merry-go-round of hype, mutual back-slapping and back-scratching; the worst kind of literary cronyism. *Private Eye* regularly skewers this nepotism in its books pages, gleefully pointing out endorsements that have been provided by people who are either friends with, related to, or colleagues of their object of praise – or even their neighbour, as this recent entry, 'Spring Log-Rolling', shows:

A ringing endorsement appears from England cricket chief selector Ed Smith on the back cover of the new book by Mervyn King, former governor of the Bank of England … This would be the same Ed Smith who is a Kent neighbour of King, who is thanked by King in his acknowledgements, and whose own book, *Luck: What It Means and Why It Matters*, is approvingly quoted by King in *Radical Uncertainty*. Lucky indeed!

This 'log-rolling' reaches dizzying heights on the original hardback edition of Dave Eggers's *A Heartbreaking Work of Staggering Genius*, the title of which, of course, parodies the hyperbolic language of blurbs.* First of all David Remnick says, 'When you read his extraordinary memoir you don't laugh, then cry, then laugh again; you somehow experience these emotions all at once – and powerfully.' Then David Sedaris says, 'The force and energy of this book could power a train.' And then David Foster Wallace says it made him forget about his fear of flying while reading it on a plane, describing it as 'terribly, terribly moving … Fine, fine writing.' So many descriptors, and so many Daves! Jobs for the boys indeed.†

One writer who put her foot down and refused to join the boys' club was Ursula K. Le Guin, who, in 1967, replied marvellously to a letter seeking endorsements with the words:

I can imagine myself blurbing a book in which Brian Aldiss, predictably, sneers at my work, because then I could preen

* One of the most notorious offenders was the blurb Nicole Krauss provided for David Grossman's *To the End of the Land*, which says that to read the book 'is to have yourself taken apart, undone, touched at the place of your own essence; it is to be turned back, as if after a long absence, into a human being'.

† Let us not forget that in 2018 it was reported there were more people called David or Steve running FTSE 100 companies than there were women or ethnic minorities.

myself on my magnanimity. But I cannot imagine myself blurbing a book, the first of the series, which not only contains no
writing by women, but the tone of which is so self-contentedly,
exclusively male, like a club, or a locker room. That would
not be magnanimity, but foolishness. Gentlemen, I just don't
belong here.

Of course, the log-rolling is nothing new. Back before book
covers even existed, writers were seeking endorsement from
other writers, sometimes in the form of dedications to patrons
such as this from the Roman poet Catullus: 'To whom should
I send this charming new little book/freshly polished with dry
pumice? To you, Cornelius!'

Fast forward to the Renaissance, and Thomas More was
taking quote whoredom to a new level, asking his friend
Erasmus to ensure that his book *Utopia* 'be handsomely set off
with the highest of recommendations, if possible, from several
people, both intellectuals and distinguished statesmen'. (He
was lucky enough to get one from Erasmus no less, praising
his 'divine wit'. Not bad.) Ben Jonson's eulogy to Shakespeare
in the Preface to the First Folio of 1623 – 'The wonder of
our Stage!' – is a perfect work of art as well as a winning
endorsement.

By the time books were an industry in the eighteenth
century, advance 'blurbs' were too, displayed at the front of
a book. These had reached such effusive heights that in the
opening pages of *Shamela*, his 1741 satirical riposte to Samuel
Richardson's smash hit *Pamela*, Henry Fielding writes a mock
endorsement from 'John Puff, Esq.'. Comic parody quotes really
are nothing new.

The first piece of praise to appear on an actual book cover

is generally thought to be for Walt Whitman's *Leaves of Grass*. When he received a letter from Ralph Waldo Emerson praising his talent after publication, Whitman had an excerpt from it printed (in gold leaf, naturally) on the spine of the second edition: 'I Greet You at the Beginning of a Great Career.' The poet who composed 'Song of Myself' lived it as he wrote it.

Things had clearly got out of control when George Orwell famously criticised book puffs in his essay 'In Defence of the Novel' in 1936, calling them 'disgusting tripe' after he was traumatised by reading a review in the *Sunday Times* that said, 'If you can read this book and not shriek with delight, your soul is dead.' Yet it is interesting that only a couple of years later, in 1938, he wrote to his friend Cyril Connolly saying:

> I see from the *New Statesman & Nation* list that you have a book coming out sometime this spring. If you can manage to get a copy sent me I'll review it for the *New English*, possibly also *Time & Tide*. I arranged for Warburg to send you a copy of my Spanish book (next month) hoping you may be able to review it. You scratch my back, I'll scratch yours.

Even the purest succumb in the end.

If we've determined that book endorsements are as old as the oldest hills, presumably they're still around for a reason. Yes, there's a lot of chumminess going on, but I'm not sure it's the 'corrupt practice' slated by Camille Paglia. Alan Bennett once said of snobbery that it was a very amiable vice, and I wonder if advance praise can be categorised in the same way. It offers a signal to the reader that the sort of writer they like also likes this thing, so perhaps they might like it too. And I don't think it's ever done in a malign spirit, but by those who genuinely rate an author and their work.* For Stephen King, a prolific endorser, it is an act of authorial camaraderie: 'I've done it only for books I honestly loved, and for a very simple reason. Early on, nobody blurbed any of mine.'†

Finally, something that may not make your soul shriek with delight. If you've ever had a niggling sense of doubt that *perhaps* the person providing an advance puff for a book hasn't actually read said book, you may be right. One of the slightly shameful secrets of publishing is that occasionally an author will really want to give an endorsement for a writer they admire, but is too busy to do it – and so they hand the responsibility over to somebody else. I confess that, yes, occasionally I have made up review quotes for a couple of high-profile authors in this manner (although luckily they did find the time to sign off on the finished piece of praise). No names given, of course.

....

* Or if they don't, they could always do what Alan Coren did when asked by his old friend Jeffrey Archer to blurb a book he really didn't like: 'Fans of Jeffrey Archer will not be disappointed.'

† His puff that appears on the front of C. J. Tudor's *The Chalk Man* just states: 'If you like my stuff, you'll like this.' What more needs to be said?

The Visual

Seeing comes before words.

JOHN BERGER

Sometimes no words are necessary. A picture is worth a thousand of them, after all, so I'm told. Our brains' visual systems evolved to process text long after images: as scientist Paolo Gaudiano says, we have a 'biological penchant for imagery'.

We all judge a book by its cover, and some of the best covers employ as few words as possible to get their point across, or turn those words into something else. One of my favourite designs of recent years is Justine Anweiler's reinterpretation of Peter Benchley's *Jaws*. Using minimalist graphics and striking colours, she makes the book's title intrinsic to the design. The bottom three-quarters of the cover is plain blue, with the blood-red word 'jaws' sitting on top of it like a boat in the sea, and the water beneath forming a fin-shape in the 'w'. It is a visual, rather than a verbal, joke that we 'get' as we look. Design here is a signifier, and a clue.

There is a lot of pressure on book covers – please refer to the Modern Toss joke cartoon where two men say: 'this novel you've written doesn't make any sense', 'that's why it's really important we get the cover right'. A brilliant design can transform a book's fortunes, especially now in the age of the online 'reveal', when a jacket must grab our attention as a tiny thumbnail on our mobile screens as well as on a bookshop table. As Faber designer Jonny Pelham says, it must 'hit hard and quick'. Every detail, every colour, matters. I remember a publishing story from several years ago about how a major retailer demanded the eye on the 1997 paperback cover of Alex Garland's *The Beach* be turned from green to blue, before it went on to become a bestseller.*

Designers play with the shape, size and position of fonts as part of their work to suit the book's market – data journalist Ben Blatt has fun noting, for example, how the size of an author's name on a front cover will increase as their fame does (for Lee Child it went from five per cent of the space to twenty-two per cent within a few books). But the covers that interest me the most are those that play with the meaning of words too, and no British designer is more renowned for this than David Pearson. He has his own studio, Type as Image, which special-ises in typography as a form of expression; turning the written word into an art form.

As he explained to me, 'When words are your only form of expression (I can't draw, I can't paint and I get clammy just thinking about cropping other people's photographs!) then you don't half focus on their meaning, on their personality, their tone, their temper and on their speed of delivery and all this informs their presentation on a book cover. Even breaking lines can dramatically change the way a cover is read and understood.'

This centrality of language can be seen clearly on David's cover designs for 'Great Ideas', a series of over 100 bite-sized books of great thought. On the front of Simone de Beauvoir's *What is Existentialism?* the title is broken up like this:

. . . .

* According to the book marketing site BookBub, covers with animals on them perform particularly well, borne out perhaps by the fox on Richard Osman's *The Thursday Murder Club*.

What
is   Ex
is   tential
is   m
?

leaving us with the eternal, echoing questions of existence. Similarly, for Peter Kropotkin's *Anarchist Communism*, the twist in the text quotation on the front cover ('Everywhere you will find that the wealth of the wealthy springs from the poverty of the poor') is enacted through the design – as its meaning becomes clear, the second half of the quotation changes to a spray-painted font on a ripped-out background. And the cover design for Robert Louis Stevenson's *An Apology for Idlers* is, very satisfyingly, half finished: perhaps the embodiment of Antoine de Saint-Exupéry's maxim that 'A designer knows he has achieved perfection not when there is nothing left to add, but when there is nothing left to take away.'

In one sense, Pearson's work continues the tradition of text-only cover designs that recalls the early days of publishing, when most jackets avoided visual representation of a book's contents (publisher Allen Lane disdained this illustrative approach because he feared it would lead to 'bosoms and bottoms', and when Penguin made the decision to 'go pictorial' in 1961, it was later compared to Dylan going electric).

But even then, many covers continued to use words as the central element of their design, including one of Pearson's favourite book covers, the 1969 design for Jean-Paul Sartre's *Words*, which foregrounds the quotation 'I loathe my childhood and all that remains of it.' As he says, 'The designer understands the power of the words, gives them top billing and then gets the hell out of the way! This elevation of the book's opening sentence sets the tone perfectly (for a book about a childhood made bearable by a passion for reading and writing) and still looks thrillingly different, over fifty years later.' Similarly, the cover of Raymond Williams's Pelican book *Communications* consists just of title and author in plain type on a white background, with a clever little instruction in the bottom right-hand corner, '*Please turn over.*'

Looked at this way, book covers are in effect, as Pearson says, 'little posters', a piece of marketing in themselves. 'They're not quite art and not quite commerce, but somewhere in-between. I enjoy occupying this space between artistic integrity and the flogging of units.'

As well as turning a book cover into a pocket-sized billboard, words can also work with or against images to create ironic tension, humour or drama. This is done to great effect on the classic 1977 cover of Michael Herr's report from the Vietnam War, *Dispatches*, where a huge, killer quote from John le Carré, 'The best book I have ever read on men and war in our time', surrounds the poignant image of a battered soldier's helmet.

From more recent publishing, I love Vintage's cover for Kurt Vonnegut's satirical novel *Breakfast of Champions* (the title is taken from an advertising slogan), which is designed like a gaudy cereal box featuring quotations from the book in flashes: 'Ideas or the Lack of Them Can Cause Disease!' 'Now it Can Be Told!' and the blurb, which unfortunately gives little clue as to what the book is about, on the side of the box. In another inspired use of the visual and verbal language of packaging, the cover of Ben Goldacre's *Bad Pharma: How medicine is broken, and how we can fix it* is designed like a packet of medicine, complete with a skull and crossbones logo and a message: 'Warning: the Pharmaceutical Industry Has Serious Side Effects.'

But for me the definitive fusion of design and copy is both in and on John Berger's 1972 book *Ways of Seeing*, based on his radical art history TV series. It is about how we look at images, and how our reading of them is influenced by our assumptions surrounding power, beauty, class and gender. Berger's essays, which meld words and pictures throughout, still have much to say about how no image is ever neutral ('Men look at women. Women watch themselves being looked at' stands as a perfect summary of the male gaze). It is also about how words change our perception of an image. For example, as Berger says, if you add the sentence 'This is the last picture that Van Gogh painted before he killed himself' below a reproduction of *Wheatfield with Crows*, it alters our view of that painting irrevocably. The picture suddenly looks more poignant, as we search for some deeper meaning that may or may not be there. In Berger's words, 'The image now illustrates the sentence.'

The book's argument – that the visual and the verbal both amplify and undercut each other – is also borne out by its front cover design. It consists of both image and words: a surreal René Magritte painting surrounded by continuous bold text, which cuts off at the bottom mid-sentence. It appears as if it will carry on to the first page when we open the book, but it doesn't. As designer Phil Baines says, 'The cover of this book is a conceit.' It plays a trick on us and makes us look twice. The words on the front tell us that 'the relation between what we see and what we know is never settled', and this is enacted by its design sleight of hand. There is no better illustration of the power of images, and the power of words; and how we read (or misread) both.

2.

IN THE BEGINNING
WAS THE BLURB

Literary History

‘A Sound Like a Publisher’
Authors, Editors, Blurbers

> Absolutely hated the cosy little domestic blurbs on my new
> covers ... So I set them on fire.
>
> JEANETTE WINTERSON

‘Don't piss off Jeanette Winterson’ is clearly one of the first rules
anyone should learn when entering the publishing industry.
When I read that she'd burned the newly re-jacketed editions
of her books in protest at their blurbs in 2021, my immediate
reaction was relief that I hadn't written them, swiftly followed
by a kind of twisted pride that those humble words should pro-
voke such passion at all.* To some authors, blurbs *really* matter.

There is a noble literary tradition of blurb-hating, which
J. D. Salinger took to a different extreme. One of the first things
I learned when I started work as a copywriter was never, *ever*
write a blurb for *The Catcher in the Rye*, under pain of death.
The famously publicity-shy Salinger, christened the ‘Garbo of
letters’, was highly protective of every aspect of his work, and
had strict rules in his contracts regarding the appearance of his
books. According to publishing director Simon Prosser in the
Guardian, ‘The only copy allowed on the books, back or front,
is the author name and the title. Nothing else at all: no quotes,

* Winterson later acknowledged that ‘The publishers are fixing the problem’
and the burning was ‘symbolic’.

no cover blurb, no biography. We're not really sure why this is.' And *The Catcher in the Rye* has managed to sell sixty-five million copies around the world without one, so what the hell do we know?

Graham Greene was another hater, writing in a letter to his editor in 1945 that 'It was because of the blurb on *England Made Me* that I insisted on no photograph or blurb appearing in *Brighton Rock*.' In this case he is referring to the 'blurb' about *him*, which he described as 'horribly chatty and personal' – and, having seen it, with its description of writing being in Greene's blood and his 'Georgian brick house on Clapham Common', I think he's dead right. In the end publisher Allen Lane had to intervene, writing that 'The ideal thing would be for you to dictate a note to your secretary of what you would like to appear.' Quite.

For most authors, however, blurbs are a necessary evil, and for a few even part of the creative process. Terry Pratchett recommended the practice: 'if you think you have a book evolving, now is the time to write the flap copy – the blurb, in fact. An author should never be too proud to write their own flap copy. Getting the heart and soul of a book into fewer than 100 words helps you focus.'

At many publishing houses, blurbs are written by the editor, or the author, or a combination of both. Authors have varying influence on the copy that appears on their books. Some are hands off; others like to write their own blurbs. After all, they know their book better than anyone else. But sometimes this becomes a hindrance. Writing tens of thousands of words of copy is a different skill from writing 100 or so, which requires condensing the work and, above all, thinking about the book's audience. This can be harder for an author or even an editor because of their closeness to the book. It can result in copy being too wordy or detailed – or, as Gelett Burgess defined the word 'blurb': 'A sound like a publisher.' As an outsider, a copywriter can offer a clearer perspective, and is able to pick out a book's salient points without wanting to throw in the kitchen sink.* But how do the authors feel about this?

One of the most curious and surprising things about being a blurb writer was, I discovered, that I was given pretty much free access to authors. What, you mean someone as low down in the food chain as me can actually write to Beryl Bainbridge to see if she likes the copy I've written? Surely this can't be true? After the excitement had worn off I soon came to realise, however, that it was a mixed blessing. Some authors are natural blurb writers, others most definitely aren't – and unfortunately those who aren't don't always realise it. Some are polite and friendly, some... aren't.

Who better to know about the joys, pitfalls and occasional terrors of copywriter–author encounters than somebody who has been both? Elizabeth Buchan is not only a bestselling novelist, with titles like *Revenge of the Middle-Aged Woman*, *The Museum of Broken Promises* and *Two Women in Rome* to her name, but also used to run the blurbs department at Penguin, a job she has described as requiring 'the hide of a rhinoceros, a nimble mind and the – occasional – box of tissues'. As soon as I read that Iris Murdoch once wrote to her saying 'blurb writing is a mini art form', I knew we had to talk. She was adamant in her views on authors writing blurbs:

....

* As Benjamin Dreyer puts it, 'The best jacket copy is attention-grabbing and inviting without being chockful of fulsome self-praise – or, to put it another way, it shouldn't sound as if the author, or the author's mother, wrote it.'

The one thing I did learn is that an author is not the person to write the blurb. For obvious reasons, they cannot see what they have written in an objective fashion. In addition, what they wish to say does not always provide the best copy for selling and marketing (hard though it is to accept). I am very happy for others to write my blurbs... with, of course, the right to make comments.*

Buchan learned her trade in the 1970s under the maverick copywriter Meaburn Staniland, who also wrote science-fiction novels – one of which, I'm delighted to discover, was a 1947 work called *Back to the Future*. She describes him as 'the most wonderful man. Clever, tricky, a little wounded, a chain smoker, he had iconoclastic tendencies and a habit of allowing his humour to go too far. He loved literature, loved publishing (although he would never say so) and also liked a battle and was constantly on alert for what he thought was pretentious or ridiculous.'

It was under the sharp eye of Staniland that she learned 'That every word must earn its place. Never phone in statements about a book from central casting.' In those days there had been an entire department called 'Cover Editorial' since the 1960s dedicated to blurbs, and writing them was considered part of the editorial process, with the copy that went on covers

....

* The fantasy writer D. W. Vogel agrees with this sentiment: 'Jacket copy should be a burlesque show. We should be left wondering, "What's under that feather?" I'm convinced that most of the time, someone else is better at finding those feather-covered bits than the author of the book in question. We either want to give you the hardcore-everything-right-now version, or we leave things so vague that you aren't sure if you're going to see a burlesque show or an actual Canadian Goose.'

coming under the same scrutiny and revision as the words that appeared inside the book.

The craft of blurb writing helped her with the writing of her own novels: 'above all, to find its backbone, or the elevator pitch. In one sentence, what is it that makes that book that book? I wrote *Revenge of the Middle-Aged Woman*. Its backbone was the adage: "living well is the best revenge". Funnily enough, it takes a bit of practice to master that mental skill.'

As for Buchan's own experiences with authors: 'My telephone encounter with Dirk Bogarde is forever etched in the memory. "I'm in London, it's raining and life's a bitch…" What could one say? Roger McGough swung into the office. Richard Adams and Martha Gellhorn were very rude about their blurbs, Kingsley Amis very nice.' (Another ex-colleague told me that the rule was only ever to phone Amis before midday, otherwise he may have been a little tired and emotional.)

And her most challenging brief? 'There was, of course, the problem of *The Satanic Verses*, which was to be processed through Cover Editorial and had to be handled very carefully. At least, I was taught how to undo a parcel and sniff it for Semtex.' I've read the copy for the paperback of Rushdie's novel, and it is like a little work of art in itself, containing the exquisite line: 'a great wheel of a book, where the past and the future chase each other furiously'.

Another blurber-turned-author I spoke to was Jini Reddy, author of the Wainwright Prize-shortlisted *Wanderland*. She described how, apart from the endless joy of seeing something she had written on a book, being a copywriter taught her to self-edit; 'to be succinct, tight, clear and economical with words'. Importantly, it helped her to put herself in the shoes of the reader and make her own book as clear as possible: 'I don't want them to have to do the labour when they read.' She also tanta-lisingly described roller-skating along Penguin's corridors one evening after work, like Peggy in *Mad Men*. It was the 1980s. Publishing was *crazy*.

Over the years I've encountered quite a few authors. Most, even those with fearsome reputations, or the mad ones (and there are a few), were both very nice and very grateful that someone had taken the time to think about their cover copy. None of them burned their blurbs, as far as I know. John Mortimer, Helen Dunmore, David Lodge, Michael Moore, Muriel Spark – all were agreeable, and sometimes charming. I was overjoyed when Seymour Hersh, the legendary American journalist who covered the Watergate scandal, responded with 'What's not to like?'

But a delightfully wry handwritten letter from John Updike, thanking me for my blurb for *Marry Me* and *sort of* approving it, is among my prized possessions:

> I went back and looked at the front flap copy I wrote for *Marry Me* and enclose it for your contemplation, as my less giddy attempt to describe its contents. Not that I wish to impose my austere style on your own copy … I was trying to remember if Ruth does sleep with Richard; it all hazily comes back to me, and I guess she did, without great passion, before Jerry and Sally got together. Oh my; have it your way.

He included a photocopy of his original hardback blurb for *Marry Me*, which starts:

> John Updike's eighth novel is subtitled 'A Romance' because, in his words, 'People don't act like that any more.' The time is

> 1962 and the place is a fiefdom of Camelot called Greenwood, Connecticut. Jerry Conant and Sally Mathias are in love and want to get married, though they are already married to others. A diadem of five symmetrical chapters describes the course of their affair as it flickers off and on through the long summer, in an atmosphere of moral twilight.

Yes, this was the old master showing me how it was done, and for once I must break my 'authors shouldn't write blurbs' rule and accept that it is a small masterpiece, elegant and modest, just like the man himself.

Most authors are far less backwards in coming forwards, and love it when their copy is plastered with positive review quotes – who wouldn't? They usually send adorable emails saying lovely things like 'Very flattering!' or 'This is terrible for my vanity!' Sometimes they slightly miss the point and want me just to pick out reviews saying how great *they* are rather than their book. And they generally get most annoyed when they've got beef with one of the reviewers and I have to seek out and destroy the offending quote. Or, as in the case of one demanding comedian-author, they ask rather grumpily why there aren't quotes from people saying nice things about their book, without realising that they have to come from somewhere and we can't just will them into existence.

At least I didn't suffer the fate of one ex-colleague, who, after writing to a particular author with his blurb, was faced with him 'ringing me up in response to my letter, very day-drunk, and bellowing the song "Hitler has only got one ball" down the phone'. An unexpected occupational hazard.

Most of the time, however, it's a civilised and genteel process, with any tugs-of-war that occur usually resolved quite amicably.

The best author-copywriters are, in my experience, those who work as journalists too, and so instinctively understand how to boil something down to a neat pitch. I nearly fainted when I received an email from the US journalist Peter Biskind actually *cutting my copy in half.* Unheard of! It's generally the other way round, with authors seeming to forget that a book jacket only has a limited amount of space on it and can't be pulled out like a concertina, instead adding hundreds of words to their blurbs – such as the author who once told me excitedly after doing just this, 'this blurb is so comprehensive no one will have to read the book!'

Sometimes, however, authors just have an instinct for what they want. Another copywriting colleague says:

> Over the years I've written a few different versions of Donna Tartt's *The Secret History.* What I love about this novel, professionally speaking, is that you can pitch it as a literary work or as a thriller or even something that sits in that difficult-to-achieve realm between the two (which is exactly what the book is, of course). However, Donna Tartt has rejected every single one of my blurbs (just as she has rejected every attempt to replace the book's original UK cover design). As an author she knows exactly how she wants to pitch her story and as the writer of one of the most critically acclaimed and bestselling books of all time, can we say she is wrong?

So much depends on relationships. I spoke to Margaret Atwood's editor in the UK, Becky Hardie, who writes the copy for her hardbacks and happily confirmed everything I had hoped about her author: that Atwood trusts her to pitch the book in the best way, and uses only the lightest of touches to change copy. This wise little deletion of 'last' is the only change she made to her hardback blurb for *The Testaments*:

> Before you enter their world, you might want to arm yourself
> with two ~~last~~ thoughts:
>> Knowledge is power
>> *And*
>> History does not repeat itself, but it rhymes.

Isn't it great when your heroes don't let you down?

I wonder, however, how the poet Louis MacNeice felt about the blurb that his editor T. S. Eliot wrote for the cover of his early collection *Poems* in 1935? This infamous copy includes the line: 'His work is intelligible but unpopular, and has the pride and modesty of things that endure.' I suspect my career might not have endured if I'd been *that* honest. It's a similar story with Eliot's copy for Robert Graves's *The White Goddess*, which states: 'This is a prodigious, monstrous, stupefying, indescribable book.'

T. S. Eliot wrote hundreds of blurbs for Faber & Faber during his time as publisher there, including works by Ezra Pound, Stephen Spender, Marianne Moore and Ted Hughes. They were often based on his numerous and rather marvellous notes from editorial meetings (sample: 'Uncle William is looney as ever' on W. B. Yeats, which sadly didn't make it to the jacket). According to his Faber colleague, founding director Frank Morley, 'Everyone admitted that he was our best blurbwriter.' Morley continued: 'Blurbs! They are the curse of publishing … They are torture to write. Eliot wrote thousands of them. I can testify, from personal knowledge both of Eliot and of blurb-writing, that during his publishing career he has turned out so many blurbs as to make it quite impossible that he should have had time or energy left over to write anything else.'

Eliot himself described the process thus: 'Every publisher who is also an author considers this form of composition more arduous than any other that he practises ... If you praise highly, the reviewer may devote a paragraph to ridiculing the publisher's pretensions; if you try understatement, the reviewer may remark that even the publisher doesn't seem to think much of this book: I have had both experiences.'

It's an interesting insight into the tension between being both writer and copywriter. It also pleases me that a poet of such genius also took the art of blurbs very seriously, even if sometimes he was too honest in his assessments.

The celebrated André Deutsch editor Diana Athill wrote in her memoir *Stet* (which contains glorious descriptions of the ramshackle nature of post-war publishing such as 'did proper publishers have to put a board over a bath in order to make a packing-bench?') that she was so traumatised by years of writing blurbs for *The Reader's Digest Omnibus* that 'I have never looked at it again since that intensive experience'.

Blurbs are clearly a minefield for all involved. But as I become an author myself, I suppose, I understand how protective they can be of their work and the way it is presented. You spend months writing a book; it consumes you – Orwell described it as 'a horrible, exhausting struggle, like a long bout with some painful illness'. Then suddenly it's born, blinking, into the world. Trying to present its best bits to other people and to condense the complexity of what you've written into a couple of paragraphs must seem a bit crass. But a good copywriter will still put care and character into those words. It's just a different kind of writing. When you've been so involved with a book, it can be easy to forget that a potential reader hasn't read it: they don't know anything about it. You can't sell them the experience of the book – you have to sell them the expectation of reading it; the idea of it. And that's when a copywriter can be an author's best friend.

One of the consistently nicest authors I have dealt with over the years is the poet Michael Hofmann, translator of *Alone in Berlin* and many other modern classics. In one exchange, he compared the 'grapple with complexity' of writing a book to the 'straight and sunny line' of writing cover copy; the perfect way, I think, of describing the linearity and economy required for those 100 words or so.

Daniel Defoe and the Dark Arts of Persuasion

> By the way if anyone here is in advertising or marketing ...
> kill yourself. No. Seriously. Go home and kill yourself ...
> you are Satan's little helpers.

BILL HICKS, 1993

If everyone took the late stand-up legend Bill Hicks at his word, history would be littered with the corpses of publishers and booksellers from the ancient world to today, stabbing themselves with quill pens and flinging themselves into printing presses. Because pretty much as long as books have existed, in fact even before they did as the hardbacks and paperbacks we know today, those who made them wanted to sell them – and used the dark arts of marketing to do so. And even before book covers existed, there were still blurbs, of a kind, using words creatively in order to convince buyers to read on. They are prototype blurbs for prototype books.

Take the very first novel in English, Daniel Defoe's *Robinson Crusoe*, published in 1719. Its title page acts as a kind of early blurb, setting out the author's stall by telling you who, where and what, and describing the events to come:

> The Life and Strange Surprizing Adventures of Robinson
> Crusoe of York, Mariner: Who lived Eight and Twenty Years,
> all alone in an un-inhabited Island on the coast of America,
> near the Mouth of the Great River of Oroonoque;

Having been cast on Shore by Shipwreck, wherein all the
Men perished but himself.

WITH

An Account how he was at last as strangely deliver'd
by PYRATES. Written by Himself.

No qualms about giving away the entire plot here. As John
Sutherland puts it,

> The early eighteenth-century novel did not have available to
> it all the peripheral information and promotional apparatus
> of the modern novel: notably, blurbs. First readers of *Robinson
> Crusoe* needed this grotesquely over-loaded title to set them up
> and get them into the novel. Partly, too, Defoe's titular surplus
> relates to how the new novel, as a commodity, was marketed
> to the public in the eighteenth century. It was normally sold
> unbound, in 'quires', and the title pages would be hung up, on
> strings, to attract purchasers.

In effect, the title page acted as the equivalent of a modern book
cover, advertising its wares and enticing a potential reader to
buy the book. It's not too much of a stretch of the imagination
to see all those displays of title pages as a precursor to the tab-
letops in bookshops or the rows of covers shown on Amazon,
with the words on the front of them acting as very early, rudi-
mentary blurbs.

When did the first blurb appear on an actual jacket? Before
the early nineteenth century books were purchased unbound,
and often had binding commissioned by their owners, sometimes out of materials such as leather or fur (or, as shock-
ingly revealed in Edward Brooke-Hitching's *The Madman's
Library*, from human skin: 'This curious little book … has been

re-dressed in a piece of the skin of a woman tanned for myself.'
Would that make a blurb a tattoo?)

The earliest known (non-skin) dust jacket has recently been
discovered in Oxford University's Bodleian Library, for an 1830
gift book called *Friendship's Offering*. And it has a blurb! (Of
sorts.) According to the Bodleian: 'Several distinctive elements
were printed on the dust jacket: the book's price of 12 shillings;
a promotional slogan stating that the volume was "elegantly
bound"; an advertisement for the first six years of the Friendship
series "uniformly done up in the improved binding"; and another
advertisement for proofs of the engravings in portfolios.' That
all sounds suspiciously like marketing copy to me. As the name
indicates, dust jackets in the past were more like wrapping paper,
used to protect the book before you unwrapped it and put it on
your shelf. Keeping them would have been weird, like preserv-
ing the Waterstones bag you bought your book in. But at the
end of the nineteenth century the jacket increasingly became an
object for design and copy in itself, printed with striking images
and words to tempt the reader to look inside.

By 1925, the idea of the dust jacket as artwork had become
firmly established with the publication of *The Great Gatsby*. Its
striking cover painting by Cuban artist Francis Cugat, picturing
a pair of eyes staring out over Coney Island at night, took the
jacket away from wrapping and to the heart of the book's identity – it even influenced the novel itself, with Fitzgerald saying,
'For Christ's sake don't give anyone that jacket you're saving
for me. I've written it into the book.' Unlike many books of the
time, which featured advertisements for other works on their
covers, there is a rather beautiful blurb, telling us the novel 'is
infused with a sense of the strangeness of human circumstance
in a heedless universe'.

Yet even before the book cover, or even the title page, existed as a vehicle for selling copy, there were plenty of other ways to reach your audience. Let me channel my inner Mary Beard and take you back to ancient Rome, where pre-codex 'books' were papyrus scrolls with a wooden rod at each end for rolling and unrolling. Papyrus was relatively cheap, and there was a large reading population, who were catered for by numerous book-shops (*taberna librarii*), mostly lining the busy streets near the Colosseum. Their fronts would be covered with advertisements for the books inside, sometimes featuring choice quotes from the books themselves – which led Martial to tell a friend not to bother going inside as you could 'read all the poets' outside anyway.

Martial, poet and inventor of the epigram, also wisely inserted a few words of puffery at the beginning of one of his volumes, to convince the reader of the quality of the work they are considering: 'I trust that, in these little books of mine, I have observed such self-control, that whoever forms a fair judgment from his own mind can make no complaint of them.' If there was no cover, presumably readers might take a look inside, so this was an ideal place to catch their attention.

Although the rectangular folded codex we recognise as a book today was initially developed in Ancient Rome – invented by Julius Caesar, according to some – it wasn't until around the fourth century CE that it really caught on and replaced the scroll entirely. Initially these were made from animal skin parchment – hence the 'spine' of a book – and were therefore rare and precious objects. Then paper came along (thanks, China), followed by Gutenberg and his printing press in 1439 (thanks, Germany) – insert 'time is passing' style montage here – and suddenly books were everywhere. For the first time in history, hundreds of readers could own the same book, and by the mid-sixteenth century readers could choose from some eight million printed books. The market was heating up.

According to a piece titled 'Medieval Spam' by the Dutch scholar of manuscripts Erik Kwakkel, 'During the last three centuries of the Middle Ages (1200–1500) the demand for books rapidly increased, in part because of their cheaper production and the growing numbers of readers. Increased demand had a major impact on supply: urban professionals took over book production from the abbeys. They started to charge money, make profit, and build the commercial book market we still have today.' And where there were books, there were adverts for books, on posters in windows ('pick a pretty letter and I'll make you a book!'), in books themselves, or in flyers posted in public. Bill Hicks would *not* be happy.

The oldest surviving printed advertisement in English was produced by the pioneering printer and publisher William Caxton, and it was for a book. It is a tiny bit of paper, or flyer, promoting a religious handbook printed by him at his Westminster workshop in *c.*1477. It tells potential buyers where to find the book, reassures them that it is 'well and truly correct', cheap to buy, and, most importantly, 'emprynted after the forme of this present lettre' (in other words printed in the same type-face as the ad): the proof of the quality is there in the reading. And the target market? Priests, of course. This is supported by the inscription in Latin, the language of religion, which says 'Supplico stet cedula', or 'Please do not remove this notice', while its small size indicates that it would have been put up somewhere quiet and unassuming, like a church porch.

And, just as today, the book itself was used as a piece of marketing. For example, in the back of one late medieval book a scribe called Herneis writes: 'If someone else would like such a handsome book, come and look me up in Paris, across from the Notre Dame cathedral.' Or in a fifteenth-century Dutch book: 'If you like this copy of the Old Testament, I can also produce a book with the New Testament for you.' Call it an early 'If you like this, try this' form of marketing. As Professor Kwakkel (I love that name) notes, 'This tempting offer has the feel of iTunes' "Complete my album" or, more appropriately, the suggestions Amazon makes for further reading.'

All these are ways of selling to a reader and using cleverly chosen words to do so. And, the more I looked at early books, the more I kept seeing prototype blurbs everywhere: especially, as with Defoe, on the front.

For example, the title page for a 1672 reprint of a book called *The Famous Game of Chesse-play* shows two nattily dressed bearded men at the board and guarantees that readers will learn 'more by reading of this small Book, than by playing of a thousand Mates. Now augmented in many material things formerly wanting.'

The book's 'Epistle Dedicatory', addressed to the Countess of Bedford, describes how the author has tried to improve on the previous version, while still respecting the original and keeping 'his Phrase and Stile whole, as farre as I might'. Dedicatory epistles, or letters, to a book's sponsor, used to express gratitude and hopes for their continued favour, were common, and in the view of writer Roberto Calasso were the 'noble forebears' of blurbs – they take pains to describe what we are about to read, and to assure us of its brilliance.*

....

* Sometimes they were used for more subversive purposes, such as Walter Scott's mock dedication to 'The Rev. Dr. Dryasdust' at the start of *Ivanhoe*, an ironic defence against those who criticised his novels' historical inaccuracies.

Even the title page of the first edition of the King James Bible gets in on the act, in 1611:

THE HOLY BIBLE, Conteyning the Old Testament and the New. Newly translated out of Originall tongues & with the former Translations diligently compared and revised by his Majesties Speciall Comandement. Appointed to be read in Churches, Imprinted at London by Robert Barker, Printer to the Kings most Excellent Majestie. Anno Dom 1611.

It is an assurance of quality; a guarantee that you are going to get the very best (and, presumably, that it's safe to read it without being burned at the stake). And, in the manner of the dedicatory epistle, the 'Preface to the Reader' by the translators states: 'Translation it is that openeth the window, to let in the light; that breaketh the shell, that we may eat the kernel; that putteth aside the curtain, that we may look into the most holy place; that removeth the cover of the well, that we may come by the water.' It uses glorious language to invite and to reassure.

This language of persuasion is also apparent on the title pages of far less lofty works. From about the mid-sixteenth century to the nineteenth, book pedlars and hawkers sold short, flimsy, pocket-sized paper booklets which became known as 'chapbooks' – or 'small books' or 'merryments'. Often crudely illustrated, this cheap form of street, or folk, literature was created for a genuinely popular readership all over Europe, and sold millions.* Chapbooks included ballads, religious stories,

---

* In an age when paper was expensive, they were often recycled, hence their nickname 'bum fodder'. For further toilet-related fun, the word 'bumf', or 'bumph', is a shortened version of this.

histories, fairy tales, cut-down 'classics' such as *Gulliver's Travels* and, above all, racy, sometimes gruesome tales of ghosts, adventure, romance, battles and crimes (sample title: *The Groans of the Gallows*), later morphing into the infamous Victorian 'penny dreadfuls' and 'shilling shockers'. Their sensational narratives were loved by readers from Samuel Pepys to Robert Louis Stevenson.

Of course, being economical to produce, chapbooks had no covers, but their title pages act as wonderful early examples of proto-blurbs. A nineteenth-century edition of *Spring Heeled Jack: The Terror of London* boasts it is 'NOW READY', and consists of 'Twenty-four plates, splendidly illustrated, in handsome wrapping.'

> The History of this Remarkable Being has been splendidly compiled, for this work only, by one of the Best Authors of the day, and our readers will find that he has undoubtedly succeeded in producing a Wonderful and Sensational Story, every page of which is replete with details of absorbing and thrilling interest.

Quality, and thrills: how could you resist?

A Glasgow chapbook recounting the adventures of Jack the Giant Killer states that it contains: 'His Birth and Parentage – His meeting with the King's Son – His noble Conquests over many monstrous Giants – and, his relieving a beautiful Lady, whom he afterward married.' (As with *Robinson Crusoe*'s title page, they don't quite grasp the concept of holding back the plot twists.)

Sometimes chapbooks had a far more urgent and serious purpose. Thomas Paine's *The Rights of Man*, written in support of the French Revolution, was reprinted in chapbook form after its initial publication and sold millions. Its first page is a textbook piece of marketing, in that it gives us a one-line 'elevator' pitch, and the author's credentials: 'Being an Answer to Mr Burke's Attack on the French Revolution. By Thomas Paine Secretary for Foreign Affairs to Congress in the American Civil War and author of the work intitled *Common Sense*.'

The seventeenth century saw the unprecedented production of pamphlets: low-cost political or religious tracts using vigorous language to convince others of their cause. They reached their zenith in the English Civil War, as historian Tristram Hunt notes: 'While books were formerly weighty tomes, pamphlets and broadsides appeared, written in easy, accessible English often shouted through the streets.' They encompassed 'some of the most fertile religious and political debate in European history ... Few periods can lay claim to such a hold on the English language.'

There was even a pamphlet purportedly composed by King Charles I and published just after his execution in 1649, defending himself from his enemies and presenting himself as a godlike martyr: 'Eikon Basilike or the Pourtraicture of His Sacred Majestie in his Solitudes and Sufferings.' Note the strength of the alliteration here. The title page also tells us that it contains 'a perfect Copy of Prayers used by his Majesty in the time of his sufferings. Delivered to Dr JUXON Bishop of London, immediately before his Death.' The genuine article, straight from the horse's mouth – what more of a hook could a potential reader need?

The pamphlets of this time are things of wonder for the richness, invention and dramatic force with which they use the English language, as royalists and Parliamentarians, Ranters,

Diggers, Levellers, Muggletonians and Quakers all shouted for attention in a war of words, which became a matter of life and death.

One particularly head-spinning example is by John Taylor, a waterman turned satirist and supporter of the king, who was engaged in a brutal and ongoing pamphlet war with the iron-monger and parliamentarian Henry Walker. As each sought to undermine the other, one of Taylor's 1641 missives included a pamphlet whose title page spits out the words:

> A Reply as true as Steele, to a Rusty, Rayling, Ridiculous, Lying, Libell; which was lately written by an impudent unsoder'd Ironmonger and called by the name of An Answer to a foolish Pamphlet Entssuled, A Swarme of Sectaries and Schismatiques. The Divill is hard bound and did hardly straine; to shit a Libeller a knave in graine.

This is rhetoric in overdrive. And it is accompanied by a wood-cut of, yes, a rather shocked-looking Devil literally shitting out Taylor's opponent.

Before the advent of newspapers, pamphlets were the ideal way to get your point across as powerfully as possible. Perhaps the greatest pamphleteer of his age was Jonathan Swift, who wrote everything from attacks on British rule in Ireland to broadsides against astrology, and, most famously, his savage satirical essay *A Modest Proposal*, which argued that poverty in Ireland could be eased by eating the children of the poor.* Compared to the

---

* Its influence could still be felt in 2020, when it was used as a tongue-in-cheek response to the UK government's refusal to extend free school meals over the holidays.

information-rich title pages of Swift's contemporaries, the front of *A Modest Proposal* deliberately holds back. It simply says: 'A Modest Proposal For preventing the Children of Poor People From being a Burthen to Their Parents or Country, and For making them Beneficial to the Publick.' That's all you get. The true horror awaits inside. In this sense, this title page fulfils the function of a good piece of copy: it piques the reader's interest and leaves us wanting more.

Coming back full circle to the time of Defoe again then, when books as we know them were still in their infancy (or maybe their rebellious teenage years), the words used to sell them give us a strange insight into the mental lives of others. Looking at these embryonic blurbs from across the ages – from medieval spam to rhetorical pamphleteering – made the past feel at once alien and bizarre to me, and yet spookily familiar too.

This was, after all, a time when printing led to a deluge of words, just as today's book market is often described as 'flooded' and readers as 'bombarded' with information. And as modern marketing and blurbs are criticised as 'hype', so the tracts, cheap books and adverts of the past were often treated rather warily, as somewhat lesser, more sensational forms of writing. Then as now, each writer had to try to shout louder than the other, to grab the attention of a potential reader. What remains constant is the power of words: to persuade and, yes, to sell, whether it's a story or an idea. Perhaps those of us involved in marketing may be Satan's little helpers, but I think trying to sell books is worth risking the fiery pits of Hell. So let us publish and be damned.

Great Expectations
How Dickens Kept Them Wanting More

Charles Dickens's children said they always knew when he was writing a book because they could *hear* him. He created characters through their voices, and would practise their verbal tics in front of a mirror. Everyone in his books has their own idiolect, or distinctive way of speaking – to the extent that when I read other authors, the dialogue sometimes becomes mush. You *always* know who is talking in a Dickens novel, whether it's the fabulous Mr Jingle in *The Pickwick Papers* ('Present! Think I was; fired a musket, – fired with an idea, – rushed into wine shop – wrote it down – whiz, bang!'), Betsey 'Donkeys!' Trotwood or the demonic Quilp in *The Old Curiosity Shop*: 'I'll scratch you with a rusty nail, I'll pinch your eyes!'* This, for me, is one of the many marks of Dickens's genius.

On the two hundredth anniversary of Dickens's birth I decided, along with some game colleagues, to read all of his novels, one a month, and in doing so realised I'd made a friend for life. Dickens creates more memorable characters in one book than most writers manage in their whole careers. He is also more experimental than he is given credit for, shifting tenses and perspectives unexpectedly, juxtaposing laughter with

* Curiously, Quilp also tries to start a fight with a dog for no reason at one point.

horror, obsessively repeating words with incantatory power, and drawing on the wellsprings of his strange, dark and frightening imagination to create an idiosyncratic reading experience that can feel unnervingly modern. As Professor John Mullan says, he is an innovator. Dickens is even, according to Mullan, 'the first novelist to make smell a narrative device'.

Yet there are still certain readers, writers and critics who look down on Dickens, seeing him as a bit silly and sentimental and not quite worthy of the serious 'greats' such as Dostoyevsky, Tolstoy or Zola. This, as far as I can tell, is for three reasons: Dickens liked plots, he was incredibly popular and, above all, he is funny. The three cardinal sins of commercial fiction.

I would like to add another element into the mix of Dickens's genius, one which also often results in a certain kind of literary sneering: he was the ultimate self-promoter. A master of marketing. Dickens knew how to create excitement, to speak to readers and keep them wanting more.

Roland Barthes wrote of the 'hermeneutic code': that is, the art of deliberately creating a question that must be answered, withholding information from the reader to create suspense. The pleasure of reading comes from finding out. Here are five reasons why I think Dickens exemplified this better than anyone:

I. HE CREATED A SENSE OF MYSTERY ABOUT HIMSELF.

When, in August 1834, Dickens decided to sign off one of his early sketches of London life with the pseudonym 'Boz',* he

....

* 'Boz' was inspired by the nickname 'Moses' that he used to give his younger brother, which, when pronounced with a pinched nose, became 'Boses'.

was, in the words of his biographer Peter Ackroyd, 'fabricating a minor mystery about the author himself'. His literary alter ego became a huge source of speculation among readers, who were desperate to discover his identity. A poem written a few years later acknowledges this:

> Who the dickens 'Boz' could be,
> Puzzled many a learned elf,
> Till time unveiled the mystery,
> And 'Boz' appeared as Dickens's self.

As well as conjuring up an authorial myth, Dickens also showed commercial nous when he rejected his publisher's rather whimsical title suggestion of *Bubbles from the Bwain of Boz and the Graver of Cruikshank* and wisely came up with the far more selling *Sketches by Boz and Cuts by Cruikshank* – at the time the illustrator George Cruikshank was far more famous than the modest young writer. Before publication he worked hard, along with his publisher, to ensure favourable puffs from reviewers, sending out advance copies to all those he knew with influence in the literary world. It was an investment that paid off, as *The Pickwick Papers* was commissioned as a result of Boz's success.

2. HE UNDERSTOOD THE POWER OF SUSPENSE IN AN ERA OF SERIALISATION.

Before *Pickwick*, many novels were published in three volumes, known as the 'triple-decker'. Dickens broke the mould. He wasn't the first to use the serialisation form, but he made it his own.

The monthly instalments of *The Pickwick Papers*, appearing in pale green wrappers at the price of a shilling (with, in place of a blurb, the traditional wordy title page), created a frenzy of excitement among readers. This reached fever pitch when Dickens, noticing sales were sluggish, introduced the comic cockney Sam Weller and saw the numbers rocket (also around the time that 'Boz's' true identity was revealed). So the form itself led to new selling opportunities and allowed him to respond directly to the market. According to Professor Kate Flint, 'The wild success of *The Pickwick Papers* is widely considered to have established the viability and appeal of the serialised format.'*

The serial was also the perfect vehicle for advertising: by the time *Pickwick* had reached its ninth instalment, its 'Pickwick Advertiser' section included more pages of ads – ranging from Rotterdam Corn and Bunion Solvent to 'Simpson's new Antibilious Pill' – than pages of text.

Which brings me to:

3. HE EMBRACED A COMMERCIAL AGE.

The nineteenth century was a time of unbridled consumerism. Advertising billboards, leaflets, posters and flyers were ubiquitous; they appeared on packaging, in magazines, journals, newspapers and books. Just like today's TV viewers, the Victorian consumer was used to having their storytelling experience broken up by commercials, to experiencing different modes of reading and to being distracted by splashy ad messages. One prime example of this is the back cover of a 'yellow-back'

....

* For anyone who thinks *Pickwick* may be a lesser work, by the way, I beg you to read it. It is hilarious, everyone is drunk *all* the time, and it contains a surprising early use of the word 'gammon' as an insult.

book (cheap, popular books bound in yellow boards with an eye-catching image on the front, portable and perfect for the new breed of nineteenth-century railway travellers who could buy them at station kiosks such as W. H. Smith). It shows an extended hand reaching out as if through the binding itself, accompanied by the greeting 'good morning' and the question: 'have you used Pears' soap?'

4. HE WAS HIS OWN BEST ADVERTISEMENT.

Dickens was a showman. He had dreamed of being an actor as a young man, appearing in a few productions. He enjoyed performing magic tricks and readings for his friends, and he *loved* performing in public, famed later in life for his sold-out reading tours of the country. Dickens amended his own texts to make them suitable for reading aloud, emphasising certain passages, inserting pauses, and noting which facial expression he should use at which point, often revising them according to audience reactions. He worked tirelessly on practising his delivery. He even lowered his reading podium so that audiences could better see his well-rehearsed gestures.

The biggest hit was his famed performance of the murder of Nancy by Bill Sikes in *Oliver Twist*, which against much advice, he chose to give the public a 'sensation'. According to biographer Claire Tomalin, 'He went on to give the murder reading twenty-eight times between January 1869 and March 1870, and the effect was just as he had hoped, exciting and horrifying his audiences.' He would lie, prostrate and speechless, on a sofa after these exertions, until revived with a glass of champagne.

Forget today's author tours. Dickens lived every moment

of his reading; he *became* his novels and they became him. And of course his writing lends itself to theatre: the sense of *grand guignol*, the voices, the force of his rhetoric ('It was the best of times, it was the worst of times'). This deliberate repetition of a word at the beginning of a sentence or clause is known as anaphora, and Dickens was a dab hand – apparently, his longest string of sentences starting with the same word is twenty-six, in his novella *The Haunted Man*. As John Mullan says, 'Other novelists might aim for eloquence, balance or wit; Dickens goes for stranger powers: incantation, intensification, repetition. He knew that his sentences were unusual.'

5. HE KNEW HOW TO ADAPT.

For many people, including me, *Great Expectations* is Dickens's greatest novel. It is dark, strange, primal, haunted and mysterious, psychologically complex (Howard Jacobson memorably described how 'the shame makes the pages curl') while at the same time tautly structured. And one of the reasons for this concision was the needs of the market. When Dickens realised that sales of his weekly journal *All the Year Round* were falling, he decided to abandon the initial plan of monthly instalments for the new novel he was working on, and instead wrote it to be serialised weekly in his publication – meaning he had to write faster and tighter. And so *Great Expectations* was born. Its narrative is of course full of mystery upon mystery, and even its title is a mystery waiting to be solved. To rack the tension up as far as possible, Dickens advertised his forthcoming book in *All the Year Round* a month before publication:

GREAT EXPECTATIONS

NEW WORK BY MR CHARLES DICKENS

In no. 84 of All the Year Round, to be published on Saturday,
December the First

GREAT EXPECTATIONS BY CHARLES DICKENS

To be continued from week to week until completed in about
EIGHT MONTHS

Great Expectations was greeted with positive reviews, one of which, from the *Atlantic* in 1861, emphasises the suspense inherent in the work: 'The very title of this book indicates the confidence of conscious genius. The felicity with which expectation was excited and prolonged, and to the series of surprises, which accompanied the unfolding of the plot ... In no other of his romances has the author succeeded so perfectly in at once stimulating and baffling the curiosity of his readers. He stirred the dullest minds to guess the secret of his mystery.'

This is it: the hermeneutic code made real. The secret is withheld, and guessing it is exquisite pleasure. The tension between mystery and disclosure – *What's happening here? What is going to happen?* – is at the heart of novel writing, marketing, advertising and blurb writing. With *Great Expectations*, as throughout his whole career, Dickens kept them waiting, kept them excited, and gave them what they wanted at the very deepest level. Satisfying our curiosity: it's the reason we buy books, and why we read.

As a final aside, there was another marketing triumph taking place across the Channel around the same time as *Great Expectations*, with the publication of Victor Hugo's *Les Misérables* in 1862. Hugo's publicity manager hit on the idea of generating some advance buzz for the novel by promoting it through a billboard campaign. According to David Bellos, 'twenty-five illustrations of the characters of the novel commissioned for the illustrated edition that would appear a year later were printed on posters and plastered all over Paris. Nothing like it had ever been done for a book.'

It sounds remarkably like a teaser campaign you might see for a new series of *Game of Thrones*, if you replace Fantine with the face of Arya Stark. The publicity manager also sent out press releases that could not go public until the day the book came out, just like today's 'event publishing', where the contents of a particularly sensational book may be embargoed until publication. In marketing, someone else always gets there first.

Hemingway's Wager

For sale, baby shoes: never worn. This is Ernest Hemingway's famous six-word story. It is a perfect miniature tragedy. There are several (longer) stories surrounding its origins, one of which claims that it resulted from a bet at a literary lunch, which Hemingway won after composing this tiny tearjerker on a napkin. According to some, he never even wrote it, and the whole thing was a fabrication by a literary agent. Wherever the truth lies, this apocryphal tale is the perfect example of using as few words as possible to achieve as much as possible – and in this sense, it is a cousin of the blurb. It illustrates not only the beauty of brevity, but also how our minds immediately turn to story, filling in the gaps and creating a whole series of imaginary events around the barest of bones.

The art of telling a story in as few words as possible, otherwise known as flash fiction, has roots going as far back as ancient fables, but is perhaps perfectly suited to our age – hence the 280-character-long 'Twitterature' phenomenon. Exploring its various forms takes you down a rabbit hole into a Lilliputian world of small pleasures. Many other writers, it turns out, have written six-word stories like Hemingway's, which are inclined towards the witty rather than the wistful:

'Longed for him. Got him. Shit.' Margaret Atwood
'Easy. Just touch the match to' Ursula K. Le Guin
'Machine. Unexpectedly, I'd invented a time' Alan Moore

Hemingway's purported original also spawned a genre called the six-word memoir, some of which were published in a book called *Not Quite What I Was Planning*, including such gems as Joyce Carol Oates's 'Revenge is living well, without you', and Joan Rivers's 'Liars, hysterectomy didn't improve sex life!'

In 2020 the *New York Times* asked readers to send in their responses to the Covid pandemic as six-word memoirs. The results are wry, often rather touching peeps into our everyday lives under lockdown: 'Bad time for an open marriage'; 'Read every book in the house'; 'Social distancing myself from the fridge'; 'The world has never felt smaller.'

Compressed fiction is playful, which is why it is often a favourite of science-fiction and fantasy writers, also lending itself well to suspense or shock, such as Colin Greenland's eight-word mini-story: 'Aliens disguised as typewriters? I've never heard such—' Or there is this 'shortest horror story in the world', which I used to thrill over when I was young: 'The last man on Earth sat alone in a room. There was a knock on the door.' I seem to remember it being a kind of playground joke, only discovering years later that it was the creation of an actual mystery writer, Fredric Brown.

Jorge Luis Borges, whose fantastical writings took him into otherworldly realms, was a fan of flash fiction. He created this eleven-word short story with his fellow countryman and writer Adolfo Bioy Casares: 'The stranger climbed the stairs in the dark: tick-tock, tick-tock, tick-tock.' The foreboding is exquisite, and the repetition suggests a nightmare that will never end.

But these little morsels are just the start, it turns out. There are also variations of flash fiction including the 'Dribble' of fifty words and, most excitingly to me, the 'Drabble', or a 'microfiction' of 100 words. Many writers have tried their hands at

Drabbles, including Neil Gaiman, who, he says, 'failed misera-bly' and couldn't get his below 102 words. Eventually he gave up, and made the first two words the title of his story, 'Nicholas Was'. It is a gleefully sinister Christmas tale. And it made me think: is the blurb the same thing as a Drabble? Have I been Drabbling all these years?

In one sense of course not, as I am writing to sell the words of somebody else rather than express my own. But in another sense, yes. Writing short, for whatever reason you do it, forces rigour, and it reminds you that words are a precious and pow-erful resource. Form both limits and liberates.

There are some writers who take precision to a peerless art. One of these is International Booker Prize winner Lydia Davis. She has been called the world's most concise short story writer, which is great news if you're a lazy reader like me, but also because she's just *so* good. Her works are the very definition of small but mighty, playing with form, mood, style and tone in a few words, like Jane Austen with her fine brush on her 'little bit (not two inches wide) of irony', except that Davis often likes to paint it black. As Ali Smith says, 'A two-liner from Davis, or a seemingly throwaway paragraph, will haunt.'

Davis's short story 'The Outing' is a mere sixty words, yet those sixty words manage to be propulsive, funny, clever, moving and slightly sinister at the same time. Plus, its sentiments will be familiar to anyone who has attempted a new walk from a Pathfinder Guide with their loved one in muddy countryside, and found their relationship tested:

An outburst of anger near the road, a refusal to speak on the path, a silence in the pine woods, a silence across the old rail-road bridge, an attempt to be friendly in the water, a refusal to end the argument on the flat stones, a cry of anger on the steep bank of dirt, a weeping among the bushes.

The honour of greatest short, short story in the world, however, has to go to Franz Kafka for 'Little Fable', which wasn't even published in his lifetime. Thank the gods that it eventually was. It's like the purest little drop of poison, but it's funny too, as is so much of Kafka's writing. Never before have the bleakness of existence and a good punchline been so winningly combined. And so I leave Kafka with the last word in how to make short say everything:

LITTLE FABLE

'Oh no,' the mouse said, 'The world gets smaller by the day. At first it was so big that I was scared, I ran and ran, and was so happy when I finally glimpsed the walls in the distance to the right and left. But these long walls hurry towards each other so quickly that I'm already in the last room, and just there in the corner is the trap I'm running into.'

'You only need to change direction,' said the cat and gobbled him up.

I talians Do it Better

Picture, if you will, a customer picking up a book in a bookshop:

> He takes a brief glance at the cover flap, hoping for some assistance. At that moment, without realizing it, he is opening an envelope: those few lines, external to the text of the book, are like a letter written to a stranger.

When I first read these words by the Italian publisher and author Roberto Calasso, I nearly wept with gratitude. Finally, somebody understood how important blurbs were. Not just that, he also described the blurb as 'a humble and arduous literary form for which there is as yet no theorist or historian' (I'm here! Call me!) and a 'cramped rhetorical space, less fascinating than that of a sonnet but equally exacting'. Now I really feel I'm in exalted company. A poet of publishing, no less.

I don't think anyone has written as eloquently on the creation of cover copy as Calasso did in 'A Letter to a Stranger', an essay in his book *The Art of the Publisher*. He saw every single element of a book – covers, paper, blurbs, publicity material, layout, design – as part of a chain in a whole, creating, in his words, 'a single text', just as all the books produced by a publishing house make up a body of work. For him, publishing is an art, and the words on the book as well as inside it are part of that art; integral to a book's history and identity.

Described as a 'literary institution of one' by the *Paris Review*, Roberto Calasso was, until his death in 2021, publisher at Adelphi in Milan, translator, expert on ancient myths and writer of mysterious, vertiginous books about art, history and civilisation. As well as all this, he also wrote the blurbs for every book he published at Adelphi – according to him, over a thousand at the time of 'A Letter to a Stranger'.

I enjoy the notion of a blurb as a letter to just one person, because that's how I think when I write. Just as Terry Wogan said of his days as a radio DJ, 'You are not talking to an audience, you are talking to one person – and they are only half listening anyway.' Whoever my solitary, mysterious reader may be, I seek to make a connection with them. They could know nothing of the book in their hand. It is the job of the words on the cover to introduce them to it – well, the best bits anyway.

Calasso is honest about the dishonesty of blurbs. He writes of how he strives to compose something that can be taken 'at face value'. But he also admits how difficult the art of praise can be, how endlessly challenging it is to use adjectives minimally and with variety ('repetition and limitation are part of our nature').

Yes, Roberto Calasso was obsessed with blurbs. If we had ever had the chance to duke it out over who was the most obsessed, at some publishing rumble in the jungle, I would have gracefully conceded. But it gets even better. In 2003 Calasso also published a book in Italian called *Cento lettere a uno sconosciuto* ('100 Letters to a Stranger'). It is *literally* a book made up entirely of 100 blurbs he wrote over the years, for works by authors including Karen Blixen, Milan Kundera and Samuel Butler, in no particular logical order. What unbridled joy, to be able to luxuriate in a book purely made of your own blurbs. Maybe I'll just staple mine together.

Unfortunately, *Cento lettere* hasn't been translated into English, but the Italian writer Daniela Cascella has translated some of its entries for the radical online journal *3:AM Magazine* (their motto: 'Whatever it is, we're against it'). It is clear from her article that Calasso's flap copy has become something of a legend in Italy. She quotes the opening of his blurb for *Lolita*: 'America *is* Lolita, Lolita *is* America', and notes that 'many Italians of my generation will still remember this sentence ... a lightning bolt of awareness'. Oh, to have one's blurbs held in such esteem.

It also becomes clear that Adelphi blurbs are completely idiosyncratic: opinionated and enigmatic, often exclamatory, rather like blurbs from a few decades ago rather than the clear, punchy copy of today: 'A nervous, phosphorescent mobility of style, an endless germination of images ... This book speaks of everything. And it leaves nothing intact ... The "sacrilegious azure" of this prose, a colour, a timbre ... give us a shock of secret euphoria.'

These blurbs don't introduce or explain, but, in Cascella's words, 'suggest possible ways of being with books, inside them'. For her, they are a mystery or a secret to be deciphered, the start of an exploration. They're not a come-on; they don't even try to persuade. They just *are*. They are more akin to mini-works of literary criticism than blurbs: 'The sexual charge that had accumulated in the end of the century, tentatively hidden in the greenhouse of Liberty where sexuality ends up censoring itself in the birth of abstraction, explodes with no precautions in Frank Wedekind.' I can't imagine myself ever describing the work of a German playwright thus. And I'm none the wiser about what's going on in that greenhouse.

This is the complete opposite of how I see blurbs: the dance between divulging and withholding, the focus on the voice of the book or author rather than my own. We hear Calasso's voice, and his opinions. And who is to say which approach is better: objective or subjective? There's probably no way of proving it. As the businessman John Wanamaker noted over a century ago, 'Half the money I spend on advertising is wasted; the trouble is I don't know which half.'

The point of Calasso's 'book of blurbs' is not to create a work of literary criticism, however. Rather, I think, it's another strand in his argument that every part of a book tells a story, and each book in turn is part of the wider story of a publisher. The blurb for *Cento lettere*, translated from Italian, supports this: 'This book is a first guide to that possible world that has manifested itself in a forest of pages under the name Adelphi … And over the course of forty years numerous readers have noticed how, to keep these books together, there is something, a tenacious bond. We have tried to indicate this tenacious bond from the beginning, in the only form in which the publisher accompanies each single book: the flap on the cover.' A blurb for a book of blurbs; bliss.

Calasso has helped me to decode the magic of the copy that appears on a book. Even though we had different methods and aims in writing blurbs, I've come to realise that they are part of a book's life and existence; a little piece of literary history in their own right.

Incidentally, the Italian word for 'blurb' is 'note di copertina'. In French, it either seems to be 'le texte de la jaquette' or 'le baratin', which also means spiel, waffle, patter or claptrap. How rude. In Spanish it's 'la propaganda', and the Greek word for blurb is 'ypervolikí angelía' (or 'excessive advertising'). 'Note di copertina' is the most sophisticated, and the kindest, description by far. As usual, Italians do it better.

The Medium is the Massage (in Three Acts)

'The classic collide-oscope of our time, a laser-beam look-around to see what's happening!' The first line of the blurb on the original edition of the cult classic *The Medium is the Massage* couldn't be more 1960s if it was wearing kinky boots and eyeliner.* So why does Marshall McLuhan's book about the rise of the mass media still matter today – and what does it have to do with blurbs?

1. As well as being fabulously of its time, this totemic 1967 book is ridiculously ahead of it. It prophesied how the 'electric technology' used to communicate information would ultimately become more powerful than the information itself. According to McLuhan, the media 'works us over completely', remaking our senses, our brains and, as Douglas Coupland later put it, 'our souls'. Anyone who's lost an entire evening doom-scrolling on Twitter might be inclined to agree. McLuhan's depiction of modern life as a global village and 'one big gossip column that

---

* The book's title is allegedly a serendipitous mistake. Apparently it should have been *The Medium is the Message*, but the typesetter made an error. When McLuhan saw it he said, 'Leave it alone! It's great, and right on target!' It *is* on target, reminding us that we are being softened up for selling.

is unforgiving, unforgetting and from which there is no redemption, no erasure of early "mistakes"' could have been written for the social media age. (Perhaps book covers – the packaging that takes precedence over the contents – are an example of this too, although I like to think of them as a fairly gentle massage.)

2. As well as its prophetic power, the language of *The Medium is the Massage* – more specifically, how it works as a visual essay – is also instructive. A collaboration between McLuhan and graphic designer Quentin Fiore, it's the perfect fusion of text and image, using the effects of film – jump cuts, shifts in scale, cropping – to drive the pace and keep you reading. Words are broken up and cropped so that our eyes dart all over the place. They are made either tiny or HUGE, Alice in Wonderland-style. There is backwards mirror writing, upside-down writing, big cartoon-like BANGS!, all spliced with photography, collage, illustration and graphic art. It disrupts language. It enhances and plays with the meaning of words, tricking and teasing us with signs and signifiers to prove its own point: that we are being manipulated.*

3. The best thing about Marshall McLuhan, however, is that he invented the 'Page 69 Test'. Forget covers, blurbs, reviews or introductions. Forget the book's first line. If you want to know if you're going to enjoy a book, open it at page 69. If you like what you read, buy the book. By then, the author has settled into their story and stopped showing off. I wondered if McLuhan just thought '69' sounded a

---

* *The Medium is the Massage* breaks the rules of what a text should do. It is also fun to read, which is always something to bear in mind when writing copy.

bit rude, but lo, I turned to said page of *The Medium is the Massage* and found a neat little aphorism nestled in there, along with a curious illustration of three men dressed like Musketeers, with geometric shapes shooting from their hands and… noses? So maybe it works – or more likely he just made his page 69 extra good to prove his point.

To find out, I thought I'd better test the theory on some of my favourite books. It worked! Each page 69 seemed emblematic of the book to me in some way. *What a Carve Up!* made me chuckle. *Tales of the City* was delightful. *A Little Life* was exquisite and chilling. *My Brilliant Friend* was intriguing, with a hint of violence. *Jane Eyre* was the best, landing on the scene where Jane socks it to the evil Mrs Reed with both barrels: 'People think you are a good woman, but you are bad, hard-hearted. You are deceitful!'

What about the books I had always meant to read, which sit there on my shelf like guilty reminders – an ever-present to-do list? Well, *Madame Bovary* (for shame) was much pacier than I'd anticipated, with some snappy dialogue and neat description. *Catch-22* sounded more knockabout and zany than the behemoth I'd feared. And Stefan Zweig's *Beware of Pity* was completely gripping – why hadn't I read this before? It's now moved from my 'pile of self-improving books' to my 'pile of books to be read for enjoyment'.

So, if the idea of reading a blurb really doesn't turn you on, baby (as somebody might have said in the 1960s), why not try the Page 69 Test, and put me out of a job?

An Odyssey Through the Classics

> Definition of a classic: a book everyone is assumed to have
> read and often thinks they have.
>
> ALAN BENNETT

When it comes to literature, the word 'classic' has connotations of eating our greens or listening to a squeaky bit of modern orchestral music: something we feel we should do because it's good for us; intellectually, or even morally, improving. The Italian writer Italo Calvino identified fourteen criteria for a book being a classic, the first of which is that people always say they're 're-reading', rather than 'reading' it: heaven forfend we should confess to never having picked up *Ulysses* or *Moby-Dick*.

My definition of a classic would be a book you were made to read, often resentfully, at school, and then realised to your annoyance either (a) at the time or (b) years later that it was actually great, and a 'classic' for a reason. As Nora Ephron says of Wilkie Collins's *The Woman in White*, 'How could I have waited so long to read this book?' I remember reading *Jane Eyre* for the first time as a teenager, and thinking, 'Oh right, now I see what the fuss is all about.' There was something about Jane's voice that was so insistent, so nakedly emotional, that it wouldn't let me go. She is the ultimate narrator as earworm.

Yet although the classics can be glorious, the experience of reading them *is* somehow different from other kinds of books. In *The Year of Reading Dangerously* Andy Miller notes that classics are 'not always straightforward or entertaining … a great book does not have to be a good read to be a great book.' They often require more effort, either in acquainting yourself with unfamiliar idioms, or in their length and pace, but the effort is rewarded.

My most important classics principle, however, is this: some of them are definitely better than others, and you don't have to like all of them. Magical realism, the Beats and most 'Great American Novels' have never done it for me, and I am at peace with that.

Classics are freighted with history; the notion that millions of other people before us have read, deciphered and internalised these books, and that the books in turn have influenced their times. Just as reading the classics is a constant process of assimilation and re-evaluation, the way we sell classics to the reader also adapts with each generation. How has the way publishers package and write blurbs for classic literature changed over the years? How do you keep attracting readers to books that they may already know the plots of or, worst of all, associate with school?

For many years, publishers took a kind of 'take it or leave it' attitude, and dispensed with blurbs entirely, presumably because it was felt that these famous books didn't need any kind of description. The Penguin Classics series, born in 1946 with the publication of retired publisher E. V. Rieu's translation of *The Odyssey*,* was designed with appropriately classical simplicity by John Overton. Book covers were colour-coded according to the work's language of origin, featuring no design other than

* He worked on this for years, reading it aloud to his wife Nellie even as the bombs fell on wartime London.

a small, circular black-and-white illustration, or 'roundel', on the front.*

There were no blurbs on the back covers, just a list of other books in the series, although this mission statement of sorts appeared inside several early editions, stating proudly (and over-patriotically): 'It is the design of this Library to provide English-speaking versions of the finest and most enduring of the foreign classics, ancient, medieval and modern. It was felt that many opportunities for enjoyment were denied to those unfamiliar with the languages concerned, by the stilted, old-fashioned and otherwise un-English style which has too often been adopted by translators.'

To avoid the dreaded 'un-English' style, Rieu, who had been put in charge of the new Penguin Classics series, deliberately commissioned professional writers, rather than academics, to translate classic works. These included Robert Graves, whose vivid translation of Suetonius' sex-and-violence fest *The Twelve Caesars* became a classic in itself, and Dorothy L. Sayers. In a rare break from the no-blurb rule, an early edition of Sayers's translation of Dante's *The Divine Comedy* features these charming words:

> By one of those happy coincidences that occasionally delight the world of letters, Miss Sayers' enthusiasm for Dante reached its climax just at the time when the Penguin Classics were launched. To bring Dante home to English-speaking people in all his moods, from the homely and humorous to the terrible

* There's a particularly excellent roundel on Lucian's *Satirical Sketches*: a woodcut showing a gruesome little gang of skeletons being ferried across the River Styx, one of whom trails his bony hand in the water in a leisurely fashion.

and the sublime, was perhaps an even greater task. It called for a poet, and it has found one.

At the time, it was rather radical to present 'classics' as being for everyone, published in the same size and format as, for example, a crime novel. The potential confusion this could cause was gleefully exploited in James Thurber's short story 'Macbeth Murder Mystery', where an avid reader of crime fiction tries to work out who really killed Duncan: 'It was a stupid mistake to make … but it was on the counter with the other Penguin books – the little sixpenny ones, you know, with the paper covers – and I supposed of course it was a detective story.'

When the 1960s came along, with sex and the Beatles and all that, things started to change further in the world of Penguin Classics. A maverick young dude (or 'half educated young upstart' as E. V. Rieu called him), Tony Godwin, had become editor-in-chief at Penguin, and commissioned Italian designer Germano Facetti, the epitome of sixties cool, to redesign the classics' covers. Facetti's designs are masterpieces, my favourite look for any classics series: black, minimalist, featuring white sans serif type and a photographed artwork – dating from the same period as the text – on the front of each cover. They are completely of their time, and yet timeless. They also feature blurbs on the back covers, some of which are idiosyncratic and, frankly, quite odd.

For example, the blurb for the ancient Welsh classic *The Mabinogion* begins: 'Nothing illustrates the strange nature of these Welsh stories better than this vertically halved tree.' Where to go from there? In fact, the more I've explored classics blurbs of yore, the more I've come to the conclusion that pretty much anything written before about 1990 is decidedly – and sometimes marvellously – unhinged.

A 1980s version of Homer's *The Odyssey* tells us: 'Odysseus' journey is scarcely straightforward: he has to undergo the wrath of the sea-god Poseidon, fight monsters, overcome sexual distractions and the loss of his crew – only to find further trials to deal with when he finally reaches his native land of Ithaca.' I suppose sexual distractions are rarely straightforward.

The Iliad, Homer's epic account of the Trojan wars, has appeared in more translations than any other classic work. A Cassell edition from 1960 features an epic blurb on the dust jacket, which states: 'For twenty-six centuries, Homer's *Iliad* has been murdered by successive generations of schoolmasters, who have treated it either with exaggerated reverence, or with no reverence at all – as a corpse for dramatic dissection. But since the original Greek text is still available, Homer can be resuscitated as a living author.' They took that corporeal metaphor and just ran with it.

Blurbs from the past, as well as being eccentric, refuse to soft-soap or talk down to their readers. The Pelican Classics edition of *The Origin of Species* states that 'no one book since the *Summa* of Thomas Aquinas has made a comparable impact'. You don't know what a *Summa* is, or haven't read Thomas Aquinas? Tough luck.

Similarly, a 1965 Oxford World Classics edition of *War and Peace* starts by telling us that 'it began as a novel about the Decembrists, developed into a story of family life (that of Count Tolstoy's own class and day) and only later assumed the vast and magnificent proportions of the present work'. Never heard of the Decembrists? Your loss.

There are so many more examples of strange, over-the-top or barking blurbs that it's hard to know where to stop. *Eugene Onegin*: 'it seems to have been born rather than made'.

A Journal of the Plague Year: '*Bring out your dead!* The ceaseless chant of doom echoed throughout a city of emptied streets and filled grave pits…' *Utopia*: 'the work of a man who drank deep of the finest spirit of his age'. *The Communist Manifesto*: 'The very essence of communism.' So good you could bottle it, comrade!

Things are just as peculiar with the classics of the twentieth century. The blurb on an elderly paperback of *The Power and the Glory* by Graham Greene informs us that 'A baleful vulture of doom hovers over this modern crucifixion story,' whereas the original hardback jacket copy is even more bats: 'Greeneland has often been described as a land bleak and severe. A whisky priest dies in one village, a self-hunted man lives with lepers in another…' I *think* I know what a whisky priest and a self-hunted man might be, but this copy is not making it easy.

There's a similar 'take it or leave it' attitude on a classic crime novel: 'This is a Lord Peter Wimsey story. Need we say more?' And for the now-canonical spy thriller *On Her Majesty's Secret Service*? 'This, the eleventh chapter in the biography of James Bond, is one of the longest. It is also the most enthralling. Really the most? *Really* the most.' *Nairn's London* tells us: 'That "there has never been a guide like this before" is a familiar boast. This time we think it may be true. Nairn's guide is an intensely subjective search for the really good things in London, described with vehement passion which flies out from a solid foundation of architectural knowledge.'*

There's something so exclamatory, so joyfully innocent, about these 'intensely subjective' old blurbs. They are at once

---

* 'This time we really mean it' is also a familiar refrain. But this really is the best book ever written about London, and I *really* mean it.

completely conscious of themselves, and utterly unselfconscious. None of them would *ever* get past a marketing team today.

But, inevitably, progress marched its march and things started to change in classics publishing. As these books became aimed increasingly towards students, it all got more sensible, sadly. Most classics blurbs now seem to attempt to strike a balance between an academic reader and a broader audience. There is usually a mixture of plot, character, scene-setting and some kind of historical or literary context. It's all very considered.

It is evidently a good thing to reach out across the barriers of something being a 'classic' and make it sound appealing to as many readers as possible. However, one of the things it's often tempting to do too is to emphasise how timeless the classics are, or 'just as relevant today as when they were first written'. Well, they all are in some way, or why would we be reading them? Can you try too hard to make classics 'relevant'? Let's use Chaucer's *The Canterbury Tales* as an experiment.

The copy that appears on the back of a 1960s Penguin Classics edition (featuring the Germano Facetti cover design) is typically out-there: 'The tone of this never-resting comedy is, by turns, learned, fantastic, lewd, pious and ludicrous. "Here," as John Dryden said, "is God's plenty!"'

An academic OUP edition from a similar time is functional, to say the least: 'This edition of Chaucer's Complete Works was edited from numerous manuscripts by the late Professor Skeat. It contains a life of Chaucer, a list of his writings and of the third editions, hints on the grammar, metre, versification and pronunciation. There is an appendix of variations and a glossarial index.' No fun to be had here. Move on, please.

Then there's a new 'retelling' by Peter Ackroyd published in 2009. I worked on this at the time but now I look at the copy, which aimed to make *The Canterbury Tales* appeal to *anyone*, I think it all went a bit 'trendy teacher': 'Love. Sex. Infidelity. Villainy. Drunkenness. Murder … The best stories ever told just got better.' Ouch.

The only thing that made me feel better about my embarrassingly overenthusiastic copy was encountering this doozy of a blurb for an American 1950s edition of Émile Zola's *Thérèse Raquin*. It starts with the immortal words: 'She listened only to the demands of the flesh. In these words lies the core of this woman's story. With Theresa's submission to her lover begins the smouldering drama that drives two people down and down the path of human degradation.' It makes me feel I'd been quite restrained in comparison.

Now that classics blurbs are generally written according to the needs of the market rather than the crazed whim of an individual editor or copywriter, I wonder, have we lost something – a flamboyant sense of fun – along the way? As the author and bookseller Martin Latham told me, 'Publishers sometimes underestimate the public taste for grainy authenticity and honesty.'

I consulted editor Henry Eliot, a man who loves Penguin Classics so much that he has written two entire books about them. He agreed that 'Blurbs have become less idiosyncratic, perhaps because the readership has widened culturally and globally, which is a very good thing. There's probably less sense now of one bookish individual (most likely white, male, middle-aged, middle-class) recommending a title to a similar, like-minded individual,' although sometimes 'I feel there could be more room for wackiness – I personally find myself attracted to unusual, singular, quirky things!'

Ultimately, he acknowledges, a blurb should try to speak to as many people as possible: 'Blurbs have played a fundamental role in the democratic project of Penguin Classics. From the beginning the series was launched in the belief that "general readers" would want to read great writers. If the cover is the front door of the book, the blurb is the greeting that welcomes you over the threshold.'

Who knows, perhaps in a few years' time the pendulum will swing back the other way, and blurb writers will stop trying to invite everyone in and instead unleash their crazed inner word maniacs once more. As long as people read the classics, they will go on being described in new ways.

I will leave the last word to the person I started with, Italo Calvino: 'A classic is a book that has never finished saying what it has to say.'

Orwell Rules

When it comes to language, are you a Berk or a Wanker? Berks, according to a waspish Kingsley Amis in *The King's English*, are 'careless, coarse, crass, gross. Left to them the English language would die of impurity' – presumably he means grocers who misuse apostrophes, as well as their 'hey chill, guys, language changes all the time' defenders. Wankers, on the other hand, 'are prissy, fussy, priggish, prim. Left to them the language would die of purity.' In other words, the pedants.

Which brings me to the worrying question, does that make George Orwell a Wanker? His six rules for writing well, listed at the end of his essay 'Politics and the English Language', have been revered by journalists and writers for decades.* Yet to some they are too prescriptive, stripping language back to a straitjacket that allows for no fun or frivolity. Author Steven Poole describes the essay as 'wildly overrated' and is especially concerned about the whiff of xenophobia in

* Orwell's Commandments are: never use a metaphor you are used to seeing, a long word where a short one will do, the passive when you can use the active, a foreign, scientific or jargon word if there is an English equivalent, and always cut a word out if it is possible – plus break any of these rules 'sooner than say anything outright barbarous'.

Orwell's dislike of 'foreign' phrases. In a gleefully contrarian article that uses such fancy terms as 'fulguration', Will Self castigates Orwell's rules as authoritarian and elitist, and his essay as 'plain wrong'. (Nice use of plain English I see there though, Will.)

I would like to defend Orwell as a non-Wanker. First, he states that his rules do not cover 'the literary use of language, but merely language as an instrument for expressing and not for concealing or preventing thought'. For copywriters or journalists, who are trying to get a clear point across within a limited word count, brevity is necessity. I find myself drawn increasingly towards the minimal, wondering not only if I can use fewer words in a sentence, but if those words can have fewer syllables. I realise the logical conclusion would be turning into a *Sun* headline writer, saying 'tot' instead of 'toddler' and 'cops' instead of 'the Police', so I try to retain some equilibrium (look, five syllables there).

I also wonder if some of Orwell's critics are just overexposed to him, forgetting how extraordinarily bracing his non-fiction is to someone reading it for the first time, how sparklingly clear and entertaining, and how original. His metaphors (England is 'a family with the wrong members in control') are still minty-fresh.

Orwell's rules made him the writer he is. When the poet Ruth Pitter, who he befriended when he was a penniless young twentysomething, was first shown his writing, she described it as like 'a cow with a musket'. She helped him polish that famous English pane of glass. According to author and editor Richard Cohen, 'Pitter may not have injected Orwell with his gift for storytelling, but she taught him to compose those stories.'

Finally, Orwell gives us his last rule ('break any of these rules sooner than say anything outright barbarous') as a get-out clause. Everyone goes rogue sometimes. I think people who mistrust fans of clear English assume they are dealing with a home-grown version of the *Académie Française*, that venerable French public body whose members (*les immortels*) aim to keep the language pure from pernicious outside influences. Yet even the Plain English Campaign (whose guidelines are clearly influenced by Orwell) say you can break the rules of grammar. Splitting infinitives, starting sentences with 'And' or 'But', ending a sentence with a preposition – according to their website, these are things they're totally down with.

All writers ignore their own advice. Stephen King is a notorious adverb-hater, yet his use of an adverb to describe his wife's smile ('severely cute') is so adorably uxorious that I couldn't forget it. In his words, 'I'm just another ordinary sinner … When I do it, it's usually for the same reason any writer does it: because I am afraid the reader won't understand me if I don't.' This need to be understood is key to 'Politics and the English Language'. Anyone who wants their meaning to be as clear as possible should use language that is as clear as possible. And if they don't want their meaning to be clear? Well, that's where the trouble starts.

For Orwell, everything was political. The corruption of language stems from the corruption of political thought, and vice versa. When people want to lie or dissemble, they search for words that will obscure their intentions. In one brilliant passage, he says that 'The great enemy of clear language is insincerity. When there is a gap between one's real and one's declared aims, one turns as it were instinctively to long words and exhausted idioms, like a cuttlefish spurting out ink.' The move from abstract idea to sensory metaphor here is classic Orwell.*

In a far grislier use of the concrete versus the vague, Orwell describes how 'villages are bombarded from the air, the inhabitants driven out into the countryside, the cattle machine-gunned, the huts set on fire with incendiary bullets: this is called pacification.' Words obscure murder. Politics is sustained by euphemism, that fig leaf of atrocity.

Albert Camus, Orwell's French counterpart in that he was also hated by many on the far left because he (a) criticised Stalin and (b) wrote clearly, notes this in his powerful polemic against capital punishment, *Reflections on the Guillotine*:

> No one dares speak directly of the ceremony. Officials and journalists who have to talk about it, as if they were aware of both its provocative and its shameful aspects, have made up a sort of ritual language, reduced to stereotyped phrases. Hence we read at breakfast time in the corner of the newspaper that the condemned 'has paid his debt to society' or that he has 'atoned' or that 'at five a.m. justice was done'. People write of capital punishment as if they were whispering.

There's always something nasty hidden by a euphemism. In season four of *The Crown*, Margaret Thatcher, played by Gillian Anderson, is refusing to agree to sanctions against South Africa's apartheid regime. She rejects the Commonwealth leaders'

---

* As is the combination of righteous anger and homely detail in his description of politicians' phrases 'tacked together like the sections of a prefabricated hen-house'. Historian Timothy Garton Ash noted, 'Only Orwell would know both how to milk a goat and how to skewer a revisionist.'

proposal every time because of the word used – 'sanctions', 'measures', 'actions' – which goes back and forth until a professional writer is brought in to help and Thatcher finally agrees to 'signals'. As well as being catnip for word lovers, this scene brilliantly shows how language that is deliberately clouded ends up having no meaning at all.*

And now, when political language has become so debased that we seem to exist in a ghastly hall of mirrors where everything (fake news, stolen election, taking back control, to be absolutely clear, all in this together) means its exact opposite, Orwell helps us both to see through the distortions of others and to search for clarity in our own words. Forget Wankers. As Jarvis Cocker sang, 'C**ts are still running the world,' and while they are, we need Orwell's rules more than ever.

Against all this, blurbs can seem a tad frivolous. But even for my 100 words of little white lies, I keep Orwell's maxims in mind. In the blurb he wrote for the first edition of *The Lion and the Unicorn: Socialism and the English Genius*, Orwell follows his own rules, keeping both his meaning and his language crystal clear. It ends: 'This is a book for those who are neither ashamed of being Englishmen, nor satisfied with England as it now is.'

Orwell evidently cared a great deal about the choice of words that appeared on his books. In a 1948 letter to his editor, Roger Senhouse, about the forthcoming publication of *Nineteen Eighty-Four*, he wrote that 'As to the blurb, I really don't think

---

* A more benign example of this professional dissembling is in the 1980s TV comedy *Yes Minister*. 'Original' and 'imaginative' are Sir Humphrey's most damning criticisms of a policy. 'Novel' is even worse. A 'controversial' decision loses votes; a 'courageous' one loses elections.

the approach in the draft you sent me is the right one. It makes the book sound as though it were a thriller mixed up with a love story.' Instead, he goes on, he would prefer to concentrate on the 'implications of totalitarianism'. The jacket copy on the first edition shows that he got what he wanted:

> 1984 is the year in which it happened. The world is divided into three great powers, Oceania, Eurasia and Eastasia, each potentially at war with the other.

The blurb goes on to describe Newspeak, the Thought Police and Big Brother, with Winston and Julia relegated to the end. Perhaps now, when these famous terms have entered the consciousness of people who haven't even read the book, we can appreciate its shabby, complicated, desperately sad love story (of sorts). But at the time Orwell's copy did what it had to do: world-build for the reader, as with any dystopian novel.

It's a similar story with the flap copy that Orwell wrote for the first edition of *Animal Farm*, published in 1945 by Secker & Warburg.* In clear, measured tones, it tells us:

> It is the history of a revolution that went wrong – and of the excellent excuses that were forthcoming at every step for each perversion of the original doctrine.

Orwell's copy was still used years later, featuring on the cover of a 1960s Penguin Modern Classic almost word for word.

....

* After famously being rejected by several other publishers who either berated its criticism of Britain's wartime ally Stalin, or, in T. S. Eliot's case, its lack of 'public-spirited pigs'.

The phrase 'the history of a revolution that went wrong' is still quoted on some current editions.*

Animal Farm has been repackaged for many different audiences over the years, most recently as a graphic novel. It has been marketed at students, at hipsters, at younger readers. Orwell's satire is not a book for children. It may be as simple as a nursery rhyme, but it is as cruel as the sea. Yet there is something about reading it that recalls childhood; that time when you feel burning injustice and powerlessness on a more visceral level that at any other stage in life.

I think this is why some of the most successful copy describing Orwell's 'fairy story' appears on editions for younger readers, using simple language such as this:

> A long time ago, there was a very special farm in England called Manor Farm. This farm was home to a lot of amazing animals that helped care for the farm, but the farm animals were not very happy…

However, by far the most powerful Orwell blurb I have seen in recent years isn't on a book at all. It is for a video game of *Animal Farm*, created to commemorate the novel's seventy-fifth anniversary in 2020. I hope that Orwell, as a lover of popular culture from *Boys' Weekly* magazines to murder mysteries, might have approved of it. The copy, which appears on the Steam website – the gaming equivalent of Amazon – uses language that anyone with a sense of fair play could understand:

* * *

* Orwell's description, in a letter to the publisher Victor Gollancz, of *Animal Farm* as a 'fairy story' was also used as the book's subtitle when it first appeared.

In Orwell's *Animal Farm*, the animals have fought off their exploitative human masters. Now they're in charge.*

It goes on to describe how *Animal Farm* has become totemic for its 'awareness of how power can be abused – and of how generation after generation seeks a more just and equal society, where the many do not suffer at the hands of the few'. But the best bit is at the end:

Play it to explore a classic tale from inside. Play it to try your hand at running the farm – or because you dream of spreading Animalism across the world. Play it because you've always wanted to oversee a construction project by a herd of cows. Play it because Boxer deserved better.

Boxer takes us straight to the heart of what matters: the child's sense of *it's not fair*. And it homes in on something small and relatable from a big idea, just as Orwell's writing does.

Orwell's greatest piece of advice for a copywriter in 'Politics and the English Language' is to let your idea choose the words; to 'get one's meaning as clear as one can through pictures and sensations. Afterward one can choose – not simply *accept* – the phrases that will best cover the meaning.' So to avoid the dreaded lack of clarity, think of something concrete from what you are describing, whether it's a fact, a number, a memorable phrase, a tangible detail or a loyal cart horse sent off to the knacker's yard. Then the words will come. Above all, work out what you really want to say before you say it.

• •

* The founder of the Orwell's Animal Farm video game project describes how 'the fate of the farm was all too real for me growing up in totalitarian Hungary'.

S tep Away from the Bonnet

Jane Austen

It is a truth universally acknowledged that every piece of writing about Jane Austen must begin with the words 'It is a truth universally acknowledged'. It is also a truth universally acknowledged that, perhaps with the exception of Shakespeare, Jane Austen has become the greatest industry ever to spring from the annals of English literature.

Margaret Drabble said that 'there would be more genuine rejoicing at the discovery of a complete new novel by Jane Austen than any other literary discovery'. Readers love her, and for good reason: those six perfect novels.

Has any other author inspired such devotion? There are societies of 'Janeites' all over the world, from Pakistan to Australia, Italy to Brazil. The bicentenary of *Pride and Prejudice* in 2013 was marked by, among other things, Austen-themed transatlantic cruises and the announcement of a new £10 note in the UK.* There are books of Jane-related recipes, dating advice, emojis, zombies, dancing ducks and, of course, guinea pigs in

....

* When it was unveiled in 2017, Janeites were delighted to point out that the quotation adorning it, 'I declare after all there is no enjoyment like reading', is spoken by Caroline Bingley, a woman far more interested in material rather than literary pursuits.

bonnets (sample copy: 'It's even more dreamy to fall in love with a furry Mr Darcy!'). And the merch is astonishing – tote bags, cookie cutters, socks and shower curtains are just a few of the ways buyers can celebrate their love for Jane.

As Austen is such big business, it follows that, like any other product, her novels have been continually repurposed and repitched over the years to keep buyers interested, and to reflect the concerns, tastes and, yes, prejudices of their times.

At the time of Austen's first published novel, *Sense and Sensibility* in 1811 (*Pride and Prejudice*, although written earlier, did not appear until 1813), novels were made entirely by hand and did not feature covers, with wealthier buyers binding them in leather for their family libraries. By the later nineteenth century, binding had become more decorative. The classic, and most beautiful, incarnation of Austen's most perennially popular novel, *Pride and Prejudice*, is generally thought to be the 1894 George Allen edition, featuring the artist Hugh Thomson's resplendent cover design of a golden peacock, chosen for its perfect symbolism of pride, vanity, outward appearances and display. These prized editions are collectors' items today, but rest assured you can also pick up an appliquéd embroidered clutch bag featuring the design for a couple of hundred quid.

The 'peacock' jacket was honoured in a 2015 edition of the same novel, designed by Coralie Bickford-Smith. Its dark faux leather binding is decorated with a repeating foil motif of swirling peacock feathers that both echoes and updates the Victorian original. In Bickford-Smith's words, 'it was a total celebration of the 1894 edition. I even own an edition of the original as it is one of my most loved covers. I had to pay homage to it.'

Vintage Classics also released new editions of Jane Austen's novels in 2014 featuring vibrant patterned designs by award-winning artist and author Leanne Shapton in bold colours, which are truly a lovely thing to behold. Shapton's covers are painterly and delicate, yet resolutely non-twee.

These gorgeous designs seem to be the exception, however. Looking at different manifestations of Austen's books over the years, they often encapsulate the uneasy tension between packaging and contents, between the way something is presented and the more complicated reality of what lies within the covers. To put it another way, they don't do Jane justice.

Many Austen book covers from the late nineteenth and early twentieth centuries, for example, show characters dressed in contemporary, rather than Regency, clothes. The bright illustration on the front of an 1872 *Pride and Prejudice* in the popular 'yellow-back' series shows a crinoline-wearing Lydia Bennet talking coyly to some suspiciously Victorian-looking soldiers. Meanwhile, a 1950 John Murray edition of *Emma* pictures a bold and slightly grumpy dame with the scarlet lipstick, nipped-in waist and hairstyle of someone resembling Deborah Kerr rather than the novel's titular heroine.

1960s and 1970s cover interpretations of Jane Austen's novels are an unfettered joy, with jackets featuring Biba-clad heroines complete with heavy eyeliner and flowing locks; a psychedelic Elizabeth Bennet; *Persuasion*'s Captain Wentworth as a sort of hipster-bearded Captain Birds Eye; beautifully manicured, red-nailed hands; and lines such as 'A frolicking comedy...'

These aren't the worst, however. The honour of best anachronistic disservice to Jane Austen belongs to the wonderfully, almost unfeasibly, bad Tor paperback editions of the 1990s, which position her firmly in the Mills & Boon category, complete with heaving bosoms and lurid taglines. *Persuasion* is emblazoned with the words 'In love, would she follow her father's advice, or her own heart?' *Sense and Sensibility* boasts 'Two sisters. Two romances. A tragic tale of love and deceit' (ah, my favourite 'repeating a number' strapline. It could only have been better if it had said '*One* tragic tale of love and deceit'.). But the hands-down, cloth-eared winner is *Pride and Prejudice*: 'Mom's fishing for husbands – but the girls are hunting for love.' No, your neighbours haven't got the builders in, it's the sound of Austen pirouetting in her grave.

The other Austen taglines that fascinate me are those on the 2011 HarperTeen range of her novels, which clearly tapped into the *Twilight* phenomenon with dark, moody covers featuring funereal flowers, vampiric fonts and lines such as 'Love is a game' on *Emma*, 'The love that started it all' on *Pride and Prejudice* and 'A love beyond measure' on *Persuasion*. The blurb copy is interesting too, dialling up the emotion and the peril to dark gothic romance proportions ('Darcy had never been so bewitched by any woman as he was by her') in a way I rather enjoyed, despite myself.

Even better, a 'Pulp! The Classics' edition of *Pride and Prejudice* from 2013 sports a deliberately garish, 1950s-style design featuring a moody, hairy-chested Mr Darcy (well, Colin Firth) smoking a cigarette and wearing a cravat, with the warning 'Lock Up Your Daughters… Darcy's In Town!' And there is fun to be had with the horror mash-up, *Pride and Prejudice and Zombies* from 2009, picturing Elizabeth with half her face fallen off.

These are all a fresh spin on a way of telling stories that have become familiar, and perhaps overfamiliar to many of us. It can leave blurb writers in a bind. Do you plunge into the plot straight away, and risk losing the reader's interest? Do you attempt to give some kind of literary context, depending on the readership?

The danger here is that you immediately transport a potential reader back to the anxiety of the classroom, such as this copy: '*Pride and Prejudice*, which opens with one of the most famous sentences in English literature, is an ironic novel of manners' (sorry, Wordsworth Editions). The cover of this book features a disembodied, pink-lined bonnet alarmingly floating in mid-air, which is definitely a feature of much recent Austen packaging: soft colours, and accessories. In 2006 Headline launched Austen explicitly for a 'chick lit' market, with the inevitable stars, birds, bonnets and flowers on their pastel-hued covers.

Many editions available today (zombies notwithstanding) feel a bit too polite and pink, and I think the language used to describe Austen's novels can often fall into this trap. Too cosy, too twee, too... bonnety. Yet when I recently re-read *Pride and Prejudice*, I was surprised by how much more pacey and modern, almost modernist, it was than I'd remembered. Many pages are pure, quick-fire dialogue, more akin to a Howard Hawks movie than polite conversation. I also remembered the mercilessness of her irony and the way that, just as in Shakespeare's comedies, her characters' happy fates often teeter on the edge of darkness before they reach their proper conclusion of marriage and harmony.

Of course, I'm probably just reading what I want into Austen, just as generations of readers have, but it's notable that themes like money, poverty and the constraints of women's lives resonate with readers and TV or film makers today. By far the best Austen adaptation of recent years was Whit Stillman's 2016 movie *Love and Friendship*, which is about as un-twee as you can get. Based on the early novella *Lady Susan*, about a scheming widow, it brings what Stuart Kelly calls the 'streak of cackling sadism' of Austen's juvenilia to the fore and, in the words of one film critic, 'reinvigorates the clichés, the breeches, buttons and bows'.

As Martin Amis says in his 1998 essay on the genius of Jane Austen, 'with every generation Austen's fiction effortlessly renews itself. Each age will bring its peculiar emphasis, and in the current Austen festival our own anxieties stand fully revealed. Collectively, we love to wallow in the accents and accoutrements of Jane's world; but for the closeted reader the response is predominantly sombre.' I've been as guilty as the next copywriter of prettiness, fluffiness and tweeness when writing blurbs for the many Austen reprints that have crossed my path, so perhaps that's why for a recent redesign, I tried to concentrate on the slightly weightier aspects of the novels as well as their glittering brightness, balancing light and shade.

As with so many classic novels, however, children's publishers do it best. I love the copy on a Scholastic edition of *Pride and Prejudice*, which begins: 'Mrs Bennet is desperate to find rich husbands for her daughters'. It gets to the point, and it shows you the money, just like Jane Austen herself.

3.

CRACKING
GOOD COPY

Writing Rules

Be a Magpie

One Detail Is Worth a Thousand Adjectives

It's an exciting moment in the humdrum life of a cover copy-writer. A customer is in the bookshop, browsing (possibly being watched by me from a distance). A jacket catches their eye. They pick the book up, maybe they flick through it, then turn it over and skim the copy that appears on the back, or inside on the flap. In that briefest of moments, which some estimate to be around thirty seconds at the most, perhaps something in that small space will make them look twice.

How does a publisher or a copywriter speak to this person and make a connection with them? We learn to accept that most of the time our words will be glossed over and forgotten, so how do we describe a character or a scene in a way that sticks in the mind? There is no 'correct' blurb, just as there is no 'correct' book, but I think one answer is: you pick out a detail.

Here is the copy that introduces the titular heroine of *Eleanor Oliphant is Completely Fine*:

Eleanor Oliphant leads a simple life. She wears the same clothes to work every day, eats the same meal for lunch every day and buys the same two bottles of vodka to drink every weekend. Eleanor Oliphant is happy. Nothing is missing from her carefully timetabled existence. Except, sometimes, every-thing.

What stood out for you? For me, it was the two bottles of vodka, and 'everything'. The copy is clear and simple, yet it contains surprising details; key signifiers that lodge in the brain. It uses short sentences and, most importantly, minimal adjectives. How much less effective it would have been if Eleanor had just been described as 'eccentric', 'quirky' or 'troubled'. Specificity is key. Vague waffle, in fact most description – whether of a character or the book itself – should be avoided.

One of the great mysteries in life is why in publishing, an industry whose business is language, the words we employ to characterise books are so often the same. We overuse adjectives such as luminous, dazzling, incandescent, stunning, shimmering, sparkling, glittering – always the light references! Or there are what I like to call the 'natural disaster adjectives': devastating, searing, powerful, shattering, explosive, epic, electrifying. Closely followed by 'I've got the flu': dizzying, dark, chilling, staggering, aching (-ly beautiful). A book is not a volcanic eruption or a virus.

One wag on social media recently compiled a 'glossary of terms' for book blurbs, including 'Enchanting: there's a dog in it. Heart-warming: a dog and a child. Moving: child dies. Heart-rending: dog dies.' We laugh because we know it's true. Why do we do it? I suspect everyone – reader, publisher, author – knows that these words act as a code of sorts. As the critic D. J. Taylor put it, blurb writing is 'a kind of semaphore between author, editor and publisher from which all kinds of extra-curricular inferences can be drawn'. Some authors like adjectives in their blurbs; as if once they've earned a 'perceptive' or a 'provocative', they've made it. But they are false friends.

If adjectives are the sworn enemies of nouns, they are often the enemies of some writers too. Hemingway mistrusted them, and Mark Twain said, 'When you catch an adjective – kill it.' Of course, all advice is there to be ignored. Dickens positively lavishes adjectives on his writing and it would be unimaginable without them. But when writing short, selling copy, reaching for a solid example makes language work harder than an adjective.* It also makes life easier for the reader, giving them a tangible point of reference, rather than a hazy abstraction.

One of my favourite blurb descriptions of a character is of Count Fosco in *The Woman in White*: 'who has a taste for white mice, vanilla bonbons and poison'. No need for a 'sinister' at all there. Another is on Patrick Hamilton's *The Slaves of Solitude*, which tells us that a young woman in a boarding house 'pecks at spam and mashed potato by night', thus making Hamilton-like descriptors such as 'shabby' or 'dreary' redundant.

Or take the more recent description of Hillary Clinton in Curtis Sittenfeld's counterfactual biography, *Rodham*:

> 'Awfully opinionated for a girl' is what they call Hillary as she grows up in her Chicago suburb. Smart, diligent, and a bit plain, that's the general consensus.

We see Hillary through the eyes of others, and immediately know she is an outsider, and an outlier.

••

* Sometimes adjectives are just inadequate. The editor Diana Athill recalls how, when working on Gitta Sereny's account of the Nuremberg trials, *Into that Darkness*, she made the decision that 'we must use no adjectives – or very few. Words such as "horrifying", "atrocious", "tragic", "terrifying" – they shrivelled like scraps of paper thrown into a blazing fire.'

In non-fiction books, facts should do the talking. They can have more impact than a thousand 'ground-breaking's or 'land-mark's. The excellent copy on Caroline Criado Perez's study of gender inequality, *Invisible Women*, picks out memorable facts and figures and uses them to great effect:

> Imagine a world where your phone is too big for your hand, where your doctor prescribes a drug that is wrong for your body, where in a car accident you are 47% more likely to be seriously injured. If any of that sounds familiar, chances are you're a woman.

On Yuval Noah Harari's *Sapiens*:

> Fire gave us power. Farming made us hungry for more. Money gave us purpose. Science made us deadly. This is the thrilling account of our extraordinary history – from insignificant apes to rulers of the world.

Those four short sentences at the start focus on the material and the graspable, distilling a big, complex book into something almost haiku-like. I would wager that the 'thrilling' probably isn't necessary, however.

I try to follow the 'minimal adjectives' advice as much as I can when writing blurbs. When I recently had to introduce the heroine of a coming-of-age novel called *The Island*, I decided it would be better to say she had been thrown out of a convent for kicking the prioress, rather than describing her as 'spir-ited' or 'rebellious'. Several years ago, I wrote some copy for an early novel by Truman Capote called *Summer Crossing* (fea-turing a kind of prototype Holly Golightly) which I was rather delighted to see quoted in John Sutherland's *How to Read a Novel*. I'm not sure if he quoted it approvingly or disapprovingly, but I felt pretty smug that my words were there at all. Then I read the description of her again: 'Grady – beautiful, rich, flame-haired, defiant – is the sort of girl people stare at across a room' and I cringed. Why hadn't I killed the adjectives and just described her as 'the sort of girl people stare at across a room'? Copywriters live and learn.

Ultimately, good copy should be able to see the wood for the trees – well, ideally, to quote a fellow copywriter, 'to step back from the trees to work out what drove us into the wood in the first place, so that others will be tempted to follow'. We should home in on sparkly details like a magpie. Chekhov said, 'Don't tell me the moon is shining; show me the glint of light on broken glass.' But preferably without adjectives.*

* Yes, I succumbed and slipped an adverb in there.

Ever-Decreasing Copy

Cut, cut, cut. Omit needless words (*The Elements of Style* by William Strunk). Kill your darlings (William Faulkner or possibly Allen Ginsberg). Slaughter adjectives (Edith Wharton). Cut your work until it bleeds (literary agent Jonny Geller). Cut like a Tory politician (me). Trim, shave, slash, hack.

It's all rather violent, the language used to describe good writing practices. A bit macho. Nick Hornby is very funny when he says that all this physical talk is an attempt to compensate for writing being such a weedy profession, 'to make writing a real job, like farming, or logging. Go on, young writers – treat yourself to a joke, or an adverb! Spoil yourself! Readers won't mind!'

Hornby is right, of course, but unfortunately the cutters are right too. The odd verbal flourish stands out more if the rest of your prose gets to the point clearly. It *is* good practice to write one day, then re-read it the next and work out what can go. Chances are, the piece of writing will be even better without it. Or, as Raymond Chandler put it so beautifully, 'Throw up into your typewriter every morning. Clean up every noon.' Delightful. And true. The aim should be, to quote James Baldwin, 'a sentence as clean as a bone'.

Blurbs require a tight structure. They need narrative progression, but on a tiny scale. Concision can be hard, but the process of stripping away forces you to focus on what you really want to say. It can also, ironically, take longer, as every word has to pack a punch. As the French mathematician Blaise Pascal wrote to a correspondent (and this is a *very* free translation), 'I would have written a shorter letter, but I did not have the time.'

I've noticed that the copy I write has become shorter and shorter over the years (apart from this book, where I get to write more than 100 words, *and* have my name attached to them!). Sometimes this concision has been my choice, more often it's been someone else's decision: usually a designer's. There's only a limited amount of space on a book cover, after all. Recently I had to write blurbs for a series of classic books that only had room for one mere sentence of copy on the back; an experience I found liberating. Never was Elmore Leonard's adage 'if it looks like writing, I rewrite it' truer. Call me twisted, but I get a strange sort of kick out of a word limit. It concentrates the mind; and the words. As they say, it's the freedom of the tight brief.

So why the recent trend for less copy? An easy argument would be that in our information-saturated age of Twitter, we have shorter attention spans.* Many of us buy books online now and the Amazon 'description' section only allows for a certain number of words to display before you press 'Read more'.

But is there more to it than that? I wonder if actually it's a case of copy coming full circle. The copy on books was generally, until a few decades ago, far briefer in the past. Much of this was to do with size. Before the 1980s, most paperbacks, whether by Jeffrey Archer or Paul Auster, were the dinky

....

* A 2021 study showed that the length of the average sentence in fiction has dropped from 12.73 words to 11.87 over the last thirty years.

'A' format, able to slip into your pocket. Then, as publishers like Picador pioneered putting 'serious' literary works in the larger 'B' format, the books got bigger, and so did the blurbs.*

Just as Parkinson's Law notes that 'work expands so as to fill the time available for its completion', there is a tendency among many publishers to fill every bit of free space on a cover with copy – and never more so than on a hardback book. Look at the jacket flaps of most hardbacks in a bookshop and you are inevitably faced with a wall of words.

The copy for one of Salman Rushdie's recent hardbacks clocked in at an astonishing 324 words, with almost that many plot points in it (the book is called *Two Years Eight Months and Twenty-Eight Nights*, which is approximately how long it takes to read the blurb). Who wants to be faced with a huge splodge of copy on a jacket, or so much information that it reads like a Wikipedia entry? No one is going to read it all.

Which brings me to the four words so cursed in publishing that they must, in my view, never be committed to paper. They are the equivalent of saying 'Macbeth' instead of 'the Scottish play', uttering the name Jehovah – or, if you're a fan of horror films, repeating 'Candyman' five times in the mirror. These dreaded words are: *Continued on back flap*.

You occasionally see them (in apologetically small print) on the front flap of a hardback jacket, when the blurb has got so ridiculously

....

* In *Kindred Spirits* Jeremy Lewis laments the loss of small-format books in the 1980s: 'I loved books that could be carried about in one's overcoat pocket … but we lived in an age of gigantism and hype. Skimpy novels looked skimpier still in a format more suitable to a road atlas, like five-year-olds swamped in their mothers' clothes.'

long that it spills over like a word avalanche. I don't spot this accursed phrase much, but when I do I want to smite it like a vengeful god.

There are many rules to remember when writing copy that sells, but a good one to bear in mind is: don't make the reader lose the will to live before they've even got to the end. Reading a blurb, or any piece of advertising copy, is different from reading a book. You're often standing up, you may not have much time, and there are many other things competing for your attention. Research has shown that we don't even read 100 per cent of a sentence when we look at it: much of the process is our brains doing guesswork and filling in the gaps, and our eyes are jumping all over the place, at three to four times per second, apparently reading in an 'F' shape rather than in a linear fashion. Be kind to a reader's eyes. They're working very hard already.

So why the word-slabs? Is there a sense readers should get their money's worth if they're shelling out on a hardback? I suspect it is to do with the publisher, and most probably the author, wanting to get the first word(s) in before a critic has their say, in effect telling them how to read it. As the journalist Tom Payne puts it, they 'produce a repertoire of sentences that publishers would like to see in book reviews'.

I hope we see a permanent return to the days of shorter copy. Most publishing is cyclical, after all. The signs are there, with chic, portable smaller formats becoming popular again, such as the Vintage Minis series, or Fitzcarraldo's beautifully slim pocket-sized books, complete with pithy copy. We may even complete the circle eventually and do away with blurbs altogether, replacing them with lists of other titles available from the publisher, as in the nineteenth century (PLEASE GOD NO. I have a mortgage.).

Any move away from 'Continued on back flap' has got to be a good thing, though, even if it threatens my retirement plans. Short is hard, but it is so much sweeter. Seneca said in *On the Shortness of Life*, 'It is not that we have so little time but that we lose so much.' What I think he meant to say was, life is short, so keep your blurbs shorter.

F**k Wisely

A Note on Successful Swearing

> The sort of twee person who thinks swearing is in any way
> a sign of a lack of education or a lack of verbal interest is
> just a fucking lunatic.
>
> STEPHEN FRY

Swearing is funny. It is also big and clever, if the scientific research is anything to go by. In 2015 two American psychologists undertook a series of experiments and determined that the participants who used a greater variety of swear words had a richer vocabulary overall. They concluded that 'A voluminous taboo lexicon may better be considered an indicator of healthy verbal abilities rather than a cover for their deficiencies.' Or, as Julie Walters's eponymous heroine in *Educating Rita* puts it: 'Educated people don't worry, do they? It's the aristocracy that swears most. It's all "Pass me the fucking pheasant" with them.'

There's also evidence that swearing uses more parts of our brain than any other form of speech. In *The Seven Words You Can't Say on Television*, psychology professor Steven Pinker argues that 'More than any other form of language, it recruits our expressive faculties to the fullest: the combinatorial power of syntax; the evocativeness of metaphor; the pleasure of alliteration, meter and rhyme; and the emotional charge of our attitudes, both thinkable and unthinkable. It engages the full expanse of the brain: left and right, high and low, ancient and modern.'

In trying to discover why, when we stub our toe or spill a glass of wine on the carpet, our vocabulary 'turns abruptly to sexuality, excretion, or religion', Pinker suggests that taboo words may tap into the deepest and most ancient parts of our brain (i.e. the bits that were there before we evolved to do things like farm, change lightbulbs and bake banana bread), notably the amygdala, the organ that invests memories with emotion. When a person sees a taboo word, their amygdala lights up – they even get a bit sweaty. If someone suffers brain damage, or even when an entire section of a patient's brain is removed in surgery, they can still swear like billy-o. (Incidentally, the seven words you can't say on television, taken from a 1972 monologue by the American comedian George Carlin, are Shit, Piss, Fuck, Cunt, Cocksucker, Motherfucker and Tits. *Tits??* Why fucking tits? I ask you.)*

Exploring why so many swear words relate to sex, bodily functions or religion, Pinker argues that the common factor is an emotional charge: feelings associated with awe, fear, disgust, hatred or depravity. Swear words also tend to be monosyllabic, and often involve harsh consonants such as 'f', 'k' or 'g'. So if you want to get someone's attention and make them feel something, swearing is a good way to do it. This is illustrated in the great tradition of literary swearing, from Chaucer's *The Miller's Tale* all the way to Philip Larkin's 'This Be the Verse' and this timeless beauty from Irvine Welsh's *Trainspotting*:

* I've often wondered if the 'seven words' were on Larry David's mind when he wrote the sublime restaurant swearing scene for Series 3 of *Curb Your Enthusiasm*, which peaks with a plummy Michael York proudly proclaiming, 'Fart, cunt, piss, shit, bugger and balls!'

> Choose life. Choose mortgage payments; choose washing machines; choose cars; choose sitting oan a couch watching mind-numbing and spirit-crushing game shows, stuffing fuckin junk food intae yir mooth. Choose rotting away, pishing and shiteing yersel in a home, a total fuckin embarrassment tae the selfish, fucked-up brats ye've produced. Choose life.

Another fine Scottish fucker is of course Malcolm Tucker in Armando Iannucci's TV comedy *The Thick of It*, who takes cursing to an art form with such classic lines as 'Fuckety-Bye', 'Shitehead Revisited' and 'Feet off the furniture you Oxbridge twat, you're not in a punt now.'

The swearing works to perfection in these examples because it's what we expect from an edgy comedy featuring the worst kind of people. (As it was said of Larkin's liberal swearing in his letters, he is 'encouraging the recipient to feel he was a member of the same secret army as the sender'.) The rest of the vocabulary used is so rich and allusive that it makes us feel clever. We're all in on the dirty joke. It's also deliberately aggressive, designed to make us squirm and gasp even as we laugh.

Swearing intentionally and extravagantly forces uncomfortable thoughts and feelings upon a viewer or reader, and as such, it can't be denied that some people just don't *like* it. More than any other piece of literary ammunition, it needs to be employed judiciously and only in real 'In case of emergency break glass' scenarios. If it's overused, or used in a phoney way, it loses its potency. I recently went to a live stand-up show where the c word was the punchline to every joke. By the end I wasn't shocked, but bored.

What about copy that's designed to sell – can swearing work well when used wisely? On book covers, fashions for rude words seem to come and go. Sarah Knight's *The Life-Changing Magic of Not Giving a F**k* worked because of the emotional frisson of a jokey swear word at the end of a traditional self-help title, and also because it was true to the insouciant spirit of the book. (It also had an ace subtitle: 'How to stop spending time you don't have doing things you don't want to do with people you don't like'.) There were a couple of 'f**k's cleverly sprinkled on the back cover too: 'Give your f**ks instead to people and things that make you happy.' The book became a bestseller and spawned a host of potty-mouthed offspring, from *Get Your Sh*t Together* to *The Subtle Art of Not Giving a F**k* and *Calm the F**k Down*.

Bullsh*t Jobs, a book by the late anthropologist and Occupy activist David Graeber, also worked as a book title, I think, because of its happy fusion of the profane and the mundane, and because he had coined the phrase himself to describe the explosion of meaningless white-collar jobs that exist purely to keep capitalism from crumbling. Authenticity is the key; and knowing your audience.

It's also worth noting the asterisk: used on book covers not because of prudishness, but because of the rules that would enable us to advertise it on Amazon, or not. Does a swear word lose its impact when it's fig-leafed like this? I think probably not; if anything, it's like a little wink-wink, an acknowledgement that this is all a bit naughty. The *New Yorker* proofreader Mary Norris describes the asterisks in swear words as 'interior punctuation, little fireworks inside the words'. And of course there are other ways to get round advertising watchdogs by playing word games, from the clothing range FCUK to a Booking.com ad that repeated the word 'booking' so many times throughout that it was obviously a substitute for something saucier.

A sweary book title, with or without an asterisk, can also just be a sign that you're going to have a really, really good time, such as the classic *Poor Little Bitch Girl* by Jackie Collins (before I started writing this section I was convinced she'd written a book called *Lucky Bitches*, only to remember that it was in fact a spot-on French and Saunders parody of the fabulous Collins sisters). There's also an inspired 1970s trilogy of books by *The Corrupted*'s G. F. Newman called *Sir, You Bastard*; *You Nice Bastard*; and *You Flash Bastard*. If these book titles don't make you do a cockney accent in your head and think of cops in Ford Granadas then, as Bridget Jones's mother said, I'm a tin of pears.

Swearing doesn't always work, however. I remember when an ill-advised brainstorm led to a book on urban legends being called *That's Bollocks*, purely because we thought it was a phrase people might use when confronted with these tales, rather than because it had anything to do with the book. It was a bit of a cynical move, and I think it backfired. Also, it was us 'showing off', which, as every child brought up in the 1970s knows, is the worst thing you can ever do. This is still not as bad, though, as a line I once saw on the front of a book: 'The Cu*t Bestseller'. I subsequently had an attack of the vapours and needed some smelling salts to revive me.

My rule for swearing on books is to be true to the words inside. And don't overdo it, or you'll be in danger of losing your edge. As Mary Norris says, 'You cannot legislate language … And yet no one wants to be pummelled constantly by four-letter words. If we are going to use them, let's use them right. Profanity ought to be fun.'

Goldilocks and the Three Blurbs
Getting It Just Right

It's not just porridge. The Goldilocks Principle, of something being *just right*, has been used to describe everything from the conditions necessary for life in the universe to a well-balanced economy. Most importantly of all, it applies to blurbs.

Every piece of copy is telling a story to somebody. A good blurb should be perfectly balanced: set the scene, include just enough detail, but not give too much information. Too little and the reader is left confused, too much and they'll lose interest. It should connect with a reader on an emotional level – whether through suspense, fascination, intrigue, fear, humour or joy – but leave them wanting more. A good blurb is a mini-drama, with a conflict and movement all of its own.

How do you do all of this? Well, welcome to possibly my three favourite blurbs of all time. (I say 'possibly' because I've written thousands of blurbs over my career and read far, far more over my lifetime.)

I salute the people who wrote these blurbs, because they made me feel something, and they made me want to read the book. They cleverly set up place, time and character, but they do it in a way that feels light and unforced. The detail is used sparingly and cleverly. And, most of all, they plunge you into their world. Here goes.

BLURB I

THE SPIRE BY WILLIAM GOLDING

Dean Jocelin has a vision: that God has chosen him to erect a great spire on his cathedral. His mason anxiously advises against it, for the old cathedral was built without foundations. Nevertheless, the spire rises octagon upon octagon, pinnacle by pinnacle, until the stone pillars shriek and the ground beneath it swims. Its shadow falls ever darker on the world below, and on Dean Jocelin in particular.

I have loved this blurb since my university years. In fact, it may well be the reason I became a copywriter. It starts with a simple premise, creates tension, employs unusual vocabulary (shrieking stones, tick, swimming ground, tick) and, best of all, it has a really ominous ending. I shuddered at the shadow falling on Dean Jocelin. The copy has risen up and up into the sky, and then suddenly comes down to earth with a bump onto one man. You know something bad is going to happen, and you just have to find out what it is.

The copy that appears on the latest edition seems to have stayed virtually unchanged since publication in 1964. Indeed, all of William Golding's current paperbacks feature copy that is either identical or very close to the original, such as the damn fine blurb on *The Inheritors*, which begins: 'When the spring came the people – what was left of them – moved back by the old paths from the sea.'

William Golding's estate told me that all his blurbs were written by his editor at Faber, Charles Monteith, who would always send them to Golding for a final check. Monteith, who spotted Golding's talent when he rescued his debut novel *Lord of the Flies* from the slush pile, remained his editor throughout his career, and by all accounts theirs was one of the most loyal and creative partnerships in publishing. Just before Golding's posthumous novel, *The Double Tongue*, was published, his widow added a dedication, 'Above all, this book is for Charles.'

BLURB 2
RIDDLEY WALKER BY RUSSELL HOBAN

'Walker is my name and I am the same. Riddley Walker. Walking my riddels where ever theyve took me and walking them now on this paper the same.'

Composed in an English which has never been spoken and laced with a storytelling tradition that predates the written word, *Riddley Walker* is the world waiting for us at the bitter end of the nuclear road. It is desolate, dangerous and harrowing, and a modern masterpiece.

That *ending*. *Riddley Walker* is hard to describe without sending readers running for the hills. It's set in Kent two thousand years after a nuclear holocaust and written in a broken-down, corrupted Estuary English that is all the blighted inhabitants of this wasteland can remember, like the ghost of a culture lost forever. It's challenging to read. I think opening up with the novel's strange language, as this Bloomsbury edition does, is the right thing to do, because you are immediately drawn into its world, and Walker's voice.

Then the blurb shows rather than tells, describing the work rather than telling a story. I don't always approve of this, but here it is done well. The adjectives are perfectly chosen and unexpected: a book, dangerous? The references to an unspoken

English and ancient storytelling traditions are just about weighty and enigmatic enough to make the novel sound important, but not lofty or off-putting. And then when you reach the end of the blurb, you've literally reached the end of the nuclear road. It's like a little sonnet, albeit an extremely doom-laden and depressing one. It also ends on a downer, which is a gamble, and one that pays off. This book clearly isn't for everyone, but if you're in the market for bleak and disturbing dystopias, then by god you're going to love it.

BLURB 3

A GAME OF THRONES: BOOK I OF A SONG OF ICE AND FIRE BY GEORGE R. R. MARTIN

This book had to appear somewhere, didn't it? I have to confess I haven't read the entire *Game of Thrones* series (seen it on the telly and all that), but I have read the first instalment, and to me its blurb is dramatic perfection. It uses the heightened, portentous language of the books and TV series. It world-builds with unusual and intriguing details to draw the reader in (winter lasting a lifetime? The iron throne?). It ends with the promise of excitement to come. And, most importantly, it implies richness and bounty in just a few words, doing the clever job of packing what feels like a whole world into a very short space:

'When you play the game of thrones, you win or you die. There is no middle ground'

Summers span decades. Winter can last a lifetime. And the struggle for the Iron Throne has begun.

> Kings and queens, knights and renegades, liars, lords and
> honest men… all will play the Game of Thrones.

Hear those stately strings and picture that spinning golden astrolabe.

I often think of these blurbs, their light and shade, their cadences and rhythms, when I'm working, even if it's on copy for a weighty history or science book. The same principles apply. Get their attention – and don't lose it. Make them feel something. Don't be lazy with your choice of vocabulary. And, whatever else you do, you'd better come up with a good ending.

Hegel Goes to Hollywood
The Pitch

Opposites – according to the wisdom of science, philosophy and 1980s singer Paula Abdul – attract. Or, as Carl Jung put it, 'There is no energy unless there is a tension of opposites.' This tension is at the heart of writing a pitch, which is at the heart of writing good copy.

The Hollywood pitch, or the elevator pitch as it's often called – that is, selling something to someone in the time it takes to ride in a lift with them – can fill the hearts of genteel publishing folk with terror, but it's vital.* One well-known literary agent said he wouldn't take on a new client unless he could pitch their book in twelve words or fewer. Every film, TV series or book can be reduced to a pitch. If you recall, the novelist Elizabeth Buchan memorably called it the 'backbone'. It forces us to think about what really matters, the kernel of a plot or idea, and the key to this should be opposition. What's that snap of tension; that point of conflict; that frisson of the unexpected? Which elements work with or against each other to spark our interest and hook us in?

I'm going to talk about the Hegelian dialectic now, but please

* Although, judging by some of the rambling elevator pitches I've heard over the years, no building is *that* high.

don't be afraid. It is simply the nineteenth-century German philosopher's theory of opposition. You have a thesis, or idea, which is countered by its antithesis, or contradictory idea, which then leads to synthesis; something new. It happens all the time. It is how we exist as humans – being changed – and consequently is at the heart of the stories we tell. In the words of the playwright David Mamet, 'Thesis, antithesis, synthesis; boy meets girl, boy loses girl, boy gets girl; act one, act two, act three.'

The screenwriter Craig Mazin, creator of the award-winning TV series *Chernobyl*, is big on the Hegelian dialectic. He talks about it as a way of approaching writing: 'constant changing. Every scene begins with a truth, something happens inside of that scene. There is a new truth at the end and you begin, and you begin, and you begin.' The ultimate aim, he says, is to 'disrupt the stasis'. There has to be an argument; a point of opposition. 'Men and women can't just be friends, well, that's an argument. Better to be dead than a slave. Life is beautiful, even in the midst of horrors. If you believe you are great, you will be great. If you love someone set them free. Those are *arguments*.'

They are also pitches, and I bet you can guess which films he's talking about here. The best Hollywood pitches embody this idea of pairings or contrasts. Among my roll-call of honour would be *I Am Legend*: 'The last man on earth is not alone'; *The Social Network*: 'You don't get to 500 million friends without making a few enemies'; and *Ferris Bueller's Day Off*: 'One man's struggle to take it easy.' Plus bonus points to *Bonnie and Clyde* for its noteworthy use of ellipses: 'They're young... they're in love... and they kill people.'

With books, this oppositional technique works well on front covers such as Robert Harris's *Conclave*: 'The power of god. The ambition of men'; and Emma Healey's *Elizabeth is Missing*: 'How do you solve a mystery when you can't remember the clues?' It is just as effective on non-fiction, including John Allen Paulos's *A Mathematician Plays the Market*: 'He figured the odds. And they still beat him.' There is something so pleasing about this formulation. It has the rhythm of a joke with a punchline.

A pithy line like this is not vital, of course. Plenty of books have become bestselling classics without any kind of snappy zinger. But they are not just there for fun. Reading them makes us laugh, or think, but trying to come up with them does more. It sets up the entire point of a book's existence, and from that, everything else should flow.

Look at the Harlequins!

Dots and Dashes

Did you look? Bet you did. The exclamation mark is, after all, the most jazz-hands, attention-seeking punctuation mark out there. I'm going to talk about the power of punctuation here, but not in the sense of how to use it correctly. There are already enough books telling you how to do that. I'm interested in using punctuation, which at its most basic level exists to help us navigate a sentence, for literary effect. This is about its function as another piece of weaponry in a copy-writer's arsenal of persuasion, and for pure enjoyment – even if it means breaking the rules. Especially if it does. As Stephen King says, 'Language does not always have to wear a tie and lace-up shoes.'

One of the greatest joys of being a teenager in the 1980s, as well as the films of John Hughes and bountiful opportunities for *really* big hair, was getting to read *Smash Hits* magazine at the height of its pomp and brilliance. An irreverent, ego-puncturing extravaganza of pop music, it also broke the rules of grammar and the English language itself with gleeful abandon. To this day I still think of Sir Paul McCartney as 'Fab Macca Wacky Thumbs Aloft' and A-ha's Norwegian lead singer Morten Harket as 'Morten Snorten Forten Horten' thanks to the genius of its writers.

Best of all was the fun it had with punctuation. Duran Duran's Simon Le Bon was described as: *'pop' 'star' Simon Le Bon*. One exclamation or question mark was never enough if three or more could be used. If a star reappeared after a quiet spell in their career, they were always 'back! Back! BACK!!!' Apart from helping me fall in love with the English language, *Smash Hits* also showed that a few dots and dashes could spark joy.

It makes sense, then, to begin with the exclamation mark, which is thought to spring from a Latin expression of joy, *io*, which would roughly translate as 'hooray!' today. It used to be known as the 'sign of admiration' or 'note of admiration' until the mid-seventeenth century. Since then it has been more commonly used to express alarm, or a warning – Stop! Fire! – but recently the digital age has seen it revert to its happier origins, becoming softer and more positive: jolly and silly, friendly and warm, sometimes a bit needy too.

Nearly everyone I know (well, I do work in publishing, where people are extremely nice) uses them in daily communication: Great, thanks! Good luck! Have a great weekend! I've even been known to use several in a row. Terry Pratchett, who once wrote: 'Five exclamation marks, the sure sign of an insane mind', would have feared for my mental health.

Many language curmudgeons seem to get very angry about the overuse of the exclamation mark, even to the point of murderousness. Mark Forsyth, author of *The Elements of Eloquence*, says: 'I'm usually relaxed to the point of torpor about punctuation, but exclamation marks are the one thing that rouses me to furious, vengeful violence. I don't mind it when it's being used for an exclamation ["Oh heavens!"] or an ejaculation ["Stop!"]. But when you use it for an amazing fact ["The pyramids are

5,000 years old!!"], I want to drown you.' Mark, leave it, it ain't worth it!

The exclamation mark has a fine literary history, in book titles and on book covers. Its immediate associations with surprise, excitement and fun mean that children's books are abundant with exclamation marks. Dr Seuss is a particular fan:*

> Congratulations!
> Today is your day.
> You're off to Great Places!
> You're off and away!

Nabokov uses it to convey this childlike playfulness in the title of his novel *Look at the Harlequins!* ('Look at the harlequins … Play! Invent the world! Invent reality'). The title of the memoir of the eminent physicist Richard Feynman, *Surely You're Joking Mr Feynman!*, immediately tells us that this scientist is going to be a fun dude cutting loose with the kids. As for Jilly Cooper's *Wicked!* and *Mount!*, well, what more needs to be said? On a more serious note, of course, there are also Willa Cather's great American saga *O Pioneers!*, which takes its title from a Walt Whitman poem, and Douglas Coupland's *Hey Nostradamus!*, which uses the exclamation mark as a counterpoint to its deadly serious subject matter.

Many feel that the exclamation mark should be used sparingly. The writer Elmore Leonard reckoned that 'you are allowed no more than two or three per 100,000 words of prose' although, according to the data, he actually used forty-nine per 100,000 words. Dickens employs tons of them, which is perhaps

....

* Dr Seuss also wrote *Green Eggs and Ham* after his publisher bet him that he couldn't use just fifty words in the whole book. Seuss won.

no shock to anyone, but, more surprisingly, James Joyce uses a whopping 1,105 exclamation marks per 100,000 words. Lolz!

I concede that, sometimes, exclamation marks can come across as a bit too shouty and jolly, like the wacky children's entertainer who is dying inside. But at their best I think they act as a sort of literary inflator, lifting up the tone of something, and elevating it to a more excitable pitch. They convey exuberance – or mounting exasperation, as Nora Ephron does to perfection: 'On the waiting list! For a purse! For a ten-thousand-dollar purse that will end up full of old Tic Tacs!'

More functional, but equally useful, are the spaced en rules,* or dashes, which can separate out a parenthesis in a sentence – in other words, an additional bit of information – and help a copywriter to break up their words in a way that both looks pleasing and adds variety and interest to a paragraph. I use them a lot; probably too much (ditto brackets).

The question mark is another handy tool, which I tend to use in three ways:

1. To start a non-fiction blurb in a way that might draw in a curious reader.
2. As part of a list within copy, to convey that a book is going to cover a wide variety of questions and topics, and that the reader is going to get the answers.
3. To end a blurb when there's nowhere else to go, usually because not much happens in the book, but I desperately don't want people to know this and instead want them to think there's much more to come.

* These are longer than a hyphen – the width of a capital 'N' – and usually surrounded by a space. Americans prefer the longer em ('M') rule.

I generally think question marks should be avoided in the titles of serious books, unless, of course, they are self-help manuals or *Do Androids Dream of Electric Sheep?* I remember working with one author who always wanted to put question marks at the end of statements in his titles, e.g. *Britain: A Democracy?* When used this way it gives off the air of a student essay, or an anachronistic 1940s 'Whither Germany?' energy. The question mark: a useful ally?

And now, on to my favourite punctuation mark... the ellipsis, those three portentous dot dot dots of doom, suspense or saucy suggestion, of things left out and unspoken. If you thought exclamation marks got a bad rap, prepare yourself for the pedant's bête noire.

The German critical theorist Theodor Adorno, who was fascinated by punctuation and described the semi-colon as looking like a 'drooping moustache', is very stern on the matter, deriding the use of ellipses as evidence of slapdash writing, as it 'suggests an infinitude of thoughts and associations, something the hack journalist does not have; he must depend on typography to simulate them'.

Many critics associate ellipses with a commercial, formulaic way of writing, a lazy shorthand for saying that something exciting or scary or dramatic is about to happen (duh duh duuuuh!), or, in the case of many romantic novels of old, that a couple are about to do something sexy which is best left to the reader's imagination. In *Eats, Shoots & Leaves* Lynne Truss quotes the Peter Cook and Dudley Moore sketch where they confess that seeing three dots still leaves them feeling 'a bit funny'.

Umberto Eco derided ellipses' 'ghastliness', and Elena Ferrante wrote recently that she had given up using them because she felt that nothing, in life or writing, should be left

unsaid (although she does acknowledge how visually and met-
aphorically pleasing they are, 'like stepping stones, the sort that
stick out of the water and are a risky pleasure to jump on when
you want to cross a stream without getting wet'.)

Truss, someone I thought would have her guns blazing for
the ellipsis, is surprisingly tolerant, but states that they should
only be used:

> To indicate words missing ... from a quoted passage.
> To trail off in an intriguing manner (which she describes as 'a
> good way to end anything').

I am of course in agreement with her on (1), as an inveterate
butcherer of review quotes, and I am even more pleased that
she approves of the trailing ellipsis at the end of a sentence.
When writing blurbs for certain kinds of books – thrillers, spy
or suspense novels, horror – it's a useful shorthand that does
indeed convey intrigue and make us feel a jolt of curiosity,
even despite ourselves. Looking at the enormous wall of Len
Deighton novels in our house, the blurbs for over fifty per cent
of them end with an ellipsis, and rightly so.

These mysterious dots can also be spotted on the front of
many thriller taglines:

> Never underestimate a woman with nothing left to lose...
> A remote island. An invitation to die for...
> You think you're safe, but what if someone is... *Watching You*

The three-spotted species is a much rarer sighting on literary fiction, but can still be seen in surprising places, such
the blurb for *What a Carve Up!*, Jonathan Coe's unsurpassed

dissection of a ruinous aristocratic family, which ends: 'Once their hapless biographer starts investigating the family's trail of greed, corruption and immoral doings, the time grows ripe for the Winshaws to receive their comeuppance...' As with the exclamation mark at the end of the title (this book is a punctuation bonanza!), the ellipsis is, I think, a sly and ironic nod to the style of the sensational comedy-horror film that inspired it. Or maybe the copywriter just wanted to create some suspense...

There's also a sense of theatrical kitsch and camp in their use on Angela Carter's blurbs: 'From the lairs of the fantastical and fabular and from the domains of the unconscious...'; 'taste the forbidden fruit of chaos...'; 'Is Sophie Fevvers, toast of Europe's capitals, part swan... or all fake?'

You could argue, quite correctly, that in all of these examples, whether commercial or literary, the ellipsis is completely unnecessary – and you would be right. These sentences would stand alone well enough without them. But, as Stephen Fry says of swearing being criticised as 'unnecessary': 'It's not necessary to have coloured socks. It's not necessary for this cushion to be here. But is anyone going to write in and say, "I was shocked to see that cushion there! It really wasn't necessary"? No. Things not being necessary is what makes life interesting.'

In other words, why the hell not embellish your prose with an exciting little ellipsis? Anything that makes writing more fun has got to be a good thing.

And now, prepare to genuflect to the goddess of punctuation. All the writers I have quoted are mere amateurs compared to the acknowledged master of the form, someone who has taken the ellipsis to the level of art. That someone is Coleen Rooney.

It happened on Twitter in October 2019, when she revealed the results of her investigation into who had been leaking private stories from her Instagram account to the *Sun*:

Now I know for certain which account / individual it's come from.

I have saved and screenshotted all the original stories which clearly show just one person has viewed them.

It's......... Rebekah Vardy's account.

Not only did Rooney's statement cause a social media storm and earn her the moniker 'Wagatha Christie', she also showed how the ellipsis can build suspense to a fever pitch more exciting than any penalty shoot-out. Yes, not one, not three, but NINE dots all in a row. Once she started pressing that full stop key, she clearly knew its power. It's *sensational*. Coleen... I salute you!

Show Me the Funny

Don't say it was 'delightful'; make us say 'delightful' when we've read the description.

C. S. LEWIS

I couldn't agree more, Clive. *Show, Don't Tell*. These words are figuratively (perhaps literally, who knows) tattooed on the chest of every writer and copywriter. They are the essence of creating character, which, the idea goes, should be through action or dialogue rather than 'backstory' or employing the services of Basil Exposition from the Austin Powers movies. In the words of James Baldwin, 'Don't describe it, show it. That's what I try to teach all young writers. Don't describe a purple sunset, make me *see* that it is purple.'

The 'show, don't tell' rule is sacrosanct when it comes to blurbs. If you want readers to think a book is fascinating and ground-breaking, show them with arresting examples of its ideas or arguments. If you want them to be scared, use language and pacing to create an atmosphere of tension and fear. Most importantly of all, if you want them to think a book is funny, for pity's sake put some jokes in your copy and make the reader titter, rather than wasting your words by saying it's 'hilarious'.

The most obvious place to start for said jokes would seem to be books by comics or comic actors. I bet the copy on those is a total gas, right? Well, not necessarily. Take John Cleese's autobiography, *So, Anyway*. The copy starts with the words 'Candid and brilliantly funny', but it doesn't contain a single joke, twist, wry aside or anything to raise even so much as a smile (sales of this book fell far below expectations and I wonder if that had something to do with it). It's a similar story with Steve Coogan's autobiography, *Easily Distracted*. The longer hardback copy begins: 'Steve Coogan was born and raised in Manchester in the 1960s, the fourth of six children,' and then continues in that vein for 200 words, reading like a CV rather than an enticing invitation to enter the world of the book, which I'm sure *is* funny. It's such a missed opportunity. Things get better on the paperback, which is written in the first person and describes Steve as 'slightly less desperate for fame than Alan Partridge, slightly less irascible than the Steve who eats his way around the Lake District in *The Trip*, and slightly less libidinous than the version of me in *A Cock and Bull Story*'. Now we're getting somewhere, but I'm still not troubling my incontinence pants.

Michael McIntyre's *Life and Laughter*? Same story: a Wikipedia entry punctuated by 'hilarious' and 'brilliantly funny's. Peter Kay's *The Sound of Laughter*? It starts: 'Peter Kay's unerring gift for observing the absurdities and eccentricities of family life has earned himself a widespread, everyman appeal.' Are we in a lecture theatre? It doesn't improve. Lee Evans's *The Life of Lee*? 'Utterly hilarious', apparently, but NO JOKES. Not a single giggle let alone a guffaw.

For jokes we need to turn to the copy on the autobiographies of Steve Coogan's alter ego Alan Partridge. Yes, these are more obviously 'comic' books, but they are essentially appealing to the same market of readers who want a chuckle, and both *I, Partridge* and *Nomad* deliver them.

Every aspect of *I, Partridge* gets it right. The copy is so good I could hug it. The pretend quotes ('Very thorough' *Norwich Enquirer*, and 'The man of the moment' *TV Quick*, 1994), the mock author biog ('Like Jesus, Alan spent much of his twenties healing the sick – he was a hospital radio DJ!', his 'award-worthy' chat show) and, best of all, the flap copy, which parodies the language, tropes and structure of blurbs to perfection:

> It is a work of heart-breaking majesty. Genuinely one of the best books of the last, what, fifteen to twenty years, *I, Partridge* charts the highs, lows and middle bits of one of Europe's most revered inquisitors … consistently putting his balls on the line for the benefit of the reader. Deeply respectful of the autobiography genre, Partridge has followed its conventions faithfully – remembering things that have happened in his life and writing about them in a roughly chronological order.

Nomad is also funny – although I would probably pat it rather than hug it.

> This deeply personal book is divided into chapters and has a colour photograph on the front cover. It is deeply personal. Through witty vignettes, heavy essays and nod-inducing pieces of wisdom, Alan shines a light on the nooks of the nation and the crannies of himself, making this a biography that biographs the biographer while also biographing bits of Britain.

What about real funny people who get it right? I loved the copy for the Glaswegian comic Kevin Bridges's autobiography, *We Need to Talk About Kevin Bridges*, which gleefully mocks the conventions of its genre:

A comedian's autobiography?

I wonder if he's ever used humour to deflect from his insecurities?

To avoid being bullied?

Is there heartache behind the humour?

I wonder if he's a manic-depressive?

Tears of a clown?

Yes, all of that.

Plus as an added bonus the blurb ends with the word 'shite', a fine piece of Scottish slang that makes me smile almost as much as the time someone wrote 'Boris Johnson is a pure fanny' on a wall in Partick, Glasgow.*

There were reports of the death of the celebrity memoir in publishing for several years, with tales of declining sales figures and a risky business model involving huge advances, hit-and-miss success and a short shelf life. Sales *had* been falling, but the last couple of years has shown that readers were sick of the formula, rather than the celebrities themselves. Like any genre, it has morphed, with a recent slew of books by famous figures that combine memoir with life advice of some kind: Caitlin Moran's *How to Be a Woman* and Robert Webb's *How Not to Be a Boy*, or those with more of a therapeutic spin, such as Simon Amstell's *Help* (tagline: 'COMEDY, TRAGEDY, THERAPY').

Just as with the books themselves, the copy for these celeb-self-help-mems is more sophisticated too – and often has jokes in it!

....

* When the council removed it, it reappeared as 'Boris Johnson is still a pure fanny'. 'Pure' is often used to mean 'really' in Scotland, in acclamations such as 'Pure dead brilliant.'

Take Sarah Millican's *How to Be Champion*, which promises that it will make you 'laugh, feel normal and probably sniff your leggings', and boasts that

> If you've ever worn glasses at the age of six, been contacted by an old school bully, lived in your childhood bedroom in your thirties, been gloriously dumped in a Frankie and Benny's, cried so much you felt great, been for a romantic walk with a dog, worn leggings two days in a row even though they smelt of wee from a distance, then this is YOUR BOOK. If you haven't done those things but wish you had, THIS IS YOUR BOOK.

Or Jo Brand's *Born Lippy* (nice pun, Jo), which has swagger and attitude, just like her:

> Sometimes it's hard to be a woman and sometimes it's time to be a hard woman… This is a book for all those times.
>
> Once upon a (very very) long time ago Jo Brand was what you might describe as 'a nice little girl'. Of course, that was before the values of cynicism, misogyny and the societal expectation that Jo would be thin, feminine and demure sent her off down Arsey Avenue.

I also enjoyed the copy for *Cunk on Everything: The Encyclopedia Philomena*, written by comic Diane Morgan's alter ego, the wondrously stupid Philomena Cunk:

> Once in a blue moon, a book comes along that changes the world. *The Origin of Species. War and Peace. 1984. The World According to Danny Dyer*. And now, *Cunk on Everything: The Encyclopedia Philomena*, by Philomena Cunk.

> Philomena Cunk is one of the greatest thinkers of the 21st century, and in *Cunk on Everything* she turns her attention to our biggest issue: why are there so many books? Wouldn't it be better if there was just one? This is that book – an encyclopedia of ALL HUMAN KNOWLEDGE, from sausages to Henry of Eight to *Brush Strokes* to vegetarian sausages.

The mock quotes are splendid too, and made me blush at my own cavalier use of reviews in the past:

> 'This is a book' Philomena Cunk
> 'Never contact me again' Professor Rupert Delgado, MBE
> '...book...' *Guardian*

All the examples I've given either use or imitate the author's tone of voice. We're not hearing a dusty publisher somewhere wanging on about this book being funny – we know it is because we've already giggled from reading the copy.

Moving slightly out of genre, Adam Kay's *This is Going to Hurt*, a med mem rather than a c'leb mem, also gets it just right. It captures perfectly the gallows humour that anybody who's ever worked, or knows someone who's worked, for the NHS will immediately recognise.

> 97-hour weeks. Life and death decisions. A constant tsunami of bodily fluids. And the hospital parking meter earns more than you.
> Welcome to the life of a junior doctor.

Analysing humour is of course, as E. B. White said, 'like dissecting a frog. Few people are interested and the frog dies,' but it hasn't stopped people from doing it over the years. Among the many theories of humour that have been around since ancient Greece – that laughter comes from the misfortune of others, or is a release valve for suppressed feelings – the one that applies best to writing copy is the 'incongruity theory', most famously espoused by Kant, where there is a disconnect between our expectations and the actual payoff (or punchline).

In this spirit, my last example of a funny blurb is one for a novel: *Bridget Jones's Diary*, part of a rich tradition of comic diaries of hapless everymen/women, from George and Weedon Grossmith's *Diary of a Nobody* to Sue Townsend's *The Secret Diary of Adrian Mole Aged 13¾*.

The back cover of my Picador edition is plastered with review quotes (including one from Salman Rushdie saying 'Even men will laugh,' *so* big of him) and just three lines of copy:

A dazzling urban satire of modern human relations?
An ironic, tragic insight into the demise of the nuclear family?
Or the confused ramblings of a pissed thirty-something?

The incongruity theory right in front of us. What more needs to be said?

Spoiler Alert!

Everyone hates a spoiler. My cinematic bête noire is the film trailer that tells the whole story, leaving me wondering, why should I bother? Fans of *Game of Thrones* were apoplectic when the infamous 'Red Wedding' episode was ruined in the papers before UK viewers had seen it, and Twitter means that even more of us have to put our fingers in our ears and sing la-la-la-not-listening in case the ending of a movie, series or book is revealed.

On books, the cardinal rule is 'never give away the ending in the blurb!', but some definitely flout it – my NYRB Classics edition of Sylvia Townsend Warner's *Summer Will Show* reveals two key plot points on the back cover, which did not go down well with Amazon reviewers at all.

On the Backlisted podcast, the fabulous publisher Alexandra Pringle recalls learning to write blurbs under the equally fabulous Carmen Callil at Virago. She remembers, 'I wept quite often over my copy.' When she let it slip in her blurb that a character dies, Callil admonished her, 'You never, ever, *ever* say that someone dies. I know what we'll say… we'll call it "the final ecstasy."' Now that's divine inspiration.

With 'ta-dah!' plot twists, the stakes are even higher than with deaths, although as someone who is an inveterate twist-guesser – I pride myself on annoying everyone I went to see *The Village* with by correctly predicting the final rug-pull just before we went into the cinema – I think it's all part of the fun. HarperCollins turned it into a selling point with their '#wtfthatending' campaign for the novel *Behind Her Eyes*. 'That ending', by the way, was so silly that it almost – almost – put me off twists for life, because it failed to respect the reader's intelligence. I see it has now been made into a Netflix series, with reviewers berating the 'what-the-hell lunacy' of that last, ridiculous reveal.

But are spoiler rules there to be broken sometimes? How many of us re-read favourite novels or re-watch favourite movies when we know what's going to happen? I find comfort in pre-dictability. Fans of Tolkien will know that his Prologue to *The Fellowship of the Ring* makes it very clear who triumphs and who is vanquished at the end of the trilogy, but it doesn't lessen our enjoyment. According to fantasy writer E. C. Ambrose, Tolkien is reassuring us, 'letting us know that things will turn out well, in spite of all the hardships these characters are about to endure'. She traces the 'spoilers up-front' tradition as far back as ancient oral epics, which began with a brief summary of what would happen before the real excitement began.

There is also Proper Scientific Evidence that perhaps spoilers don't matter as much as we think they do. A 2011 experiment at the University of California San Diego gave readers a series of short stories by famous writers including Roald Dahl, John Updike, Anton Chekhov and Agatha Christie. Some stories were presented as they were written, some with a spoiler paragraph at the beginning, and others with a spoiler paragraph embedded in the text. To everyone's surprise, participants significantly preferred the spoiled versions, especially in the stories with ironic plot twists. Perhaps the world of a book, its atmosphere and characters, is even more important than suspense? Maybe our parents were right and the journey really is part of the fun (a notion severely tested when stuck on a motorway somewhere in the Midlands with only a Michelin *I-SPY On the Road* guide for comfort. I spy an industrial chimney!).

One writer who uses spoilers as part of her art is Muriel Spark. A Catholic convert fascinated by the notion of free will and the godlike powers of the author, she would often casually disclose the destiny of a particular character early on in a novel, jumping forward in time to reveal their invariably unhappy ending. It is a kind of fatalism that both illustrates her narrative command* and gives the reader a delicious frisson of doom and death. She called these her 'flash-forwards'. In keeping with this dark spirit, the blurb on the back of her novel *The Driver's Seat* deliberately ends with, or at least foreshadows, the death of the heroine (Chapter Three tells us she will be murdered): 'Infinity and eternity attend Lise's last terrible day in an unnamed southern city, as she meets her fate.'

The word 'fate' is key here, illustrating how Spark's art is an echo of Greek tragedy, with her authorial interjections acting as the chorus. Ancient dramas, as well as brimming with avenging Furies, naked satyrs, incest, blindings, patricide, infanticide, suicide, mass homicide and about any other 'cide you could think of, are also filled with spoilers, making a character's destiny clear from the start. Then the wheel is set in motion and the pieces start moving. We know there is nothing we can do to stop it; the release comes from watching the inevitable car crash unfold in front of us. It's the same with Shakespeare, who

....

* The teenage Spark studied the now lost art of 'précis writing' at college, learning how to extract the key meaning from a longer text, which helps explain the sharp perfection of her sentences.

uses a chorus at the beginning of the play to tell us that Romeo and Juliet will die.

I still contend, however, that when describing a literary work, there is a responsibility not to give the whole game away. There may always be someone, somewhere, who doesn't know how things turn out. So the blurb I wrote for a scholarly edition of *Romeo and Juliet* describes the play as 'a warning of death', *King Lear* talks of 'a wretched wasteland of insanity' and *Titus Andronicus* eschews kids in pies for 'a murderous revenge of barely conceivable cruelty'. Euphemistic, possibly, but it's always good to cover your back where plot is concerned.

Some people will deliberately *not* read an entire book when they're writing copy for it, so they're left in as much of a state of suspense as the person who will read the blurb. I can see the merits of this approach, as it is easy to become overwhelmed with plot detail. However, I prefer to read to the end if I have time, especially with fiction, often skipping to it before I've read the whole thing (I realise this is the act of a philistine). I want to get the full picture, to know where I'm going and what grisly fate or happy outcome I might at least want to *hint* at – plus, as Harry Burns says in *When Harry Met Sally*, 'in case I die before I finish, I know how it ends'.

$\mathbb{T}$riangle, Diamond or Hourglass?

The Shape of Copy

Mighty is geometry; joined with art, resistless.

EURIPIDES

Everything has a shape, even blurbs. Especially blurbs. I don't mean their physical layout on a book cover, I mean their underlying geometry. They have a structure, just like stories, with different moving parts. And the order you put these elements in determines their hidden shape.

Albrecht Dürer called geometry the foundation of all painting, and the same can be said for writing. Even the baggiest of monsters has a kind of shape. Laurence Sterne riffed on this in his 'cock and bull story' *The Life and Opinions of Tristram Shandy, Gentleman*, a rambling shaggy dog story if ever there was one. A piece of metafiction centuries before the term existed, this fictional 'autobiography' subverts the form of the novel, at one point marking the death of a character with an entirely black page. But the best part is where the narrator announces he is going to continue his story 'in a tolerable straight line', then illustrates what's happened so far with a series of wiggly, bendy, winding diagrams of all his plot digressions. As critic John Mullan puts it, 'This is a book that provides its own self-mocking diagrams of itself.' I enjoy the notion of capturing narrative with shapes.

Which brings us to the geometry of blurbs. This idea isn't mine; it was given to me by a fellow copywriter who has kindly allowed me to play with it here. The shape is not to do with how a piece of copy looks, but what it focuses on. So it may concentrate on something very small (a character, a plot detail) and then move to something big (an overarching theme, a world), or vice versa, or in a different order. Looked at this way, the famous opening of Stanley Kubrick's film *2001: A Space Odyssey* would be an hourglass shape, moving from the big (the sun rises over the earth) to the specific (a prehistoric tribe discover how to use bones as weapons) and widening out again to the universal (space, the final frontier!).

And what about the blurb for Arthur C. Clarke's own novelisation of the film? Pretty excitingly (if you like this sort of thing), it's an hourglass too, moving from wider context to plot detail and out to big ideas again:

> Written when landing on
> the moon was still a dream, and made into
> one of the most influential films of all time,
> *2001: A Space Odyssey* remains a classic work
> of science fiction. The discovery of a black
> monolith on the moon leads to a manned
> expedition deep into the solar
> system, in the hope
> of establishing contact with an
> alien intelligence. Yet long before the
> crew can reach their destination, the voyage
> descends into disaster. Brilliant, compulsive and
> prophetic, Arthur C. Clarke's timeless novel
> tackles the enduring theme of mankind's
> place in the universe.

Has that whetted your appetite for more blurb geometry? Of course it has. Here's a diamond blurb for Tolstoy's *Anna Karenina*, moving from the specificity of one woman's predicament to the whole of society, and then back to an individual story:

Anna
Karenina seems
to have everything – beauty,
wealth, popularity and an adored son. But
she feels that her life is empty until the moment she
encounters the impetuous officer Count Vronsky. Their subsequent affair
scandalises society and family alike, and soon brings jealousy and bitterness in
its wake. Contrasting with this tale of love and self-destruction is
the vividly observed story of Levin, a man striving to
find contentment and meaning – and
a self-portrait of Tolstoy
himself.

And now, last but by no means least, may I present one of the most popular blurb models, the triangle. It starts with a moment and then broadens out to encompass story, more characters and big themes:

The
Woman
in White opens
with Walter Hart-
right's eerie encounter
with a strange, solitary woman
on a moonlit London road. Engaged
as a drawing master to the beautiful Laura
Fairlie, Walter becomes embroiled in the sinister
intrigues of Sir Percival Glyde and his 'charming' friend
Count Fosco, who has a taste for white mice, vanilla bonbons and
poison. Pursuing questions of identity and insanity along the corridors of
English country mansions and the madhouse, this is the first and most influential of the Victorian genre that combined Gothic horror with psychological realism.

With geometry, the fun never stops. You can also have an upside-down triangle, or a messier, zig-zag blurb – but when copy gets into the realm of the wobbly, it is perhaps a sign that it isn't as well structured as it could be. The shape of copy can be a good way of testing whether words are working as hard as they can, and also of rewriting something that isn't quite there yet. I'm not sure Laurence Sterne would approve of this simple symmetry, but it can stop a few sentences from turning into a big mess.

There are other ways you can change the story you are telling too. Which brings us to…

THE LITERAL SHAPE OF COPY

I once read an interview with Salman Rushdie where he spoke about writing his children's book, *Haroun and the Sea of Stories*. He showed the first chapters to his young son, who complained that 'it doesn't jump up enough'. I knew exactly what he meant. Good writing should be 'jumpy', moving along and keeping the reader engaged, and well-structured copy should jump too, moving from one element to the next as swiftly as possible. It should also look 'jumpy' on the page, which brings us to its physical shape.

Some back cover blurbs are written within the constraint of a design template, which only allows for a certain number of words in a particular format. But if not, it's a good idea to consider how the words will look when they appear in print. Copy can be made 'jumpy' with short sentences, creative punctuation, chopped-up paragraphs and, above all, not being frightened of empty space.

Thrillers often go to town with the look of the copy on the back cover, to keep the pace up, such as Lucy Foley's 2021 bestseller *The Guest List*:

EACH HAS A SECRET

EACH HAS A MOTIVE

Off the windswept Irish coast, guests gather
for the wedding of the year.

Old friends
Past grudges
Happy families
Hidden jealousies
Thirteen guests
One body

One guest won't leave this wedding alive…

But it can work effectively for weightier subjects too. The back cover of Felicity Lawrence's *Shopped* has been cleverly designed so that the copy looks like a shopping list, in order to pull out punchy details and highlight them visually, with each item 'ticked' off:

SUPERMARKETS. NOT SO SUPER AFTER ALL?

High streets killed by megastores ✓
Bullied suppliers ✓
Fake choice ✓
Pesticide-covered fruit and veg ✓
Third world producers exploited ✓
Local jobs destroyed ✓
Massive profits and rock-bottom pay ✓

AND THAT'S JUST THE START…

There is no opportunity to be bored with this copy, as its layout keeps us engaged, all the way to the bottom of the list.

The moral of these tales of metamorphoses? Words are there to be mucked about with. Shifting the shape, either figurative or literal, of a piece of copy can make language fizz. And, finally:

Don't be scared of white space.
Space is your friend.
It makes everything you write
Look better.

The Ultimate Bliss of Bad Blurbs

Oh bad, bad blurbs, you make me feel so good. I'm not talking about blurbs that are bad because they're too long, too boring or the writer fell asleep before they got to the end – please refer to the copy for Thomas Piketty's *Capital* if you really want to put yourself through that. I'm after some cheap thrills; the kind of blurbs that would be *Showgirls* or *Cats* if they were a film. There are several deranged abominations dotted throughout this book, but I thought a few more bad, mad or sad blurbs deserved their little cabinet of horrors here too. Each is its own special brand of nonsense, but I've tried to categorise them because not only do they add to the gaiety of nations, they can also teach us what *not* to do in copywriting.

Welcome to the Seventh Circle of Copy Hell. Oh, who am I kidding? I *love* these blurbs.

I. ENGLISH, BUT NOT AS WE KNOW IT

Sometimes copywriters take it upon themselves to use words in their own special way, one that bears no resemblance to the way an actual human might use them. It's as if they translated their copy into a foreign language on Google, and then translated it back again, like this description on a lurid Panther pulp edition of Jack Kerouac's *Maggie Cassidy*:

175

The vibrant, demanding, woman-bodied girl who fascinated and confused the man she yearned for.

Woman-bodied? Creepy *and* nonsensical. Double points there. The copy on Kerouac's *Tristessa* is almost as good:

A new and hauntingly different novel about a morphine-racked prostitute.

It does what it says on the tin, I suppose, if you like that sort of thing?

Pulp classics often take leave of their senses, such as a 1940s edition of Zola's *Nana*:

At the head of the scarlet list of literature's most vivid courte-sans stands Nana. Rich men left their fortunes, their titles, and their honour at her feet. Poor men left their love and even their lives. Voluptuous and violent, she created a world of luxury which revolved about her person.

There are definitely some words here, they are in some kind of order, but perhaps not the right order. I feel rather alarmed for scarlet Nana's person, what with a world revolving around it, as well as various men.

While we're in the realm of objectifying women, there's a great 1970s 'missing the point' edition of Edna O'Brien's break-through feminist classic *The Country Girls*, which features some soft-focus boob photography on the front, along with a tagline that is cryptic, to say the least: 'Green as Ireland, Cait and Baba, *The Country Girls*.' Any clue? No, me neither.

Then the back is just baffling:

> When Irish eyes are smiling, here's what's hidden behind them – a fresh, gay assessment of a world where the wolves still roam.

I'm still none the wiser. But I am a little scared.

Before we move on, an honorary mention is also needed for this copy on a novel by Tom Robbins:

> In *Fierce Invalids Home from Hot Climates*, his seventh and biggest novel, Tom Robbins brings on stage the most complex and compelling character he has ever created ... there is nothing remotely wishy-washy about Switters. He doesn't merely pack a pistol. He is a pistol.

Such riches. I don't know what I prefer – 'biggest novel' or 'He is a pistol'. The blurb also later talks about his 'strangely elevated heels'. It's English, but in the loosest possible sense. A quote on the front of the cover tells us: 'You'll burn your brains trying to remember all the one-liners.' That's if you haven't already melted it trying to decipher the copy.

2. HAVE THEY READ THE BOOK?

These are the blurbs that bear no resemblance to the book you are reading. I often wonder who wrote them, exactly what book they had in front of them, and what kind of loopy juice they were on.

I've already touched upon the lunacy of the 1990s Tor covers for Jane Austen's novels, but the blurbs are on another level entirely. This one for *Pride and Prejudice* displays a tin ear of magnificent proportions:

What's a Girl to Do?
Scatterbrained, social climbing Mrs Bennet makes one demand
of her five daughters.
Marry. Marry well. Marry RICH.

It ends by giving away a plot point too:

Mrs Bennet's in hysterics. Mr Bennet's in his study. Lydia's
eloped with a soldier and Jane's heart may well be broken. Will
any of the Bennet girls find true love and fortune?

It is terrible. But also amazing.

Classics are a rich seam of good-bad blurbs, possibly because
when we know the plot it's even better when the writer just
gets it wrong, such as this 1950s Pocket Cardinal edition of
Wuthering Heights:

Heathcliff – man or devil?
It was a question which haunted Catherine like a malignant
disease. When she looked into Heathcliff's wild, glittering eyes,
she could only turn away in horror…

I don't remember *Wuthering Heights* being a horror novel.
Neither do I recognise *Brighton Rock* from this 1948 description.

Front cover: Mad killer prowls a summer resort
Back cover: A story of stark terror on the blood-drenched sands
of Brighton. Author Graham Greene takes you behind the glittering façade of a holiday resort town, deep into the twisted
soul of a fiendish murderer.

I don't think Brighton ever glittered in the 1940s. I don't think the copywriter has been there. And I don't think they read the book.

Another 1940s edition, this time of *The Great Gatsby*, has a similarly hysterical vibe:

> Wild Fabulous Parties
> WITH A HOST NOBODY KNEW!
> Riotous orgies, with careless women and maddening music and flowing champagne. Yet in all this crowd *nobody knew the host*.

The anonymity of the host is *really* annoying this copywriter, isn't it.*

My final 'blurb that weirdly concentrates on the wrong thing' is the jacket copy on the first edition of *The Catcher in Rye*, from 1951: 'Anyone who has read J. D. Salinger's *New Yorker* stories will not be surprised by the fact that his first novel is full of children.' Full of children, is that *really* the main selling point? It goes on to describe Holden Caulfield thus, in a big 'screw you' to the reader:

> The boy himself is at once too simple and too complex for us to make any final comment about him or his story.

I wonder if this was part of the reason Salinger insisted on no copy appearing on his books for ever-more?

....

* It also has an air of one of those 'bad book descriptions' that do the rounds online. *The Great Gatsby*: 'Man sells drugs, buys mansion to impress one night stand from five years prior.' *Rebecca*: 'Second wife unfazed by husband's needlessly complicated murder of first wife.' *Crime and Punishment*: 'Man talks about an axe for three chapters, you put the book down, never to return.'

3. ANTI-BLURBS

On occasion, a copywriter will do everything in their power to put readers off a book. This can be done in a number of ways. One technique is to depress the hell out of them, such as this blurb on a 1980s edition of Jean Rhys's *Good Morning, Midnight*, beginning:

> Back in Paris for a quiet, sane fortnight, Sasha Jansen has just been rescued by a friend from drinking herself to death in a Bloomsbury bedsitter … Streets, shops and bars vividly evoke her Paris past, feckless husband Eno, her dead baby, sundry humiliations in abject jobs.

As a general rule, I would say abject misery, dead babies and suicide in a bedsitter are not the best ways to lure a reader in.

Yet this copy is positively flaunting itself compared to the blurb on the back of an old edition of John Steinbeck's adolescent coming-of-age story *The Red Pony*. It is clearly aimed at children, but I'm tempted to call social services:

> This is the poignant story of a boy, Jody, who above all wanted a pony. It is the story of how he got it, and how it died…
>
> But Jody waited, hoped and prayed for another pony and, finally but tragically, he got it…

To top it all off, there is a review from *School Librarian* saying that it 'contains most of the ingredients of a great children's story'. 'Most'. Apart from dead ponies.

Remember: don't make your audience want to slit their wrists before they even open the book.

Another method is to tell the reader that the book will send them to sleep, such as the copy on the Chapman & Hall 1961 first edition of Evelyn Waugh's *A Tourist in Africa*: 'a very pleasant bedside book (which should induce sleep in all but the most stubborn insomniacs)'.

Or if that doesn't work, you can just tell them the book is rubbish, as on this aged Penguin Modern Classic edition of Henry James's *The Ambassadors*:

> *The Ambassadors*, though it was the author's own favourite among his novels, is one of those (his last three) which have abruptly divided critics. In them Walter Allen finds 'the final splendid flowering of James's genius' and Graham Greene groups them together as his 'three poetic masterpieces'. On the other hand: 'We are asked to admire *The Ambassadors*,' writes F. R. Leavis, 'and *The Ambassadors* seems to me not only *not* one of his great books, but to be a bad one.'

Do take a moment if you need to after that. I know the copy of the past is often less 'selling' than today's, but who thought this was a good idea? Were they attempting some kind of Brechtian alienation effect through the medium of blurb? Were they just a massive snob? We shall never know.

4. DIVINE MADNESS

Now on to fabulously bad blurbs. They are to copywriting what Ed Wood was to films, taking copy to a level that is godlike in its camp. And to enjoy them at their fullest we must travel to the 1960s and 1970s.

The supernatural or weird provides rich pickings from this period, when one could enjoy books such as *How to Become a Sensuous Witch* by 'Abragail' and 'Valaria' (sample copy: 'keep your cauldron steaming!'); *Tales of the Unexpected* ('Roald Dahl can stand you on your head, twist you in knots, tie up your hands and leave you gasping for more.' Exhausting); or *Killer Crabs* ('A bloody carnage of human flesh on an island beachhead!' I love the geographical specificity of 'beachhead'.). Or maybe you're in the mood for some psychotic leprechauns lurking in the cellars of a castle? The copy on the 1966 horror novel *The Little People* informs us: 'ELVES? DEMONS? They speak German. They carry whips…' A review from the *New York Times* says this is 'carefully laid-on horror'. Careful? I'm not sure *they* read the book.

This copy, for the original UK edition of Jacqueline Susann's 1966 saga *Valley of the Dolls*, is as garish and kitsch as one of the author's Pucci pantsuits:

> From Broadway to Hollywood, this is one of the fastest-selling, most whispered about novels ever. And no wonder! It reveals more about the secret, drug-filled, love-starved, sex-satiated, nightmare world of showbusiness than any book published.

I actually believe every word of it. A round of applause, please.

But my winner is an early edition of Jilly Cooper's 1978 romance *Imogen*. I worship at the altar of Cooper's sexy sagas, and this copy delivers raunch in spades. If the front cover tagline is the tease ('The Path of a Jet-Set Virgin Was a Hard One!') then the blurb is positively orgasmic:

> Girls like Imogen, tied to dreary jobs in provincial towns, are apt to dream of romantic escapes to sun-drenched beaches and

to conjure up visions of ultimate bliss in the bronzed arms of the athletic heroes of their night-time fantasies. Seldom, however, do they have to face up to their dreams coming true. In *Imogen*, a rustic Yorkshire ingénue finds her dreams coming true rather faster than she can cope with them. How she parries the advances of Nicky Beresford, the lecherous tennis ace, and copes with the gropes of the rest of the Riviera drones, will bring a warm glow of reassurance to all those nervous Mums whose daughters' tender bosoms have been over-exposed to the St Tropez sun.

There is *so* much to love here: rustic ingénue, tender bosoms, gropes. Take a bow, Jilly's inappropriate blurb writer. You have made me very happy.

You. Yes, you. I'm talking to you.

'This is your brain,' says a man holding an egg. He points at a frying pan: 'This is drugs.' He breaks the egg and fries it: 'This is your brain on drugs. Got any questions?' Now considered a classic, this 1987 American anti-drug advert is an example of what psychologists would call 'self-referencing messages', which employ the second person to engender empathy and identification. 'You' is a powerful word and, as we all know from Spider-Man, with great power comes great responsibility.

We're often told that 'free' and 'new' are the most influential words in advertising, but 'you' is a strong contender too. You can see it again and again, in campaigns for the *Independent* ('It is. Are you?'), Marmite ('You either love it or hate it') and of course Lord Kitchener's finger-pointing recruitment poster, 'Your Country Needs YOU' – which, like all famous ads, has been resurrected several times, most recently in an ill-judged campaign targeted at millennials ('Snowflakes, your army needs you and your compassion,' 'Selfie addicts, your army needs you and your confidence'). Way to insult your target audience, armed forces.

When used wisely, the second person can engage and create sympathy, such as the classic 1980 Chivas Regal ad, which used long-form copy to express the writer's love and admiration for his father:

Because I've known you all my life.
Because a red Rudge bicycle once made me the happiest boy on the street.
Because you let me play cricket on the lawn…

And so on, until we get to

Because I don't say thank you as often as I should.
Because it's Father's Day.
Because if you don't deserve Chivas Regal, who does?

Twenty-five 'becauses' in total. Yes, it's sentimental, but it works because it manages to be intimate and universal at the same time, and it creates feelings of familiarity and fondness.

But when it is used clumsily, 'you' can sound hectoring and domineering. According to psychologist James Price Dillard, if this formulation is used to 'imply a relationship in which the hearer is subordinate', it can be counterproductive. Take the recent email that popped up in my inbox from Ocado, titled 'Have you watched it yet?' and directing me to a video 'celebrating' what I'd bought that year. I love Ocado, and I know everyone's boredom threshold is very low at the time of writing, but no – I haven't and I don't want to, thank you. It was the 'yet' which irked me with its bossy, presumptive tone. In effect, what 'you' really must say is 'we'. If it doesn't, it can misfire.

Addressing the reader directly can work in blurbs, when used to intrigue rather than accuse.* Take the copy that appeared on

* For an excellent example of using the *first* person in a blurb, check out the chef's-kiss-perfect copy on Andy Weir's *The Martian*: 'I'm stranded on Mars. I have no way to communicate with Earth … I'm screwed.'

the original trade paperback edition of Eric Schlosser's *Fast Food Nation* when it was first published in the UK:

> You are what you eat. But do you really know what you're eating?
>
> Britain eats more fast food than any other nation in Europe. It looks good, tastes good, and it's cheap. But the real cost never appears on the menu.

It was written by my old boss, and I think it pitches the 'you' question at exactly the right level – plus its acknowledgement that fast food is attractive stops the copy from bashing the reader over the head with guilt.

The second person can also invite a reader in with a nod of recognition, such as the copy on the book *Why Do Men Have Nipples?*:

> You know how it is… you're at a party, you've had a drink or two, and then someone introduces you to a friend. He's a doctor. And it seems like the perfect time to ask all those strange questions you've always wondered about, but never had the courage to ask.

The inviting copy on the first edition of *Tinker Tailor Soldier Spy* uses the universal 'you' to emphasise the anonymity of le Carré's hero:

> You could meet him any day on the Underground. Hundreds of him. Mr George Smiley, small, podgy, and at best middle-aged, is one of London's meek who do not inherit the earth.

'You' works when it could be replaced with 'any of us'. It can also implicate us too, and stop us in our tracks. The blurb for Afua Hirsch's *Brit(ish)* is a brilliant example of how to use 'you' both to universalise and make a point:

> You're British.
>
> Your parents are British.
>
> Your partner, your children and most of your friends are British.
>
> So why do people keep asking you where you're from?
>
> We are a nation in denial about our imperial past and the racism that plagues our present. *Brit(ish)* is Afua Hirsch's deeply personal and provocative exploration of how this came to be – and an urgent call for change.

The gut punch of the fourth line is perfect, and its casual tone is the ideal counterpart to the serious copy that follows.

The copy on Laura Bates's *Girl Up* works in a similar way, but with a clever switcheroo from second to first person at the end (this copy is adapted from the opening of the book):

> They said you need to be thin and beautiful.
>
> They told you to wear longer skirts, avoid going out late at night and move in groups.
>
> Wear shoes you can run in more easily than heels.
>
> Dress to flatter your apple, pear, hourglass figure, but don't look like a slut.
>
> They said if you're strong or opinionated, you'll be shrill, bossy, a ballbreaker.
>
> They said 'That's not for girls.' 'Take it as a compliment.' 'Don't rock the boat.'

They told you 'beauty is on the inside' but you knew they didn't really mean it.

Well screw that. I'm here to tell you something else.

This copy, in my view, is *mighty*. Like *Brit(ish)*, it provokes a cry of recognition in the intended reader and, one hopes, a nod of empathy even in those who aren't.

What about those few books that are written in the second person – do they get blurbed in a similar way? The copy for Jay McInerney's *Bright Lights, Big City* starts promisingly using lines from the book, but pulls its punches halfway through:

> You are at a nightclub talking to a girl with a shaved head. The club is either Heartbreak or the Lizard Lounge. All might become clear if you could just slip into the bathroom and do a little more Bolivian Marching Powder. Then again, it might not… So begins our nameless hero's trawl through the brightly lit streets of Manhattan…

A little frustrating, I feel.

Now this is more like it. It is the copy on the back of Andrew Hankinson's *You Could Do Something Amazing with Your Life [You Are Raoul Moat]* and to my mind it is the perfected use of the second person in a blurb:

> A letter arrives. You've got an appointment with a trainee clinical psychologist on April 29, 2008.
>
> You don't attend.
>
> Another letter arrives. It says they don't normally reschedule appointments, but they know this is hard for you, so they're offering you another appointment. It's on May 13, 2008.

You don't attend.

Two years later you shoot three people and shoot yourself. You will be called a monster. You will be called evil. The prime minister, David Cameron, will stand up in Parliament and say you were a callous murderer, end of story. You have nine days and your whole life to prove you are more than a callous murderer.

Go.

When I first read this blurb, I gazed upon it in awe and wonder like a medieval peasant in front of Chartres cathedral, thinking that the copywriter or editor who had created it was a genius. The 'Go' at the end is chilling and sickening. Then I discovered it was taken directly from the book (as I've said elsewhere, sometimes you just have to accept that another's words are better than yours) and that Andrew Hankinson was the genius. He uses the second person throughout to force us into the mess of self-pity, delusion and toxic masculinity that is the mind of Raoul Moat, the Newcastle bodybuilder who shot three people before killing himself amid a media circus.

I don't think Hankinson's method necessarily creates empathy, or even sympathy, and I don't think it is intended to. Instead, by rewriting a murderer's own words (from transcripts and records) in this way, it makes us realise that there are countless Raoul Moats out there, and that just one bad decision – let alone a lifetime of them – could result in this happening anywhere, at any time. It is the ultimate use of 'you' as 'anyone'.

As this copy shows, the second person, when used with care, can do something completely different. It can be shocking, or welcoming, or thought-provoking. But it should always be employed with an awareness of who your reader is going to be, and the effect you want it to have on them.

4.

BLURB SPOTTING
IN THE WILD

Book Species

Come and Have a Go if You Think You're Hard Enough

Literary Fiction

> I have a joke about literary fiction. Well, less of a joke, more of a 'compelling meditation on love and loss, couched in prose of pellucid beauty'.
>
> JONATHAN COE

'Does anything actually happen in this book?' 'No, not really – is it that obvious?' This type of exchange often occurs with my fellow Penguin copywriter when we meet to look at each other's blurbs. It tends to happen when one of us has written a blurb for a literary fiction title. You know the kind of book. They win prizes. There generally isn't much in the way of a plot. Or if there is, it's something along the lines of woman goes away and finds herself, someone thinks about an event from their past, or sad middle-aged man has an affair – or even just considers said affair and doesn't go through with it. It's all about character and atmosphere. In other words, to paraphrase comedian Frank Carson, it's the way they tell 'em. Which is fine. Many people like this kind of thing. (Although, according to John Carey in *The Intellectuals and the Masses*, they actually don't, and modernism was invented by cultural snobs such as Virginia Woolf just so that the newly literate classes wouldn't get it.)

The blurbs for literary fiction need to entice the reader into the world of a novel, and assure them that it is a work of quality.

This is where copy can be guilty of publishing hyperbole, or as one writer nailed it, 'bullshit superlatives'. It's never moving, always 'deeply moving'. See 'deeply personal' too. It's never a story (heaven forfend), it's a meditation, an exploration, a reflection. It is a 'tour de force'. The writer is at 'the height of their powers' – which begs the obvious questions, is it all downhill from here onwards, and was everything they wrote before this a bit crap? Another word I've noticed a lot recently is 'liminal'. Books are always occupying liminal spaces between things these days. Are they though, really?* And then of course we have 'In the tradition of…', which just sounds like they're ripping off another writer.

Most people in publishing have been guilty of using these formulae at some point: I know I have. There are only so many words in the world and, let's be honest, sometimes we're in a bit of a rush.† US publishing insider Will Schwalbe says, 'I would love flap copy that says "this isn't the author's best book, but there are some modest pleasures to be found in the pages."' As if. We chicken out, and we all climb aboard the merry-go-round of superlatives, which Jeremy Lewis describes in his charming publishing memoir like this:

••

* A shout-out for 'haunting' too, which according to one journalist appeared in the descriptions of thirty-six books published by Macmillan in the US in 2020.

† Or perhaps publishing, as so many other industries, just has its own jargon – like the law with its baffling Latin, business with its 'matrix hubbing', tabloids with their 'flauntings' and 'beddings', the art world with its 'conceptualisations', as skewered by Jonathan Meades in a recent invective against jargon: 'centrifugal, evasive, drably euphemistic, unthreatening, conformist … language that speaks to itself'.

> The good publisher must – and not entirely cynically – per-
> suade himself and others, if for a season only, that a particu-
> lar novel is 'the most amazing thing I've read for years' ...
> This momentary quite genuine readiness to make, and believe
> exaggerated claims is essential to the workings of the literary
> business and to the well-being of those who depend upon it.

So how do you describe and sell a book where not much happens, without resorting to the bombastic language of literary
fiction? As my co-copywriter and I have concluded, you *have*
to give the appearance of a story, even if there isn't one. People
really, *really* like to know what a book is going to be about.
Humans have always loved listening to and telling stories,
from troglodytes to telly. As Jonathan Gottschall says in *The
Storytelling Animal*, 'We are, as a species, addicted to story. Even
when the body goes to sleep, the mind stays up all night, telling
itself stories.' Stories are a hard habit to break. It's natural, as
this beauty from Twitter shows:

> Me, begging, tears in my eyes: Please just tell me what the book
> is about. The plot. Please.
>   A book cover, unfazed: A Subversive Masterpiece. A Deep
> and Touching Story. The *New York Times* Bestseller. Go Fuck
> Yourself.

Whenever I ask people what they hate most on the back cover
of a novel, it's a list of review quotes with no blurb. Readers are
crying out for even just a *hint* of what happens, and you have to
give them something.

One way of making a story out of no story is to pick out
memorable, unusual details about characters or places (see 'Be

a Magpie'). Another is to keep the vocabulary simple. I love the description 'This new novel is a speaking picture' from the blurb for Hilary Mantel's *Bring Up the Bodies* (of course this novel has a sensational plot, but it is one that is familiar to many). I also like the ending of the blurb for Anna Burns's *Milkman*: '*Milkman* is a tale of gossip and hearsay, silence and deliberate deafness. It is the story of inaction with enormous consequences.' Isn't that list of solid, anchoring nouns far more appealing than wasted adjectives? Plus 'inaction' is such an unexpected, counterintuitive word.

My failsafe technique for describing literary fiction, however, is to create a point of tension. In other words, even if nothing really happens, imply that it *might*, somehow. Set up an opposition (even if it's just with a couple of words, such as the description of Flora the 'golden tyrant' on Elizabeth Taylor's *The Soul of Kindness*). Hint at a future action. Ask a question. Introduce a twist of wit or surprise. A good example of this is the blurb on the first edition of Ottessa Moshfegh's *My Year of Rest and Relaxation*. On one level, this novel is the very definition of a book where nothing happens. A troubled young New Yorker decides to spend a year in a prescription drug-induced state of near-constant sleep and, in a sense, that is it.* Stripped to its bare bones the plot is minimal. The blurb gets round the lack of action nicely – as long as we politely avert our gaze from the well-worn 'three adjectives and an adverb' formula at the start:

> A shocking, hilarious and strangely tender novel about a young
> woman's experiment in narcotic hibernation, aided and abetted
> by one of the worst psychiatrists in the annals of literature. Our

* I loved this book and, unlike most people who read it, found my insomniac self envying the heroine and her Sleeping Beauty-like year of being zonked out.

narrator has many of the advantages of life, on the surface. Young, thin, pretty, a recent Columbia graduate, she lives in an apartment on the Upper East Side of Manhattan paid for by her inheritance. But there is a vacuum at the heart of things, and it isn't just the loss of her parents, or the way her Wall Street boyfriend treats her, or her sadomasochistic relationship with her alleged best friend. It's the year 2000 in a city aglitter with wealth and possibility: what could be so terribly wrong?

I like it because of the psychiatrist joke, the ironic and tantalising question at the end, and the daring use of 'thin' as an aspirational adjective to describe our heroine, which feels rather wrong in its honesty. Later on the blurb also sickly describes the book as 'dangling its legs over the edge of 9/11', which I enjoyed for its discomfort.

Another excellent example of making something out of not much is this blurb for *Embers*, by Sándor Márai. In this book, two men sit down and have dinner, and that is it. Really. But the blurb manages to turn a little into a lot, through pacing, drama and suggestion:

As darkness settles on a forgotten castle at the foot of the Carpathian mountains, two men sit down to a final meal together. They have not seen one another in forty-one years. At their last meeting, in the company of a beautiful woman, an unspoken act of betrayal left all three lives shattered – and each of them alone. Tonight, as wine stirs the blood, it is time to talk of old passions and that last, fateful meeting.

'Unspoken', 'that last, fateful meeting' – by saying what isn't, rather than what is, this copy leaves me wanting more.

Julian Barnes's novel *Flaubert's Parrot* is essentially about a bloke looking for a stuffed bird, but the cover copy gets round this very well:

> *Flaubert's Parrot* deals with Flaubert, parrots, bears and railways; with our sense of the past and our sense of abroad; with France and England, life and art, sex and death, George Sand and Louise Colet, aesthetics and redcurrant jam; and with its enigmatic narrator, a retired English doctor, whose life and secrets are slowly revealed.

I approve of the sensible, business-like 'deals with' at the start of the copy, which enables a pick 'n' mix to ensue and, with 'slowly revealed', we have the promise of action.

What about another male stalwart of prize-winning literary fiction, Ian McEwan? *On Chesil Beach* is not an action-packed book and, unfortunately, I think the blurb on the current paperback perhaps makes this a bit too clear:

> It is July 1962. Edward and Florence, young innocents married that morning, arrive at a hotel on the Dorset coast. At dinner in their rooms they struggle to suppress their private fears of the wedding night to come and, unbeknownst to them both, the events of the evening will haunt them for the rest of their lives.

I'm just not sure what a reader is going to get out of this, and you want to think you are going to get *something*. It reminds me of the 'blurb' for a French film I recently saw on Netflix: 'A passionate middle-aged philosophy professor rethinks her already much examined life after an unforeseen divorce.' Even before my husband and I sat down to watch it, we looked at each other and said, 'Nothing's going to happen, is it?' And lo, it didn't. The heroine hung out in the countryside discussing philosophy with some students for a while, she got a cat and that, genuinely, was that. I still got something out of the film: the lovely Parisian scenes, Isabelle Huppert slamming doors chicly. But I think the Netflix copy could have done a little more to welcome us in, just as a blurb should help us out. If the 'nothing's going to happen' alarm bell is ringing before they've even opened the pages, why should they bother?

And now we come to novels that deliberately eschew the notion of plot altogether; that cut up narratives and experiment with form in an episodic, deliberately disorienting way. With these books, you just have to go with the flow and make the lack of plot an asset, such as the blurb on Flann O'Brien's freewheeling metafiction, *At Swim-Two-Birds*, which tells us it's 'a jumble of ideas, mythology and nonsense'. But one of my favourite pieces of cover copy, on the hardback of Alasdair Gray's historical parody *Poor Things*, makes itself meta. There are actually two blurbs, one headed 'BLURB FOR A HIGH-CLASS HARDBACK' and, below it, 'BLURB FOR A POPULAR PAPERBACK' – I'm delighted to report that the latter now graces the paperback edition. Gray also created mock quotes ('yet another exercise in Victorian pastiche' *The Times Literary Implement*) and cod textual apparatus, turning every aspect of his book into a tongue-in-cheek riff on itself.

The challenge of blurbing postmodernism is acknowledged in a different way by the copy on Thomas Pynchon's notoriously 'difficult' (in other words, mainly read by show-offs) novel *Gravity's Rainbow*:

> We could tell you the year is 1944, that the main character
> is called Tyrone Slothrop and that he has a problem because

bombs are falling across Europe and crashing to the earth at the exact locations of his sexual conquests. But that doesn't really begin to cover it.

Reading this book is like falling down a rabbit hole into an outlandish, sinister, mysterious, absurd, compulsive netherworld. As the *Financial Times* said, 'you must forget earlier notions about life and letters and even the Novel.'

It works well, although there's a lot that niggles me. The 'We could…' section implies that if I want a story, I'm a bit basic. The rabbit hole comparison just makes me think it's not going to be as good as *Alice's Adventures in Wonderland*. And I don't want to forget 'the Novel', thank you, if it's all the same to you. But then maybe I just have to assume I'm not the market for this kind of book. I wonder how many people have read it and then *not* told anybody they've read it? Zero, I suspect. Because the point of books like these is that they are an Iron Man literary challenge, and once you've been macho enough to read them you can boast about it. This copy says 'come and have a go if you think you're hard enough', which is, after all, a come-on of a kind. At least it doesn't say it's a 'meditation', so we must be grateful for small mercies.

Each Peach Pear Plum

I have found it. The blurb to begin and end all blurbs. The Ur-Blurb. It is so perfect it could have sprung fully formed from a rock or a tree like a being from Greek mythology. It is the copy on the back of a children's picture book called *Dave's Cave*, and it goes like this:

> Meet Dave, Caveman Dave.
>> Dave live in cave.
>> Dave cave *perfect*.
>> But Dave not happy…
>> Dave want *new* cave.

If anyone wants a lesson in how to write an effective piece of copy, they should study *Dave's Cave*. Maybe someone somewhere has written a thesis on it. It does everything a blurb should, in both its tone and its structure:

1. It sets up the lead character.
2. It gives you a sense of time and place.
3. It reflects the language of the book in a way that is funny and enticing.
4. Most importantly, it has dramatic tension. The story immediately goes somewhere, gives us a mystery, and we have to know what will happen. Will Dave get his new cave?

The story is a delight too. You guessed it, Dave leaves his cave and tries out all sorts of new ones, where he encounters bats, a sabre-toothed tiger ('Dave not like pets') and a man called Jon, until he comes full circle and realises there's no place like home. And it's all written in a brilliant 'ug ug' primitive caveman idiom, which is tons of fun to read to kids.

'GOOD STRONG WORDS THAT MEAN SOMETHING'

Like the best children's books, and the best children's blurbs, *Dave's Cave* speaks to a young reader directly in a language that they will understand, but that also brings them joy. As Jo March says in *Little Women*, 'I like good strong words that mean something.' This is where the language of picture books, where we all start our reading journey, really sings. The words used both inside and outside the books are simple, yet, at their best, put together with charm and warmth: a voice that says 'come inside and take a look', and makes young readers laugh, listen and learn. The perfect way to do this is with rhymes.

On *Each Peach Pear Plum* (doesn't the fruity title alone make your heart leap with joy?) by the children's author-illustrator team Janet and Allan Ahlberg* – once described as 'to children's books what Fred and Ginger were to dancing' – the back cover blurb simply says:

⋯⋯

* Allan Ahlberg once said that 'Just because a book is tiny and its readers are little doesn't mean it can't be perfect. On its own scale, it can be as good as Tolstoy or Jane Austen,' and the Ahlbergs' books exemplify this.

In this book
With your little eye
Take a look
And play 'I spy'

It's almost impossible not to read it aloud; a fine reminder that children's picture books are the continuation of the oral tradition in literature. Rhythm and rhyme are instinctive to us, and children enjoy them even before they understand what words mean. I may not have known what a 'velveteen' rabbit or a 'slithy tove' were when I was young, but I loved the sound the words made. As poet Clare Pollard says, 'Take the earliest art form babies enjoy, the lullaby. They are listening, but it is probable that they are not understanding.' Just as well, maybe, what with the bough breaking and the cradle falling.

Julia Donaldson, author of *The Gruffalo*,* is the undisputed Queen of Rhymes, which is why children love her books so much. The back covers of her books often feature her bouncing, musical lines of verse, such as:

We're the ugly five, we're the ugly five.
Everyone flees when they see us arrive.

Or…

Oh help! Oh no! A Gruffalo!

---

* Apparently several names were discussed for her creation, including Snorgle and Margelchimp, before Gruffalo was picked because it sounded like a growling Buffalo, and rhymed with 'know'.

Or...

> Superworm is super-long.
> Superworm is super-strong.
> Watch him wriggle! See him squirm!
> Hip, hip, hooray for SUPERWORM!

As well as making language dance, children's picture books are also totally meta, in that they draw awareness to the book itself as an object.* The front cover of the pop-up book *Haunted House* by beloved author and illustrator Jan Pieńkowski – not only the greatest pop-up ever created but possibly the greatest children's book – is the door of the house itself, green and mouldy-looking, with a strange sea-creature's tentacle wriggling out through the letter box and a note saying 'Let yourself in' attached to the doorknob. The back cover is, of course, a back door, padlocked and boarded up, with another tentacle sliding out of the bottom.

The books of Richard Scarry, with their exuberant illustrations of bustling, everyday American towns where animals (Bananas Gorilla was a particular favourite) drive cars, work on construction sites and generally get on with their busy lives, are objects of wonder. The back cover of *Busy, Busy World* is a bus, and the blurb is the advert on the side of the bus: 'Travel around the world in ninety-two pages! Hop Aboard, and read about these thirty-three exciting adventures in [IMAGES OF FLAGS] and many other countries.' The back of *What Do People Do All*

---

* One of the first tactile books for children was *Pat the Bunny*, 1940, which featured different textures inside, and was advertised with the great line '*For Whom the Bell Tolls* is magnificent – but it hasn't any bunny in it.'

Day? shows a mouse flying a plane (naturally) pulling a banner that shouts 'Books are fun!', while the copy for his *Biggest Word Book Ever!* – featuring another favourite, Lowly Worm in his Tyrolean hat, on the front – boasts that it is 'as tall as a toddler and packed with fun!'

The glorious distractions of Richard Scarry aside, my favourite picture book when I was growing up, by a country mile, was *The Butterfly Ball*. This 1973 prize-winning masterpiece is like a psychedelic steampunk fever dream made real in book form. Based on a poem from 1802,* it describes the preparations for a huge feast attended by insects and creatures from all over the land. It is illustrated by Alan Aldridge, a graphic designer who created crazy, kaleidoscopic album covers for The Beatles and The Who, and also ran the art team at Penguin Books for a time. The pictures – of a dormouse in her party frock, a fox on a train dressed as Mr Punch, snails being pulled through the air by butterflies on reins, a caterpillar in a pig mask, a worm in an elephant mask! – enthralled and disturbed me in equal measure. Everything felt rather odd: the strange gloaming, half-light of many of the scenes, the level of detail on the insects' spindly joints, claws, fangs and antennae, the feeling of unease. I also loved (and still love) the fact that it features a blurb in the form of a party invitation:

....

* Written by the MP William Roscoe for his ten children and first published in the *Gentleman's Magazine*.

The pleasure of your company is requested at
The Butterfly Ball
and
The Grasshopper's Feast
to be held beneath the Broad Oak Tree
Fancy Dress optional.

(Wasps, Hornets and Bees are requested to leave their stings at home.)

There's even a hint of the sinister here, with the reminder that not only are insects creepy, they can hurt you. But once I'd accepted my invitation, I couldn't tear myself away.

You're never more aware of books as objects than when you are a child, chewing them, loving them, taking them to bed, looking at them until they fall apart,* noticing every little detail on them and inside them (hence the bounteous opportunities for fun in the end pages of children's books, with quizzes, facts and games softening the blow of the story ending) and then later reading and re-reading absolutely everything, including, in my case, the blurb.

I was so cheered by Lucy Mangan recalling her excitement at reading a hardback blurb for the first time – for *Goodnight Mister Tom* – and knowing it wasn't just me: 'Two days before the declaration of war in 1939, began the blurb on the inside flap. How exciting! I'd never had an inside flap before!' School children today are taught about how books are made and written – and, yes, they tell them about blurbs! Although obviously I made sure my niece knew about these when she was a toddler.

....

* The blurb for the first edition of Tove Jansson's *Finn Family Moomintroll* even encourages young readers to destroy the dust jacket: 'If you want the Snork Maiden on your mantlepiece cut her out'.

So it makes perfect sense that book covers should draw attention to their 'bookiness' in this way, having fun with our expectations and playing gleefully with our ideas of the form.

A great example is the cover of Raymond Briggs's *Fungus the Bogeyman*, the now-classic tale of a morose, snot-ridden being whose job it is to scare humans in the night. While current paperback incarnations are plastered with review quotes in a slimy typeface, the back of the original hardback offered a sort of illustrated field guide to a bogeyman ('Bogey anatomy is adapted to wetness and cold') and the equipment they need to survive dry, sunny conditions, including 'IMPERMEATOR: a contrivance for lubricating the interior surface of a Bogeyman's trousers by the pumping in of oily slime.' Uggghhhh! This copy is unexpected because it is not scared to use odd or unfamiliar words (it is a picture book for older children), and brilliant because it appeals to the child's love of all things disgusting.

The other thing to bear in mind about copy on picture books is that it is often speaking to two separate audiences: the child, who may be learning to read and sounding out the words on the back, and the parent, who is going to buy the book. In fact, it could be more if you consider teachers and librarians too. So often you will get a kind of double blurb working on two levels, with copy appealing to a young reader, and a line of acclaim or a quote to assure the parent or relative of the book's quality ('classic' is a favourite word in these, as I think adults like to believe they are passing on something of lasting value). So, for example, on Judith Kerr's *The Tiger Who Came to Tea*, we have:

> The doorbell rings just as Sophie and her mummy are sitting down to tea. Who could it possibly be? What they certainly don't expect to see at the door is a big furry, stripy tiger!

'A modern classic' *Independent*

The multi-million selling picture book no childhood should be without.

All bases neatly covered.

A word on Beatrix Potter too, before I leave picture books behind. Well, the inimitable Clive James's words, because they capture beautifully how hard language works in writing for young children:

> Her stories are never winsome in themselves, mainly because of her tactile, yet quite tough, feeling for language … Beatrix Potter got her poetry from prose: which is to say, from speech, concentrated. Children like to hear good things said a thousand times, so it helps if the good things are as good as this.

Many of us will have our first encounter with strange, long, unfamiliar terms in the books of Beatrix Potter – 'superfluous', 'implored' and 'affronted' were just some that intrigued me as a small person – because she deliberately included at least one difficult word in each story. It takes us back to rhythm and rhyme: even when we don't understand a word, we can both enjoy it on a sensual level, and grasp for its meaning. The blurbs on Beatrix Potter's books are deliberately simple, either a list of other titles or a very short quotation from the text – why try to improve on perfection?

What about when children get a bit older, and can start helping to choose the books they want? Well, this is where the fun and games with copy *really* start.

KWEEEEEEEEEEEEEEEEEEEEEEP!

This, in case you were wondering, is the noise that a Pig Siren (or 'alarm squeal') makes. Of course it is! How could it be anything else? It is just one of the delightful words used by children's copywriter Sarah Topping, in this case at the start of every blurb for a series of books called *Pigs in Planes*. She has been copywriting for over fifteen years, working at Puffin Books and later as a freelancer on everything from Road Dahl to Harry Potter. I asked her about writing children's blurbs, and this is what she said:

> Oh it's such fun! There is a lot of scope for being playful by pulling out particular words or phrases that are just fun to read and exclaim out loud. I think this is particularly true of young comedy fiction – some books lend themselves to making silly expressions a real focus of the blurbs and covers. I've started a blurb with 'Oh, dungle droppings!' (Steven Butler's *The Wrong Pong*), spent many a happy hour scouring Jeremy Strong's stories for phrases like 'FANTASTIC-BUBBLY-CRUMBO' and words like 'Squiggly! Splurrggghhh! Hooey-hoo!' and kicked off every *Pigs in Planes* blurb with the alarm siren 'Kweeeeeeeeeeeeeeeeeeeep!' These books are made to make us smile, and I'm all for making the prospective reader smile from the moment they look at the cover.

How does she ensure she is speaking to a young reader in their language, and working out what makes them tick?

> When I read a manuscript for blurb writing, I look for extracts filled with details that reflect the voice of the author, that provide a charming and evocative taster of what you're going to

discover inside. I'm often asked if I have to read every book I blurb, and most often the answer is yes. I can't write the cover copy properly if I don't know what happens. It also serves to ensure I'm completely familiar with the tone, which I can echo in the blurb, without ever talking down to the reader.

It's clear from this that a lot of work and care goes into words that, on the surface, seem so casual and light. Take the blurb Sarah wrote for Jeremy Strong's *Batpants!*, a book aimed at readers around seven to nine years old, the age when, I think, you're most receptive to silly things that make you giggle. The back cover design pops with colour and action and works perfectly in harmony with the copy:

NA-NA-NA-NA-NA-NA-NA-NA
    BATPANTS!
    BATPANTS the orang-utan is completely, wildly HAIRY. She loves swinging through trees, and apple crumble. But most of all she loves her family, the Loveharts, and all their madcap adventures...
    CRAVING MORE SILLINESS? Join Jeremy's KRAZY KLUB at...
    FANTASTIC-BUBBLY-CRUMBO!
    (Warning: Side effects include split sides, aching cheeks and tears of laughter)
    TOMATOES! LIGHTS! CAMERA! BATPANTS!

I love the zany, madcap tone here, and it also makes me a bit sad that blurbs on grown-up books don't begin by making us imagine the Batman music. Maybe it's only on children's books that language can be at its most free, exuberant and exclamatory.

Take the popular Mr Gum books by Andy Stanton. I don't know what 'Shabba me whiskers!' at the start of the copy even means, but it just makes me giggle. As an aside, Andy's author biography is a scream too, as so many in the genre are: 'Before becoming a children's writer he was a film script reader, a market researcher, an NHS lackey, a part-time sparrow and a grape.'*

As well as the excitable exclamation, another technique the openings of many children's blurbs use is the imperative: 'Howl with laughter', 'Go back in time', 'Laugh your socks off', 'Explore the deep dark wood', 'Beware! Do not open this coffin!' Or 'Hold on to your broom for magical mayhem!' adorning the front covers of Jill Murphy's classic *Worst Witch* series – which showed kids learning magic at boarding school way before Harry Potter got in on the act, except that poor Mildred Hubble is really rubbish at her craft. These copy lines get straight to the point, and say, *come on, join in!*

The copy often plays visual games too, such as the blurb on the back of Andy Shepherd's *The Boy Who Grew Dragons*, which is a checklist of all the things dragons do ('Poo in your dad's porridge? TICK'). While the back cover of a book by Andy Griffiths, *Just Stupid!*, takes the form of a questionnaire:

Is this the right book for you? Take the stupid test and find out!
Do you push doors marked pull and pull doors marked push?
Do you think that being able to stuff your mouth full of marshmallows is a sign of superior intelligence?

* There are also some brilliant quotes from kids inside the book: 'If you love books with huge dogs, mad people and large poos this is the book for you' – Katy, aged 9. I don't know about you, but I'm in!

Do you automatically turn around when someone shouts 'Hey Stupid!'?

Score: one point for each 'yes' answer.

3: You are extremely stupid. You will love this book.

As well as featuring a disconcerting number of authors called 'Andy', these examples show none of the reverence that adult books do for the constraints of punctuation, grammar rules, or language itself.

In the words of the BFG, they…

GOBBLEFUNK AROUND WITH WORDS

> If you want to remember what it's like to live in a child's world, you've got to get down on your hands and knees and live like that for a week.
>
> ROALD DAHL

No writing about children's books would be complete without mentioning Dahl: children's literature behemoth, spy, pilot, creator of *Tales of the Unexpected* and, above all, linguistic genius, inventing words like scrumdiddlyumptious, frothbungling, gloriumptious, jumpsquiffling, lixivate, snozzcumber and fizzle-crump. (There's Enid Blyton too, but I love her so much she's getting her own whole section: see 'Simply Wizard!') Everyone has their favourite Dahl book; mine is *Danny the Champion of the World*, mainly because of its unforgettable description of an enormous pork pie containing 'hard-boiled eggs buried like treasures in several different places'. As a greedy child (and grown-up), this has stayed burned in my brain.

Since the publication of *James and the Giant Peach* in 1961,

Dahl's children's books have sold hundreds of millions of copies, with numerous cover looks along the way, from the delicate, intricately detailed Faith Jaques illustrations of my childhood to Quentin Blake's whizzpoppingly kinetic designs. In addition to the very brief blurbs that appeared on the back of old Puffin editions, there was also an inviting longer blurb on the first page of the book. The one in my original *Charlie and the Chocolate Factory* ends with the words 'Ages unlimited, but guaranteed pleasure for anyone old or young enough to enjoy Hot Ice Cream, Eatable Marshmallow Pillows or Mr Wonka's Three Course Dinner chewing-gum.' Francis Spufford remembers 'how securely authoritative Puffins seemed, with the long, trustworthy descriptions of the story inside the front cover, always written by the same arbiter, the Puffin editor Kaye Webb'. I agree: they are the equivalent of being taken by the hand and into the book.

What about the copy that appears on Roald Dahl's books now? How does it both reassure and entice? Children's copywriter Sarah Topping has worked on dozens of Dahl blurbs over the past few years, and she was kind enough to tell me about it.

Every so often, book covers are refreshed and redesigned, to bring them to a new audience, to highlight a big anniversary or celebration, and to create a new talking point. I have had the pleasure of writing three rounds of blurbs across Roald Dahl's children's stories – that's thinking of three entirely different ways to describe each of his books. How to mix the synopsis up for a different cover each time?

Round one – to tie in with the inaugural Roald Dahl Day in 2006, the brief here was to pull out some fun, enticing words – or in the case of *The BFG*, some Gobblefunk – and set the scene. I also wrote a new mini-biography of Roald Dahl to introduce him to young readers.

Round two – this time, the copy would focus on the one or two most central characters in the story. For *Charlie and the Chocolate Factory*, for example, the blurb opens with Charlie Bucket, leading into Mr Willy Wonka, those Golden Tickets and the wondrous chocolate extravaganza that awaits.

Round three – for the new cover look to tie in with Roald Dahl's centenary in 2016, my brief was to focus on the mischief and mayhem, on the darker side of Dahl. This time, a quote from the story went on the back cover, with the blurb inside the book. This gave me a bit more space and freed me up to include some extra deliciously dark details.

It's a bold move, I think, just having Dahl's own gloriumptious words on the back cover, as some children may not be aware of the stories, but perhaps the heroes are now even bigger than the books, bigger than I realise. It's interesting to note that, over the three iterations of the covers Sarah mentions, Dahl's name has got smaller every time, from completely dominating the design to having equal weighting: a sign, perhaps, that his creations now have lives of their own, as musicals, films and cultural icons.

What also shines out from listening to Sarah talk about children's blurbs, apart from it clearly being the Best Job Ever, is that you have to respect your audience. She has also worked at Pottermore (now Wizarding World), the official website of all things Harry Potter, and notes that:

It was important to remember when writing for Pottermore that the devotion of its fans knows no bounds. Their love for Harry Potter and the Wizarding World is palpable, the depth of their knowledge and passion immeasurable. Everything that is created has to be perfectly pitched, entertaining and factually correct. Writing features for the website involved a detailed level of research into my subject, re-reading the books or watching scenes from the films, seeing what the fans have to say online, to create an insightful, entertaining piece with new angles.

I can't think of a more demanding audience than young Harry Potter fans. There's a weight of cultural expectation that comes with writing about the books of certain authors. You have to acknowledge their status as modern classics, while still assuming that every reader could be coming to them for the very first time. But what about 'classic' classics? How do you make a book from the nineteenth century sound fresh, exciting and relevant for a young reader today, rather than old-fashioned, hard to relate to, or something that makes them think of school?

Sarah's way of approaching the Puffin Classics for a series rebrand is instructive. She decided that what really matters to young readers is the characters they encounter while reading, and by using the theme of 'Discover a new friend for life today', she wrote an 'A–Z of Adventure' featuring some of the most famous characters in kids' books, to appear inside every edition. This idea also formed the theme of the blurbs across the series. This is the A to Z:

Alice, Black Beauty, the Cheshire Cat and the Dormouse, Estella, Fagin, Gulliver, Huckleberry Finn, It, Jim Hawkins, King Arthur, Long John Silver, Mowgli, Nancy, Oliver, Pip, the Queen of Hearts, Ratty, Sarah Crewe, Tom Sawyer, the Unicorn, Rip Van Winkle, the Wizard of Oz, the SphinX, the Yahoos and Zeus...

Some of these you might know. Others you won't. Some of them you'll recognise from films or TV. They're from a cast of classic characters – boys and girls, pirates and thieves, creatures and legends who have travelled through time in their ships or motor cars, tumbled down rabbit holes, journeyed across high seas and fantastical lands – to come to life for your great-grandparents, your grandparents, your parents and now for you … And it's completely up to you what they look like.

Great, right? I especially like the last line, which puts the child in charge and reminds us that we decide a character's appearance in our head as we are reading. It's an acknowledgement of what a heightened, imaginative experience reading at a young age is, and how the books we read then can stay in our hearts forever. Until we get older, that is, and things get even *more* intense…

DARKER MATTERS

Young Adult fiction is a genre unto itself, yet it chimes with so many other things I've looked at so far: namely, use words inventively to capture your audience's imagination, and *never, ever* patronise them. What I remember from my own teenage reading is that it is a serious business. You don't want to be talked down to or wrapped in cotton wool. The blurb on the original edition of Barry Hines's *A Kestrel for a Knave* tells us that 'This book is a slap in the face to those who think comprehensives are all about free school milk and orange juice.' No mollycoddling here.

As a teenager you are ready for big, earth-shattering ideas, grand passions, death, sex, destruction and just tons and tons of doom – Robert Swindells's *Brother in the Land* is about a nuclear apocalypse and has cannibals in it, for heaven's sake. As Super Hans says to Jeremy when they form a band in *Peep Show*, 'What we really need to do is create a powerful sense of dread … we need more dread.'

Jeopardy is key. When you're a teenager, *everything* matters, so there has to be something big at stake in the copy. The blurb on my old edition of the aforementioned dystopia doesn't beat about the bush, and begins: 'A survivor of a nuclear holocaust, Danny is one of the lucky ones – or is he?' You can almost hear the duh duh duuuuh! In a different vein, the copy on Susan Cooper's *The Dark is Rising* omnibus uses the prophetic poem from the book to great effect:

> When the Dark comes rising, six shall turn it back;
> Three from the circle, three from the track;
> Wood, bronze, iron;
> Water, fire, stone;
> Five will return and one go alone.

It creates foreboding, just as the sinister rhyme engraved on the ring in *The Lord of the Rings* does ('One ring to bring them all', etc.). It's like a doomy incantation or a spell, reminding me of how much I loved all things portentous at a young age. Similarly, the blurb for the first volume of Philip Pullman's *His Dark Materials* trilogy, *Northern Lights*, starts: 'Without this child, we shall all die.'

But more than demons, dragons or Sauron himself, the one thing that scared us most as teenagers was, of course, the thought of Actual Sex. Thank goodness, then, for Judy Blume, a truly excellent human being and a writer who genuinely seemed to understand our hang-ups and worries – about boobs, periods, boys – and, not only that, wrote about them in a way that made us laugh and feel reassured and, above all, understood. The cover of the current edition of *Forever*, her cherished and at the time rather scandalous story of – gasp – a couple of teenagers enjoying a sexual relationship without guilt or punishment, before they break up amicably, is a far more sophisticated affair than the one on my much-shared and much-giggled-over edition. It's sleek and simple and shows the image of a cherry, accompanied by the strapline: 'There's a first time for everything.' The blurb is rather good, I think, and says:

> Do you remember the first time?
>
> *Forever* is still the bravest, freshest, fruitiest and most honest account of first love, first sex and first heartbreak ever written for teens. It was a book ahead of its time – and remains, after forty years in print, a teenage bestseller from the award-winning Judy Blume. With a contemporary cover, *Forever* is a teen classic ripe for a new generation of readers.

Apart from loving how they took that 'losing your cherry' metaphor and just ran with it, I also enjoy its positive, upfront tone, with just a little hint of jeopardy and heartbreak. I also wonder if it is aimed at a mother buying the book for a teenage daughter, with the 'do you remember' line suggesting an older woman keen to educate a younger one. Or maybe I'm just assuming all mums were like mine, buying me books called things like *Where Do I Come From?* and *What's Happening to Me?* while I was in junior school, when I was so embarrassed I had to hide them under the bed.

It is a far cry from the innocence of *Dave's Cave*, but that's what childhood reading is: a journey, where the writers and characters we love hold our hand along the path called growing up. Words matter, but perhaps when we are young they matter more intensely, more crucially, than at any other time in our lives.* They help us decide who we are and who we want to be, and the words that appear on books, as well as inside them, help us on the way.

* According to Dr Daniel J. Siegel in *The Whole-Brain Child*, words are also essential for articulating children's fears and worries: 'Name it to tame it.'

Make Me Better
Self-Help

> The spirit of self-help is the root of all genuine growth in the individual.

These are not, as you might be forgiven for thinking, the words of a tanned, relaxed Californian wellness guru sporting loose linen clothing. They are from a Scotsman, Samuel Smiles, who coined the phrase 'self-help' with his bestselling book of the same name in 1859, showing his readers how to be industrious go-getters. Self-help has been around for a long time; you can trace its roots as far back as ancient philosophy. Like many genres, it is nebulous, often sliding into business, spirituality, health or, more recently, tidying. And, above all genres, it is easy to mock: 'Can you just shut up please, darling, because I'm trying to do my mindlessness' (Edina in *Absolutely Fabulous*).

It is also changing. When I spoke to the communications director of a successful self-help publisher, I realised that my notions of the genre – ugly white books plastered with huge lettering and even bigger snake-oil guarantees to make readers happy, rich, thin, popular, better – were hopelessly out of date. Those hoary old bestsellers are still around, but the genre is moving on.

Nowadays, with celebrities and even royals talking about mental health, the stigma of a genre typified by Bridget Jones knocking back the vodka and reading *How to Make Men Want What They Don't Think They Want* has gone. It's all about self-care. The goal is 'living well'. Gone are those garish, cheesy covers, and in their place is a desirable, covetable book you wouldn't be ashamed of reading on the tube. If these books are a source of comfort and inspiration, then buying one can be seen as the first step to looking after yourself.

But although the look of these books has got subtler (think Fearne Cotton's *Happy*, with its pastel watercolours), the copy follows the same pattern of old: set up a problem, offer a solution and, above all, make a promise. This promise should be the key to everything – and prove that, up to the moment of picking this book up, everything else you thought was wrong. It explains why so many books in the genre are called things like *The Key*, *The Secret*, *The Greatest Secret* ('Once you know, freedom is yours'). It needs to be a combination of audacious, yet worth aiming for too, such as the rather brilliant last line of the blurb on Gyles Brandreth's *The 7 Secrets of Happiness*: 'This book won't simply enhance your life: it will extend it.' The promise should also press the right emotional buttons. 'We once put the word "stress" on the front of a book,' the comms director told me, 'but then realised we shouldn't highlight the problem. We should talk about calmness, not stress. It's all about how the reader will feel.'

The crime writer Sophie Hannah is such a fan of self-help that she not only wrote her own guide called *How to Hold a Grudge*, but also one about her love of the genre – *Happiness, A Mystery: & 66 attempts to solve it*. I asked her what she thought about the unsubtle nature of the promises made on these books:

> I think the blurbs have to be in your face because they're, in some
> ways, more like plumbers than they are Anita Brookner novels.
> You buy their services to help you solve a problem, therefore

they must promise (via the blurb) to solve that problem, just as a plumber promises to fix your leaky tap, otherwise you'd never pay his call-out fee in advance! So, the blurbs are doing exactly what they should. And they don't have to worry about plot spoilers.

I'm going to show you in three steps (as a self-help blurb might say) how the problem/solution/promise set-up works across different types of books in the genre. Starting with:

THE BODY BEAUTIFUL

I use this as an umbrella term for anything to do with physical health. Many of these books appeal to what the publicist I spoke to calls the 'Bro audience: young men who are into self-optimisation through physical betterment'. They run triathlons and go to the gym. They like the crunchy detail of no-bullshit books like Joe Wicks's *Lean in 15* or Matt Morsia's *The 24/7 Body* ('The UK's No. 1 Fitness Vlogger').

Numbers are the key to so much self-help. They make change feel achievable and digestible, like the copy on *Atomic Habits*, which promises that 'tiny changes' such as 'doing two push-ups a day, waking up five minutes early' can transform your life, or Dr Rangan Chatterjee's *Feel Better in 5*, whose front cover is a case study in promises, with Chris Evans telling us that he is 'one of the most influential doctors in the country' and a little roundel saying '30+ 5-minute tips to lose weight, improve sleep and move more'.*

....

* Compare these friendly promises with the naked aggression of the subtitle for diet book *Six Weeks to OMG: Get Skinnier Than All Your Friends!* Dodgy in the extreme.

Personal trainer James Smith's No.1 bestselling *Not a Diet Book* (followed up by *Not a Life Coach*) takes the masculine energy up a notch. The title says this isn't your usual namby-pamby wet lettuce sort of stuff, but the copy follows the traditional pattern. The promise is there in the subtitle: *Take Control. Gain Confidence. Change Your Life*; the blurb sets up a problem in a down-to-earth way ('Are you sick of always wearing black and getting undressed in the dark?') and it offers a whole bullet-pointed list of solutions, plus an extra promise at the end ('This book will put you back in control'). It's bro heaven, and it's textbook self-help.*

But it's not all about the testosterone. Healthy eating guides such as the enormously successful *Pinch of Nom* are centred around real, relatable women and covered with words like 'light', 'easy', 'slimming', and lots of numbers. Meanwhile, books in the 'hyper-wellness' genre are aimed at a young, female audience with time and money to care for themselves (I know it's stereotyping; don't shoot the messenger). They are typified by Goopy Gwyneth Paltrow† in all her freshly douched glory. Her books are lifestyle disguised as cookery, and the covers show her beaming, wholesome and as well scrubbed as her dreamy kitchenware, surrounded by words such as 'clean', 'glow', 'home' and 'heal'. There's barely any food in sight. Let's face it, it's not really about the food. We are being shown that by eating like Gwyneth, we can become pure, perfected and complete.

....

* I love Charlie Brooker's take-down of the trope in *I Can Make You Hate*: 'Would you like to eat whatever you want and still lose weight? Who wouldn't? Keep dreaming, imbecile.'

† Or, as Marina Hyde memorably described her, 'turbocapitalist fanny egg pedlar Gwyneth Paltrow'.

I discovered, by the way, that there's also an anti-Gwyneth book called *Is Gwyneth Paltrow Wrong about Everything? How the Famous Sell Us Elixirs of Health, Beauty & Happiness*. But what thrilled me even more was that the blurb still followed the self-help rules, reassuring us of the author's credentials ('health law policy researcher Timothy Caulfield'), laying out a problem ('our health decisions and goals are influenced by celebrity culture') and promising us 'a practical and evidence-based reality check on our own celebrity ambitions'. Blurb bingo! Who needs self-help when you can get this kind of joy from copy? Which brings us to…

THE SEARCH FOR HAPPINESS

If my last section was a catch-all umbrella, then this is a really big tent. It encompasses everything from mindfulness to relationships, coping with anxiety to general all-round betterment, but it all points towards the same thing: the human condition, and how we cope with it. The eternal question, packaged in a different way every time.

What I noticed most about this genre is the language used. These books tend to be aimed at a slightly older, often female, audience. There's a forgiving, calm, comforting 'been there seen it' tone to much of the copy. It's chatty and conversational. It's inclusive, with lots of 'we's. The force of celebrity is also strong.

So on Ruby Wax's *A Mindfulness Guide for the Frazzled*, we're told:

We are all frazzled…

Five hundred years ago no one died of stress: we invented this concept and now we let it rule us. Ruby Wax shows us how to de-frazzle for good by making simple changes that give us time to breathe, reflect and live in the moment.

Let Ruby be your guide to a healthier, happier you…

I can actually feel my blood pressure lowering as I read those words.

It's the acknowledgement of our frailty and fallibility that is the copy key here, such as Elizabeth Day's *How to Fail*, inspired by her hit podcast:

This is a book for anyone who has ever failed. Which means it's a book for everyone…

It ends:

Because learning how to fail is actually learning how to succeed better. And everyone needs a bit of that.

I enjoy the way this copy turns a negative into a positive. It's in the fine tradition of books promising us we can find happiness in the unlikeliest of things, from Russian novels to Roman philosophers, architecture to not giving a f**k. Above all, cleaning. Guides such as those by the wildly popular Mrs Hinch and, most recently, Stacey Solomon's *Tap to Tidy: Organising, Crafting and Creating Happiness in a Messy World* are ostensibly books about housekeeping, but really about managing anxiety. When we feel the world is in chaos on a macro level, these books go micro and focus on what is within our control.

The back cover copy on *Tap to Tidy* shows this in spades:

If you're reading this, then we have something in common…

I find it hard to sit still, but losing myself in a craft project or tidying a drawer is my form of meditation. It's a chance for me to forget about the things going on in the world around me for a minute.

I hope this book helps you to lose yourself for a moment, too – and that you enjoy reading it and even, maybe, having a go at some of the bits inside.

You are in a judgement-free zone, and the author is a friend squeezing your hand. Which is what everyone needs sometimes, especially in times of change. A neat segue into:

THE CIRCLE OF LIFE

By this I mean birth and death. Life stages seem to be the one area where people who 'don't read self-help' *do* read self-help, especially parenting books.

In *The Poetry Pharmacy*, William Sieghart says that the two overwhelming emotions of parenthood are love and fear. 'That love, which is one of the most wonderful things in the world, is also deeply frightening.' To be a parent is to be afraid from pregnancy to around the time your child can afford to take you out for dinner. Because of this, parents seek reassurance from experts. Experience, authority and longevity are valued. And said expert should be a proper, qualified professional rather than the suspect 'Master Certified Coach' or 'Instagram Visionary' I've seen knocking around in self-help.

Perennial, practical-looking bestsellers like *What to Expect When You're Expecting* ('The world's bestselling pregnancy manual') reassure with numbers:

With 18.5 million copies in print, *What to Expect When You're Expecting* is read by 93 per cent of women who read a pregnancy book and was named one of the 'Most Influential Books of the Last 25 Years' by *USA Today*.

A softer-looking guide, *How to Grow a Baby and Push It Out* (great title), still bigs up the author's credentials in the same way, with 'MIDWIFE' in big letters under the author's name. Another midwife appears in her uniform on the front of one book to allay those fears even further.

But once parents have got through the essential work of producing the child and keeping it alive, then the other anxieties kick in: namely, am I going to screw them up forever?

The fear is very strong in the title of Oliver James's *They F**k You Up: How to Survive Family Life*. The title and subtitle are both excellent; brazen and brave. But the blurb – 'Do your relationships tend to follow the same destructive pattern? Do you feel trapped by your family's expectations of you? Does your life seem overwhelmingly governed by jealousy or competitiveness or lack of confidence?' – made me feel stressed, possibly not the desired effect.

Far better is the copy on Philippa Perry's *The Book You Wish Your Parents Had Read (and Your Children Will Be Glad That You Did)*. It is a masterclass in kind words and non-bossy advice:

> Every parent wants their child to be happy and every parent wants to avoid screwing them up. But how do you achieve that?
>
> Instead of mapping out the 'perfect' plan, Perry offers a big-picture look at the elements that lead to good parent–child relationships.

The rest of this copy uses phrases such as 'sage and sane advice'. It calms and reassures parents that everyone gets this stuff wrong sometimes.

Apart from being someone's child, the other thing we can guarantee about life is the end of it.

Self-help books that deal with grief have many things in common. They use a subtle palette on their designs – much like condolence cards – with flowers, leaves and feathers, pale colours and soft type.

Their copy foregrounds experience, such as that on *Grief Works*:

> Death affects us all. Yet it is still the last taboo in our society, and grief is still profoundly misunderstood. Julia Samuel, a grief psychotherapist, has spent twenty-five years working with the bereaved and understanding the full repercussions of loss. This deeply affecting book is full of psychological insights on how grief, if approached correctly, can heal us.

But with these books, the reassurance also comes from personal understanding; the guarantee that the writer knows how you feel, from Sheryl Sandberg to C. S. Lewis, Julian Barnes to Joan Didion. The back cover of her *The Year of Magical Thinking* features just a few words that show how a death upends life:

> Life changes fast. Life changes in an instant. You sit down to dinner and life as you know it ends.

Grief books, you sense, are therapy for the writer as well as the reader. The blurb for *The Madness of Grief*, written by the Reverend Richard Coles after his partner David died suddenly in 2019, homes in on personal, intimate details that will resonate with anyone who has lost a loved one:

> Much about grief surprised him: the volume of 'sadmin' you have to do when someone dies, how much harder it is travelling for work alone, even the pain of typing a text message to your partner – then realising you are alone.

We may have come a long way from clean eating now, but there is a golden thread running through all self-help books. It is that, as my Yorkshire mother-in-law says, 'We've all got our barrow to push.' And when it is done well, the copy on their covers should tell us: You are not alone.

$\mathbb{R}$ead, Rinse, Repeat

The Comforting Thrills of Genre Fiction

ALAN PARTRIDGE: Shoestring, Taggart, Spender, Bergerac, Morse. What does that say to you about regional detective series?

TONY HAYERS: There are too many of them?

ALAN: That's one way of looking at it. Another way of looking at it is, people like them, let's make some more.

Alan, who is trying to pitch a new TV series to a BBC executive here, is of course right (although perhaps his other ideas of Inner-City Sumo and Monkey Tennis aren't so convincing). In this comic exchange lies the rub of genre fiction: it repeats the same pattern again and again, but we can't get enough of it. We use terms like 'comfort reading', 'relaxing' and 'curling up with' these kinds of books. They are the literary equivalent of a duvet and some Heinz Cream of Tomato soup.

George Orwell sums up this feeling of blissing out on extreme reading perfectly in his essay 'Decline of the English Murder':*

> It is Sunday afternoon, preferably before the war. You put your feet up on the sofa, settle your spectacles on your nose, and open the *News of the World*. Roast beef and Yorkshire, or roast pork and apple sauce, followed up by suet pudding and driven

* I know, I know, more Orwell. But he's so damn quotable.

home, as it were, by a cup of mahogany-brown tea, have put you in just the right mood. Your pipe is drawing sweetly, the sofa cushions are soft underneath you, the fire is well alight, the air is warm and stagnant. In these blissful circumstances, what is it that you want to read about? Naturally, about a murder.

Why do rollicking tales satisfy us so much? Francis Spufford offers the explanation that they provide something akin to the certainties of childhood reading: 'All genre writing is a natural counterpart to the controlled world of children's fiction. Pick up a romance, a Western, a thriller, a Wodehouse comedy, a horror novel or a detective story, and you know in advance what sort of synthetic experience you are about to be offered. Genre writers are in the business of delivering sensations for which their readers have already at least half-formed a wish.'

According to author Martin Latham, they satisfy a dark kind of yearning that is already within us at the most basic level. 'This is why fairy tales and myth keep crashing back into mainstream culture like a minotaur charging into a genteel restaurant … we've always been geeks, dreaming of the forest, of half-beast men, discarnate entities, ambiguous Loki-types and messed-up families; it's just that contemporary highbrow novels don't seem quite grown-up enough for our quaking collective unconscious.'

I love reading genre fiction (although I'm not a fan of the limiting label), and writing copy for it too, when I get the chance. The idea of these books as lesser works, or 'guilty pleasures', is baffling to me. As Marian Keyes, who knows all about the perils of labels, says, we must never apologise for the things we enjoy:

In my 20s and 30s, I obediently read the books widely touted to be works of genius. I was repulsed by their depictions of women but I thought the fault must be mine. Maybe I just wasn't clever enough? These days I trust my own judgment. There are far too many 'shoulds' attached to reading – I read for pleasure, for escape, for insight into the lives of others. I don't read to learn a lesson and my heart breaks for readers who feel a book should be 'worthy'.

Or, as Cathy Rentzenbrink puts it in *Dear Reader*, 'I don't think I realised that some books were supposed to be better than others, and I had no concept of highbrow versus lowbrow.'

When the bestselling and brilliant crime author Tana French was asked which books influenced her writing, her answer was: 'Probably *Mystic River* by Dennis Lehane and *The Secret History* by Donna Tartt. They brought it home to me that the supposed boundary between literary and genre fiction is complete bollocks.' Preach.

There is no such thing as a 'good type' or 'bad type' of book, just good and bad books. And just like literary novels, genre fiction has both good and bad within it. Emotion is key to these works, whether it's joy or fear, and it should be key to the copy too. It must attract the reader with genre cues: a combination of the familiar and the unexpected, with patterns, tropes and codes that are anticipated by them, yet with something new offered every time (as John Wyndham has been described: cosy catastrophe).

In *Hit Makers*, Derek Thompson explains why 'the same but different' succeeds: 'Most consumers are simultaneously neophilic – curious to discover new things – and deeply neophobic – afraid of anything that's too new. The best hit makers are gifted at creating moments of meaning by marrying new and old, anxiety and understanding. They are architects of familiar surprises.' By tweaking a genre – just a little, not too much – writers hit the sweet spot.

I'm going to look at various types of genre fiction (like most categories, the edges are often blurred) to work out how to offer the reader something old and something new every time. As with the books themselves, it's often more complicated than it at first seems.

BOO!

Do I believe in ghosts? No, but I am afraid of them.

MARIE ANNE DE VICHY-CHAMROND

The fingers under the bed waiting to grab your ankle. The nameless menace lurking in the abandoned house, the lonely underpass or the deep, dark woods. A loved one returned from the dead, horribly changed. Satanic offspring, demonic possession, flesh-eating clowns, killer rats and vampires tapping at the window (*never* invite them in). Take my (cold, skeletal) hand and enter the cursed world of horror fiction…

I spent most of my youth being terrified. Trolled by public information films that resembled snuff movies, we children of the 1970s were warned about the dangers of, among other hazards, rabies, quicksand, electricity pylons and *things* in stagnant ponds (Donald Pleasence as 'the spirit of dark and lonely water' scarred a generation for life). Put a rug on a polished floor? 'You might as well set a man trap.' Thanks to this, and my beloved great-aunt's bookshelves groaning with supernatural tales, horror was my favourite teenage genre (I include ghost stories in this category too). Stephen King, James Herbert, Clive Barker, Graham Masterton, William Peter Blatty, I worshipped and feared them all – and the more lurid, the better.

Horror covers from the 1970s and 1980s are often horrifying in themselves. My battered Corgi edition of Fred Mustard Stewart's soul-swap story *The Mephisto Waltz* promises 'A DIABOLICAL SPELLBINDER. A novel for every addict of the satanic and the supernatural', and features a naked lady dancing on a piano keyboard. A quote on *Rosemary's Baby* describes it 'squeezing my heart with fingers of bone'. The feast of terror continues with black and bloody designs for *Satan's Spawn*: 'Little Andrew will capture your heart... and devour your very soul.' Or sinister sibling saga *Twice Blessed*: 'Their innocent blue eyes were twin mirrors of evil!' It's easy to mock, and also rather fun, as the cover of *Paperbacks from Hell: The Twisted History of '70s and '80s Horror Fiction* shows. The back cover copy parodies the shrieking language of horror fiction blurbs so well that I had to include it in full:

Demonic possession! Haunted condominiums! Murderous babies! Man-eating moths! No plot was too ludicrous, no cover art too appalling, no evil too despicable for the

PAPERBACKS FROM HELL

Where did they come from? Where did they go? Horror author Grady Hendrix risks his soul and sanity (not to mention yours) to relate the true, untold story of the

PAPERBACKS FROM HELL

Shocking story summaries! Incredible cover art! And true tales of writers, artists and publishers who violated every literary law but one: Never be boring. All this awaits, if you dare to experience the

PAPERBACKS FROM HELL

But this glorious schlock aside, how do you get fear right, without being silly? As anyone who's stayed up far too late reading these books (and then can't sleep because of what might be outside the bedroom door) knows, anticipation is the mother of palpitation. It is the things unseen, 'things terrible and unguessable', as the young governess in Henry James's *The Turn of the Screw* says. All the true masters of the macabre use it to perfection, and effective copy should do the same.

The opening of the blurb on William Peter Blatty's *The Exorcist* is a great example. The succession of short sentences builds fear, as do the increasingly unnerving details:

> The terror begins quietly. Noises in the attic. In the child's room. An odd smell. The displacement of furniture. An icy chill. Easy explanations are offered. Then frightening changes begin to appear in eleven-year-old Regan...

To say that the language of horror copy is all about setting up scares, though, is simplistic. It is also about a kind of visceral, physical shudder – the 'dull yellow eye of the creature' opening in *Frankenstein*, the moment in *The Haunting of Hill House* when Eleanor says, 'God God – whose hand was I holding?', or the 'face of *crumpled linen*'* in M. R. James's short story 'Oh Whistle and I'll Come to You, My Lad'. In his genuinely haunting memoir *Ghostland*, Edward Parnell writes that '[M. R.] James's tactile nature is reflected in his stories, in which the protagonists often experience the touch or feel of something that causes them revulsion'.

....

* Never have italics been deployed to such sinister effect.

Philosophy Professor Noël Carroll agrees that the key to horror is 'Disgust. The monsters in horror fictions are not only fearsome, they are typically disgusting. You would shrink from the touch of the Mummy; to be kissed by him would make you gag. Nor would you want to pet the Fly. In short, horrific monsters induce revulsion. Why? Because they are not only dangerous but *impure*. Horrific monsters violate our norms.'

Impurity is the killer word here – it's why so much horror features children; the idea of innocence threatened or corrupted by evil forces. There is an instinctive *wrongness* to it. A literal translation of the German word for 'the uncanny' as Freud described it, *unheimlich*, is 'unhomely'.

The copy on Neil Gaiman's *Coraline* is an object lesson in unhomeliness:

> There is something strange about Coraline's new home.
>
> It's not the mist, or the cat that always seems to be watching her, nor the signs of danger that Miss Spink and Miss Forcible, her new neighbours, read in the tea leaves. It's the other house – the one behind the old door in the drawing room. Another mother and father with black-button eyes and papery skin are waiting for Coraline to join them there. And they want her to stay with them. For ever.

The creepy button eyes! Unlike other thrill genres, horror offers us the adrenaline of terror, but without the predictable reassurance of resolution. At the end we are left uncertain, with the dead, looking into the abyss, or perhaps in Hell itself. There is no closure. As the medium in Hilary Mantel's *Beyond Black* says of spirits, 'They don't become decent people just because they're dead. People are right to be afraid of ghosts.'

And now, as the fire dies and the night draws in, I want to tell you about the scariest story I have ever read. It is the last tale in a children's anthology by Jan Mark, *Nothing to Be Afraid Of* (oh never was a book titled with such bitter irony). The blurb describes 'the kind of horrors that follow you upstairs in the dark and slide under the bed, and there they stay'. The cursed story is called 'Nule'. It is about a boy who becomes convinced that the newel post at the bottom of the bannisters has come alive and is going up to get him. Its chilling last line confirms the dark truth of horror fiction: that it is a genre without happy endings. Everything is *not* going to be all right.

CAN YOU EVER FORGET YOUR FIRST LOVE?

The ultimate aim of all love affairs is more important than all other aims in anyone's life.

ARTHUR SCHOPENHAUER

Even the pessimistic German philosopher Schopenhauer realised how important love is. It changes everything, it lifts us up where we belong, it's all you need, it's a dangerous drug – and readers just can't get enough of the stuff.

'Romance' is an elastic term, encompassing Mills & Boon category romances, 'chick lit', erotic fiction, Aga sagas and bonkbusters by the likes of Jilly Cooper (they're getting their own section, though, because they deserve it). It is also the most despised genre, presumably because it is written by women for women, and sells in its millions.* As the romance and suspense

---

* *The Times* 'Best Books of 2021' was slammed by many writers for boasting that it covered 'every genre' of book – while leaving out the most successful category, romantic fiction.

novelist Nora Roberts (who sells, it is estimated, thirty-four books every minute) said, 'A woman writes it, and it's just one of *those* … a guy writes it and they call it something else. And it gets reviewed.' As she asks, 'Novels that celebrate love, commitment, relationships, making relationships work, why isn't that something to be respected?'

Romance has probably evolved more than any other genre too, reflecting how women's lives have changed over the twentieth century. When the publisher Harlequin began distributing Mills & Boon novels in North America in the 1950s, editorial control was enacted through a strict 'decency code'. Heroines were innocent, virginal and, if they worked at all, were nurses or secretaries. The men were older, richer and more experienced. A chaste kiss was as racy as it got. Roberts brilliantly describes the formula that still reigned when she started writing in the 1980s:

> He was often a Greek tycoon; she was often orphaned and raised by an aunt. She's on her way to a new job, working for the richest man in the free world. In the airport, she's rushing through with her battered suitcase. She runs into this man and the suitcase falls open, revealing a pitiful wardrobe – it's all neat and well-mended but sad. And he calls her a clumsy fool and helps her stuff her clothes back in the suitcase and storms off, and the next day she goes into the offices of the richest man in the free world and who should be there but the man she ran into in the airport?

I confess I really want to read this book. I also note that it sounds depressingly similar to *Fifty Shades of Grey*, which is effectively a regression to the old days of virgin and conqueror –

Ana is even described as 'unworldly and innocent' in the blurb.*

For the most part, however, romance novels moved with the times, with female characters becoming more independent and working in a variety of high-powered jobs. They took the lead in the stories too, which became more about self-discovery and self-worth – bestsellers of recent decades such as Cecelia Ahern's *P.S. I Love You* and Jojo Moyes's *Me Before You* eschew a happy ending for emotional catharsis, with the greatest love story being between the heroine and herself, or even the reader and the heroine (although they are good old-fashioned weepies too). The genre is slowly becoming more diverse, with romance occurring between characters who aren't just straight, white, young or beautiful, and novels like Ingrid Persaud's *Love After Love* and Sara Jafari's *The Mismatch* shooting up the charts.

To show how our tastes have changed, there's a comparison of two blurbs for different editions of *Venetia* by Georgette Heyer (the doyenne of exquisitely witty Regency romances) on the Backlisted podcast. The 1970s blurb goes like this:

> Lord Damerel found Venetia to be the most truly engaging and wittily perverse female he had encountered in all his thirty-eight years. Venetia knew her neighbour for a gamester, a shocking rake and a man of sadly unsteady character. It was therefore particularly provoking to find that given the occasion Damerel could make up his mind to be quite idiotically noble…

* Sadly, *Fifty Shades* does nothing to dispel the late feminist Andrea Dworkin's contention that the genre is 'rape embellished with meaningful looks'.

And this is the blurb on the contemporary edition:

> In all her twenty-five years, Venetia Lanyon has never been
> further than Harrogate. Nor has she enjoyed the attentions
> of any man aside from her two wearisomely persistent suitors.
> Then, in one extraordinary encounter, she meets a neighbour
> she only knew by reputation – the infamous Jasper Damerel.
> Before she realises it, Venetia is encouraging a man whose way
> of life has scandalised the North Riding for years.

The woman has taken centre stage, and we see the action
through her eyes. Although, of course, we know instantly that,
just as in *Beauty and the Beast*, Damerel's inner goodness will be
revealed, and they will fall hopelessly in love. This is the crux of
romance. It is the one genre where the reader knows, or hopes
they know, *exactly* what is going to happen even before the novel's central characters do. We want to savour the obstacles before
the (mostly) happy ending, so the blurb has to send a different
kind of signal. It must convey jeopardy.

What could be more of an impediment to love than God?
Way before Fleabag and her hot priest, Colleen McCullough
set the world on fire with *The Thorn Birds*, an epic 1970s saga
set in the Australian outback, which centred on the forbidden
love between a young woman, Meggie, and Father Ralph de
Bricassart. The copy on the first edition is brimming with
emotional peril, describing 'the intense joining of two hearts
and souls over a lifetime, a relationship that dangerously over-
steps sacred boundaries of ethics and dogma'. Is it all a bit sexy
too? 'Dark passions … hard land … secrets that penetrate their
family … the novel explodes.' The earth moved.

Germaine Greer rather meanly called *The Thorn Birds* 'the

best bad book I ever read', but I note that it was reissued as a Virago Modern Classic recently. In her Introduction, the romance novelist Maeve Binchy writes: 'Here was the first popular novel where the heroine knows that there is no other man for her except the priest, and that one day she will get him … We know they will get together and it's not so much a question of if but when. It gives the story an almost unbearable sense of urgency.' As always with romance, it's not the outcome – it's getting there that is such wonderful agony.

Looking at the copy on more contemporary romances, such as the hugely successful novels of Katie Fforde, there are similar themes of obstacles or opposition at play. Someone moves to a new town, encounters an old flame, or is thrown into a new situation. It's that old three-act structure: a set-up, a change, a resolution. Fforde's novels all feature questions on the front, putting the tension right out there: 'Which should you trust: your head, or your heart?', 'Will her heart melt this winter?', 'Can a holiday romance become happy ever after?', 'Can love be about to bloom?'

The answer to all of the above is, of course, yes, yes, YES! (to quote Sally Albright in *that* scene). But that's not the point. It doesn't matter if it's predictable; it's all part of the fun. So if reading a romance novel is like sex, ending in a satisfying resolution with a good time to be had on the way, I guess that makes the blurb foreplay: something to get the reader going before they get going.

WHODUNNIT?

Mysteries make life better.

SOPHIE HANNAH

There is a body. There has to be a body. There are short sentences. Very. Short. The story loop is as tight as a noose. There is a dark, dark cover. A *huge* title. IN CAPITALS. And, above all, there is a promise. Something makes this murder different from all the others. And solving it is going to test our protagonist to the limit… (ellipses are also good).

Crime is the genre that satisfies our need for both novelty and reassurance like no other. Reading a crime novel is solving a puzzle: no detail is insignificant, you look for clues throughout and thrill at the solution. Unlike horror, everything *will* be all right in the end, more or less.

Crime novelist Anthony Horowitz describes murder mysteries as 'the only form of literature that deals in absolute truths. When you read a whodunnit, the joy of it is that you know that at the last chapter every "i" will be dotted, every "t" will be crossed, everything will be solved. Perhaps now, more than ever, when we often don't know what to believe, there is enormous comfort in a world in which everything is completely explained and closed off.'

But, as they sang in *Gypsy*, you've gotta get a gimmick if you're gonna get ahead – there needs to be a new twist, a new hook, every time, whether the novel is a traditional police procedural, a psychological thriller or a 'whydunnit'. The copy should signal each novel's point of difference as efficiently as possible – what makes *this* book stand out in an overcrowded field?

The copy for Horowitz's *The Word is Murder* has a nice hooky beginning:

A woman is strangled six hours after organising her own funeral.

The gimmicks keep on coming as he includes himself as a character in the novel:

Daniel Hawthorne, a recalcitrant detective with secrets of his own, is on the case, and he's found himself a sidekick – popular crime novelist Anthony Horowitz, who's struck a deal with Hawthorne to turn his latest case into a true crime bestseller…

P. D. James's *Unnatural Causes* and Val McDermid's *Killing the Shadows* both feature murdered crime writers. So meta. And while we're on Val McDermid, the copy for her first novel featuring Tony Hill and Carol Jordan, *The Mermaids Singing*, makes its hook clear: men are being mutilated and tortured by 'a serial killer unlike any the world of fiction has ever seen'. Here is the promise of something we haven't had before.

In Henning Mankell's *Sidetracked*, one of the greatest Scandinavian crime novels, Kurt Wallander witnesses a teenage girl set herself on fire in front of him, and must hunt down 'a killer who scalps his victims'. In Susie Steiner's *Remain Silent*, my new favourite detective DI Manon Bradshaw encounters a young immigrant worker found 'hanging from a tree in Cambridgeshire, a note attached saying "The dead cannot speak".' In *Dissolution*, the first novel by C. J. Sansom featuring Matthew Shardlake (and if a Tudor hunchback lawyer-turned-detective isn't enough of a hook for you then there's just no pleasing some people), one of Thomas Cromwell's henchmen is slaughtered in a monastery 'accompanied by equally sinister acts of sacrilege – a black cockerel sacrificed on the altar'.

And on it goes; each murder mystery highlights its Unique Selling Point (Unique Killing Point?) for the next insatiable reader. We also know that the best crime writing will bring us a vividly realised sense of place, and touch on the darkest aspects of society – and ourselves. Probably nobody does this better than Ian Rankin, whose Rebus novels are as much about the grim underbelly of Edinburgh – gang violence, illegal immigration, political corruption – from the 1980s onwards, as the crimes themselves. The latest Rebus, *A Song for the Dark Times* ('Family comes first, even before the truth'), sees his daughter become suspected of murder.

The recurring detective is the perfect way to keep things the same but different. It's no accident Agatha Christie is the Queen of Crime. Not only do her novels feature fiendishly ingenious plots and recurring investigators, but gimmicks too: ten victims bumped off one by one in accordance with a nursery rhyme, a killer working his way through the alphabet or, in one of the latest reincarnations of the Poirot series by Sophie Hannah, a murderer who places a cufflink in each victim's mouth.

We want our detective to be godlike, a saviour with magical problem-solving powers who sees that one thing nobody else can, yet at the same time as horribly flawed as we are – in fact more so, like some tragic hero of ancient myth. We make the journey with them, and read crime to savour character as much as plot.

This is why identification is key in crime blurbs: either with the world-weary/jaded/maverick detective, or with the victim. It's telling that so much crime is written and read by women. We are aware from childhood that we are vulnerable, warned about going out alone. Part of the thrill, I think, is that jolt of 'there but for the grace of God go I'.

The front covers of thrillers often lay out their scares with a shoutline speaking directly to our fears – 'You don't know her. But she knows you' on *The Girl on the Train*; 'Be careful who you let in' on *The House Swap*. The blurbs do it too. *Land of the Living*, by Nicci French, was written a few years ago, but the beginning of the back cover copy has stayed with me:

> You wake in the dark, gagged and bound. A man visits you, feeds you. And tells you that he will kill you – just like all the rest.

My potted rules for crime blurbs, then? Identify your Unique Killing Point. Remember character. And make the reader identify. A good crime blurb should be like a really creepy version of the National Lottery slogan… 'It could be you.'

IN A GALAXY FAR, FAR AWAY…

> Science fiction is no more written for scientists than ghost stories are written for ghosts.
>
> BRIAN ALDISS

Science fiction, as anyone with a nanoparticle of sense knows, is not about spaceships. It is about big ideas, and the human condition. It deals with life, death, time, fate, consciousness and belief. It plays with gender, perspective, language and reality itself. Science fiction reflects the anxieties of its times, whether surrounding the rise of technology, environmental catastrophe (hence the 'cli-fi' phenomenon) or our fear of ourselves and what we are capable of. Ursula K. Le Guin was a feminist SF trailblazer, and as a whole the genre is becoming less conservative, with works like Namina Forna's African mythology-influenced *The Gilded Ones*. In her words, 'I wanted to put Black and brown people at the forefront of this world; and women, who have so often been pushed to the periphery of fantasy, at the very centre.'

Like all genre fiction, science fiction is treated with more than a whiff of snobbery by the literary world. Some novelists happily and willingly dip their toes into it with spectacular results, like Kazuo Ishiguro's *Klara and the Sun* or Michel Faber's *Under the Skin*. But some shy away from the label. When Ian McEwan, talking about his latest AI-themed novel *Machines Like Me*, seemingly disparaged the genre, he incurred the wrath of fans: 'There could be an opening of a mental space for novelists to explore this future,' he said, 'not in terms of travelling at 10 times the speed of light in anti-gravity boots, but in actually looking at the human dilemmas.' As if science fiction hasn't been dealing with these dilemmas for decades.

In a gloriously grumpy exchange with an interviewer who says science fiction isn't 'serious literature', Terry Pratchett mounts a faultless defence of what he calls a 'ghettoised' genre:

> The first fiction ever recounted was fantasy. Guys sitting around the campfire telling each other stories about the gods who made lightning. They did not complain about the difficulties of the male menopause while being a junior lecturer on some Midwestern college campus. Fantasy is the ur-literature, the spring from which all other literature has flown. Fantasy can carry a serious burden, and so can humour.

As Michel Faber noted: '*Under the Skin* was discussed on BBC Radio 4's *Open Book* recently and the three presenters tried their best to argue that it wasn't really sci-fi because it was beauti-fully written and had such strong characterisation and profound themes. On the one hand it's lovely to be appreciated, but on the other you can see the institutionalised disrespect for the genre and understand why it drives sci-fi writers mad.'

I am also going to risk offending purists by touching on fantasy and speculative fiction here too, although I know they are different beasts. But the techniques are similar, namely that the writer is creating a world. World-building means giving your fictional universe – however fantastical – an inner logic, from its landscapes and mythology to its language (Tolkien called it a 'Legendarium'). So, good copy for science fiction, fantasy or dystopian fiction should build a world too – only it has fewer words to convey new, unfamiliar or potentially confusing infor-mation to a reader.

The copy for Aldous Huxley's landmark dystopia *Brave New World*, spruced up to accompany the (ill-fated) recent TV series, does this rather well:

EVERYONE BELONGS TO EVERYONE ELSE

Welcome to New London. Everybody is happy here. Our perfect society achieved peace and stability through the prohibition of monogamy, privacy, money, family and history itself. Now everyone belongs.

You can be happy too. All you need to do is take your Soma pills.

It's a neat, unexpected way into ideas that could sound stale if they had been described differently, and I like the way it mimics the deadened language of a society that has lost its purpose.

However, the best world-building copy I have read is for the first volume of Terry Pratchett's Discworld series, *The Colour of Magic*:

> *In the beginning there was… a turtle.*
>
> Somewhere on the frontier between thought and reality exists the Discworld, a parallel time and place which might sound and smell very much like our own, but which looks completely different.
>
> Particularly as it's carried through space on the back of a giant turtle (sex unknown). It plays by different rules…

It works because it gets across unusual information in an easy way, and because it is funny.

An example of how not to do it is the copy for Frank Herbert's *Dune*, which also aims to tell us about the novel's universe, but does it through too many details and names, which just leave me reeling in the space-time continuum:

> When the Emperor transfers stewardship of Arrakis from the noble House Harkonnen to House Atreides, the Harkonnens fight back, murdering Duke Leto Atreides. Paul, his son, and Lady Jessica, his concubine, flee into the desert. On the point of death, they are rescued by a band of Fremen, the native people of Arrakis, who control Arrakis' second great resource: the giant worms that burrow beneath the burning desert sands.

This isn't even a third of it, yet it makes my head hurt. It makes the mistake of concentrating too much on plot. As Francis Spufford says when describing his love affair with science fiction, plots are often secondary. What he remembered was the 'sensually vivid and specific detail ... plot plus tone plus ideas plus visuals'.

One of the most important qualities of science fiction is influence. Each book is part of a family tree, inspiring subsequent titles, and each book both reflects and shapes our view of the world. The copy on William Gibson's *Neuromancer* highlights its famous first line and makes a claim for its place in our culture:

> *The sky above the port was the colour of television, tuned to a dead channel.*
>
> William Gibson revolutionised science fiction in his 1984 debut *Neuromancer*. The writer who gave us the matrix and coined the term 'cyberspace' produced a first novel that won the Hugo, Nebula and Philip K. Dick Awards, and lit the fuse on the Cyberpunk movement.

This brings me to another key element of science-fiction copy: taking your audience seriously as intelligent beings.

The copy on the three-volume hardbacks of *The Lord of the Rings* that I inherited from my grandmother (there's even a fold-out map of Middle-earth!) goes in very high – perhaps too high, I admit. It begins: '*The Lord of the Rings* is not a book to be described in a few sentences.' It compares it to heroic romance, Edmund Spenser's *The Faerie Queene*, Norse mythology and science fiction before concluding that it has 'a flavour of all of them and a taste of its own'. The blurb on the latest edition takes things down a notch, ticking off Sauron, the One Ring, Frodo and the Shire in as few words as possible, while still conveying the novel's literary significance. And the cover uses Tolkien's original artwork, showing the eye of

Sauron inside a ring of Elvish writing, which gives it a nice feeling of continuity.

Science fiction has produced some of the most inventive design in publishing, such as David Pelham's classic creations for the Penguin Science Fiction series, featuring black backgrounds, a purple logo and out-there psychedelic illustrations. The 1974 edition of Alfred Bester's *Tiger! Tiger!* is emblazoned with a surreal 'composite portrait made out of debris' and a rather marvellous back cover blurb from esteemed copywriter (and part-time SF writer) Meaburn Staniland, describing the novel's protagonist as 'liar, lecher, ghoul, walking cancer. Obsessed by vengeance, he's also the twenty-fourth century's most valuable commodity – but he doesn't know it.'

When reviving this series in 2020, art director Jim Stoddart retained the purple logo, but went for something more restrained on the covers, employing minimal line drawings by the likes of Picasso and Le Corbusier to suggest rather than represent. The effect is cool and calm compared to the busy, frenetic look of much of the genre. In Stoddart's words, 'These books are existentially mind-bending and the action best takes place in the imagination. It felt right to let the role of these covers be simply to allude to the pages held within, rather than illustrate them.'

That's why the best science-fiction copy is short and spare, world-building in as few words as possible. As it's such a *big* genre, in story as well as ideas, sometimes you need to go small to compensate.

Simply Wizard!

Blurbing Blyton

Oh, Enid, how I love you. Let me count the ways. There are the unfamiliar words and phrases I learned from you: Wizard! Brick (as in, 'you're a'). Jolly. Mam'zelle (this was my first encounter with French). San (sanatorium). Dormy (dormitory). Racket press. Curl papers. Health certificate (what was this mysterious thing the girls always had to give to Matron at the start of a new Malory Towers term?). And, naturally, midnight feast.

As well as introducing young readers to the strange thrill of unfamiliar language, and the enlightening knowledge that people spoke and acted differently in the past, Blyton's books are, of course, 100 per cent pure storytelling crack. One of the silver linings of lockdown was reading the Malory Towers school stories to my then six-year-old niece on Zoom. Admittedly she was a little young for them, but they were the only children's books that I owned a full set of – my original early 1980s Dragon Granada editions, which are uniformly brown and feature anachronistic illustrations of girls with Lady Di 'flick' haircuts on the front covers.

Thank goodness I'd kept them. My niece is still *transfixed* by them. As soon as I start reading, the thumb goes in the mouth, the label inside whatever piece of clothing she is wearing is grabbed (labels are very important to Nancy), and she is hooked.

She likes the feasts best, and she *has* to know what happens next – according to the data, Enid Blyton has one of the highest authorial rates of cliffhanger chapter endings. Nancy has already learned about French lessons, lacrosse, playing tricks, bronchitis and how bad colic can be for a horse ('if it lies down it can die!') from our Malory Towers outings, among many other things, and the experience has been life-affirming for me.

However, there's no denying that Enid can be... problematic. I've found myself self-censoring (for example, because I thought girls going round slapping each other in a fit of anger was probably a bit much for such a young child). And then of course there are the charges of sexism, racism and class snobbery that have been levelled at her over the years, for good reason – although Malory Towers more than passes the Bechdel Test with flying colours.* On any argument about censoring works from another age I would usually come down on the side of 'the past is another country, they do things differently there', yet elements of Blyton's stories do feel very old-fashioned today.

We met children's copywriter Sarah Topping earlier, and I'm welcoming her back because she was recently given the task of rewriting the blurbs for several Enid Blyton series. What an enviable joy! I spoke to her (while swallowing down my jealousy) about how she went about pitching Blyton's books to a modern audience, and how she found the elements from the stories that would still appeal across the years to a child today,

* The Bechdel Test is used to measure the positive representation of women in a film: if its female protagonists (a) number more than one, (b) are talking to each other and (c) talking to each other about something other than men, it passes the test.

despite their unfamiliar vocabulary. Here's what she said about the Famous Five books:

> Once I overcame my squealing excitement at being invited to work on another brand I adored as a child, I spent a while pondering exactly what I'd loved about them as a young reader. It all came down to two things – freedom and adventure. Thinking about The Famous Five for example, parental figures are very much in the background, while the children and Timmy the dog are off chasing smugglers, catching criminals and solving mysteries galore. Rather than considering this as something that would feel alien or remote to today's reader, I concentrated on the excitement of it all – no strict parents, no teachers, no rules… a dream come true!

Part of Sarah's brief was also to write copy for 3-in-1 sets of the Malory Towers books (my envy is getting unbearable now).

> I had to re-read each book (SUCH JOY!) and try and describe it in a sentence or two. This was quite hard – there is so much going on in the stories and we had such limited space. I wanted to pull out the feeling of going off to boarding school, particularly one in such a glorious location as Malory Towers – for me, the school itself was as memorable as the main characters. These stories felt so important at that age, in terms of becoming independent, forming new friendships, having fun, understanding right and wrong, dealing with strict teachers – yet at a comfortably safe distance. In the end I started my blurbs with:

Welcome to
MALORY TOWERS
Fun, friendship and adventures at school by the sea

This gets it just right. I also notice that the copy for the Malory Towers books on Amazon focuses on similar things: the fun and adventure of it all, rather than the schoolwork:

> There's more to life than lessons at Malory Towers, Enid Blyton's best-loved boarding school series.

It's interesting that nobody finds the idea of boarding school alienating to young readers. As a timid child, I found the idea of being sent away from home terrifying, but, as we all know, the best children's books always get the grown-ups out of the way, and what better way to do it than through this device?

The key to Blyton's stories, especially her school stories, is camaraderie, and the importance of being a Jolly Good Egg – and is that really such a bad thing? Yes, her insistence that girls who are outliers get ruthlessly cut down to size is horribly judgemental, and she has very dubious views on a particular nation's characteristics (Americans = brassy and vulgar. French = naughtée). There's a delightful passage in Barbara Trapido's *The Travelling Hornplayer*, where her giggling twin heroines tell their father why they love Malory Towers so much more than the 'proper literature' they are meant to admire:

> 'What on earth goes on in these frightful books you read?' he'd say, and that was all the invitation we needed.
>
> 'Oh, but they're brilliant,' Lydia would say …
>
> 'The French teachers are always terrified of mice …'
>
> 'And the American girls,' I pitched in. 'They come to English schools so that they can learn to speak properly.'
>
> 'And their fathers are called "Pops", and they drive huge cars, and they're all road hogs,' Lydia said …

'And the French girls are always cheats.'

'They have to come to English schools to learn a Sense of Honour, but they never do, they can't,' Lydia said.

'Why can't they?' our father said.

'Because they're French,' Lydia said, 'of course.' …

'Do you two learn these books off by heart?' Father said.

'No,' Lydia said. 'It's just that they're so good they stick in our minds.'

It nails triumphantly what makes Blyton's stories slightly suspect and so vivid at the same time. I think they are also more morally complex than they're given credit for. In *Bookworm*, Lucy Mangan perfectly expresses her mixed feelings about Blyton, honouring her 'balm to the soul' while also lamenting the books' 'simple psychologies'. I suppose, given that Blyton wrote ten thousand words a day at her peak of productivity, there wasn't a lot of time for depth.

This is definitely true of much of her output, but I think Malory Towers offers something a little more sophisticated. Readers are introduced to a dizzying array of multiple plot strands, with several stories kept spinning at once. We learn that people can be complicated too. Someone (such as Sally Hope, jealous of her new baby sister in Book 1) can be giving the outward appearance of one thing, while a whole mixture of emotions is churning away underneath: envy, insecurity, anger, anxiety. In *Second Form at Malory Towers*, the glamorous new girl Daphne is actually a thief, stealing money from her schoolmates, yet she is forgiven because of a single act of selfless bravery. As the cool, assured headmistress Miss Grayling says, 'You think that if someone does a brave deed quite suddenly, then he or she could never do a mean one? We all have good and bad in us.' One day I would like to be as wise as Miss Grayling.

Through Malory Towers we appreciate that it's much better to be kind than to be brilliant, to have character rather than look pretty, to face up to unpleasant truths about ourselves, and others. We discover that emotions are unpredictable and confusing things.

Enid, I have realised, is not to be underestimated. I've also found that perhaps we worry too much in publishing about making things 'relevant'. There's always something to love and learn from in a book, especially if it lasts as long as these books have, and part of the job of people like me is to pick out what makes it special and pass it on.

'Which one of you bitches is my mother?'

Ah, the great words of the great writers… 'It is a far, far better thing that I do, than I have ever done.' 'Who controls the past, controls the future.' 'So we beat on, boats against the current, borne back ceaselessly into the past.' Too many to choose from, surely? Well, admire their literary majesty, and gird your loins for something less lofty. In my unscientific opinion, 'Which one of you bitches is my mother?', appearing at the end of the first chapter of Shirley Conran's *Lace*, is probably the greatest line in the history of the written word. It has graced every incarnation of the book's blurb since it was published, and it is burned onto the hearts and minds of every woman who was a teenager in the 1980s.

You prise my copy of *Lace* from my cold dead hands. An epic saga of friendship, sex and ambition published in 1982, it has sold over three million copies in thirty-five countries and was the zenith of the 'sex and shopping' or bonkbuster genre. These books were flamboyant, gripping and utterly suited to their times; huge, brash tomes dominating the period between the 1970s feminist revolution and the 1980s consumer revolution like glittering colossi. My friends and I were obsessed with *Lace*, especially the dirty bits – just say the word 'goldfish' to a woman in her late forties and she might go a bit funny (and when you search for the book online, 'Shirley Conran Lace goldfish' comes up second).

Other leading lights in this noble genre include Judith Krantz's *Scruples*,* Jackie Collins's *Hollywood Wives*, both set in glamorous Los Angeles, and Jilly Cooper's *Riders*, which swapped the States for romps in English stables with the rakish Rupert Campbell-Black – it's even set in a fictional county called 'Rutshire'.

The novels of Shirley Conran's contemporaries are all hugely enjoyable, era-defining books, but *Lace* still has the edge for me because it is a truly feminist work. Its story of four girls who become friends at a Swiss finishing school, sticking together as they make it to the top in their chosen careers, is a celebration of women at work, and of female friendship – while touching on issues like abortion, equal pay and the porn industry in a way that felt shocking at the time.

Shirley Conran lived it as she wrote it, famously stating in her 1975 book *Superwoman* that 'life is too short to stuff a mushroom'. In her Afterword to the thirtieth-anniversary edition of *Lace* (which is the very definition of fabulous, containing throwaway lines such as 'the Duke of Bedford explained to me', 'one of France's most eligible young bachelors', 'as I was being served breakfast in my four-poster bed'), she recounts how '*Lace* is based on my own life, my own experiences and my own friends … in fact, I watered it down a bit.'

Lace was originally intended to be a guide to sex for teenage girls, in response to the many letters Conran received while a

---

* One of the best hatchet jobs I've ever read is Clive James's 1980 review of Judith Krantz's *Princess Daisy* in the *London Review of Books*. Sample burns include: 'all Mrs Krantz's carefully garnered social detail gives way to eyes like twin dark stars, mouths like moist fruit and breasts quivering with indignation … the first breasts to have done that for a long, long time' and '*Princess Daisy* reads like *Buddenbrooks* without the talent.'

newspaper columnist. She says, 'I spent 18 months researching it. But then I got so bored I thought I might as well have a go at writing a novel. So *Lace* is really intensely researched sexual information dressed up as a novel.'

Don't worry, Shirley – it *was* a sex guide. The dirty bits (what Nabokov called the 'O.S.S.' or obligatory sex scene) were our teenage *Joy of Sex*, but without the hairy people. I was slightly crestfallen to learn from Richard Cohen's *How to Write Like Tolstoy* that Conran actually paid another writer to dream up these delights. According to Cohen, she 'hired fellow-novelist Celia Brayfield to contribute twelve erotic scenes, two of which featured a goldfish and a diamond in unusual settings, paying her £500 for her work'. It gets better, as the two women fell out over this, resulting in a literary rivalry that could have come out of Conran's (or Brayfield's) pages. But, wherever its origins lie, the point remains that sex in Shirley Conran is fun, and that women feel desire.

By comparison, weedy, virginal little Ana in *Fifty Shades of Grey* is a milksop. In Conran's words, the twenty-first-century incarnation of the bonkbuster is 'Infantile. You have to wait until page 200 for any sex at all. She doesn't get her bottom spanked until page 400.' Well quite.

I love this description of the power *Lace* had over teenage girls around the world by Irene Sabatini, author of *The Boy Next Door*:

I first read *Lace* as a 16-year-old schoolgirl at Dominican Convent High School in Bulawayo, Zimbabwe, in the 1980s. I remember that chunky, glitzy novel being passed around during math, biology, religious education classes ... under our desks, pages earmarked as it moved along ... *for your reading pleasure* ... To whom the book belonged remains a mystery, but in a sense it belonged to all of us convent girls in that sleepy town. We were having our eyes opened in more ways than one. We took turns taking it home, like a beloved class pet.

My extremely well-read 1980s edition of *Lace* uses the classic 'bitches' quote at the start of its back cover copy. The front cover features a soft-focus image of a sultry woman wearing red lipstick and a natty pillbox hat with a black lace veil, and the line 'The bestselling novel that teaches men about women – and women about themselves.' I remember being deeply impressed by the profound truth of this tagline, and couldn't wait to find out all about myself inside. This is the blurb:

> Which one of you bitches is my mother?
>
> The question sears through the thoughts of the four women summoned so mysteriously to a glamorous New York hotel apartment, unlocking the past and a secret – a secret that has enmeshed their lives and dogged their success – that lies at the heart of this scorching, sensational novel.
>
> The story of four women, Judy, Kate, Pagan and Maxine, who took life as they found it and dared to make it a success. Against an international backdrop of the rich, the famous and the depraved, these women – bound together by ties stronger than love itself – created legends.

It's rounded off with a review from the *Sunday Express*: 'Riches, bitches, sex and jetsetters' locations – they're all there.' I loved this blurb, and still do. It was so propulsive, so outrageously sexy with its use of 'scorching' and 'depraved', and I thrilled at the boldness of women 'daring' to be a success and creating legends.

The cover of the thirtieth-anniversary Canongate edition features a riotous design that the journalist Rachel Cooke describes thus: 'cross an old Duran Duran video with a 1980s billboard for Rimmel cosmetics and you're about halfway there'. Very wisely, it retains the 'bitches' line, but the blurb is pared back and simplified to make room for quotes of homage from the likes of Helen Fielding and India Knight, rightly worshipful of the novel's status. Still, I miss the over-the-top copy of old.

Why does the line 'Which one of you bitches is my mother?', used as the opening of all the *Lace* blurbs I can find, work so well? It is a classic hook, plunging the reader into a moment, presumably mid-conversation, and it throws up a whole load of questions: who's saying it? Why doesn't she know? Who are the bitches? It demands answers. But it also tells us immediately what the novel's voice is going to be: rude, brash, fun. You are going to have a good time here. It has irresistible energy, just like the novel itself. What kind of maniac would *not* want to read on? It is a reminder of how important tone is.

In fact, it's so memorable that the heavy lifting of the blurb is already done. It may feel like cheating to use an author's words, but when a line of genius comes along, you have to stand back and take a bow. The legendary advertising copywriter David Abbott famously said, 'Sometimes the best copy is no copy.' Well, sometimes the best words are not your own. On occasion, the wisest thing a copywriter can do is to accept defeat.

X-Rated

Lolita and Other Dilemmas

> No one will ever succeed in describing it fully on a book jacket. But how wonderful that so many have tried.
>
> MARY GAITSKILL ON *LOLITA*

That's fighting talk, Mary. I like to think that no book is indescribable. But it does raise the question, are some books and characters so problematic, so 'difficult', that any attempt to capture them is bound to go wrong? How do you approach the cover and copy of a novel such as *Lolita*, a work of divine comedy and also, in the stark words of Professor Ellen Pifer, 'a threnody for the destruction of a child's life'? Some very silly things have been written about *Lolita* over the years, but Nabokov was always emphatic that his narrator Humbert Humbert was 'a vain and cruel wretch', 'a hateful person'. He is a verbose monster, but the novel is also extremely funny – he's called Humbert Humbert, for goodness sake. So how do you solve a problem like *Lolita*?

There have been hundreds of jacket designs for Nabokov's novel over the years, in fact so many that an entire book has been dedicated to them: *Lolita – The Story of a Cover Girl*. As the book's Introduction says, 'If there ever were a book whose covers have so reliably gotten it wrong, it is *Lolita*.' Lolita herself has continually been misinterpreted and misrepresented, made into an object of sexual desire – partly due to the Kubrick film adaptation of 1962, with its 'maddeningly indelible' image of the teenage girl in heart-shaped sunglasses. Mary Gaitskill's brilliant essay in the book notes that 'a high percentage of the covers go for cute: whimsical buttons on bright red, an ejaculating pink plastic gun, a crenelated candy-pink shell, a pale-pink plastic necklace spelling the titular name, that name elsewhere spelled with a bobby sock L, a paper-doll leg, a crushed red lollipop'.

The best cover, according to Gaitskill, is the US Vintage paperback edition of 1997, which features a black-and-white photograph of a young girl's legs, knock-kneed, with short socks and lace-up shoes. I agree it's effective: the pose looks awkward rather than coquettish – in her words, 'it expresses fear … she is cringing.' But she is not happy about the quote that appears on the front cover, from *Vanity Fair*, proudly stating that *Lolita* is 'The only convincing love story of the century.' In her view, 'it is quietly outrageous that a main-stream publisher would choose to put it on the cover, directly over those understandably frightened legs … *Lolita* is about obsession, which is never, ever love, and Nabokov himself was disappointed that people did not understand this and take away the right message.'

Rather ickily, the US Vintage fiftieth-anniversary edition from 2005 still uses the offending *Vanity Fair* quote on the back cover, along with this copy:

> Awe and exhilaration – along with heartbreak and mordant wit – abound in *Lolita*, Vladimir Nabokov's most famous and controversial novel, which tells the story of the aging Humbert Humbert's obsessive, devouring, and doomed passion for the nymphet Dolores Haze. Most of all, it is a meditation on love …

Not only does the copy employ the language of romance ('doomed passion', 'heartbreak'), but it also uses Humbert's word for Lolita, 'nymphet', as if it is an objective truth. Yuck.

Nabokov took a keen interest in cover design, and was concerned about how his novel would be represented. The first edition of *Lolita*, published in France by Olympia Press in 1955 as two paperbacks, had a very simple, olive green typographical cover. The book went under most people's radars until a review by Graham Greene brought it to the attention of the public, as a result of which customs officers were instructed to seize any copies entering the UK – it was banned until 1959. For the 1958 American edition, Nabokov wrote to his US publisher Walter J. Minton, at Putnam, about the cover. 'What about the jacket?' he asked:

> Who would be capable of creating a romantic, delicately drawn, non-Freudian and non-juvenile, picture for LOLITA (a dissolving remoteness, a soft American landscape, a nostalgic highway – that sort of thing)? There is one subject which I am emphatically opposed to: any kind of representation of a little girl.

Nabokov rejected all of Minton's proposed designs. 'I have just received the five designs and I quite agree with you that none of them is satisfactory,' he wrote. 'I want pure colors, melting clouds, accurately drawn details, a sunburst above a receding road with the light reflected in furrows and ruts, after rain. And no girls. If we cannot find that kind of artistic and virile painting, let us settle for an immaculate white jacket (rough texture paper instead of the usual glossy kind), with LOLITA in bold black lettering.' This is a pretty accurate description of the final cover design that was used.*

Looking at other incarnations of the novel over the years, some just plump for typographical designs, such as the US edition which made me laugh uncontrollably with its bathetic tagline 'The second most-often cited title in Book Week's poll of distinguished fiction, 1945–1965.' Another features the rather gnomic line 'MOST TALKED ABOUT NOVEL OF OUR DAY.' Why bother with the definite article, eh?

Most of them, however, ignore Nabokov's original request not to picture a little girl. They represent Lolita herself, either using stills from film adaptations, or artwork – usually showing a girl who looks older than twelve, as if the covers can't quite bear the grim truth. The Penguin Modern Classics edition used a photograph of a young girl lying in grass, inspired by the 1997 Adrian Lyne film, which has now wisely been replaced by an oil painting of fruit and flowers that sidesteps the issue of representing Lolita entirely. The copy that has been on this edition for several years is pretty good, I think, and it starts with the first line of the book to show that this is as much a book about language as it is about lust, then continues:

> Poet and pervert, Humbert Humbert becomes obsessed by twelve-year-old Lolita and seeks to possess her, first carnally and then artistically, out of love, 'to fix once for all the perilous

* Annoyingly, Nabokov later appeared to ignore his own advice. There's old footage of him looking through a shelf of foreign editions of his book, including a French Livre de Poche picturing the face of a girl, which he calls 'very pretty'. Perhaps principles go out of the window when authors land a foreign rights deal.

magic of nymphets'. This seduction is one of many dimensions to Nabokov's dizzying masterpiece, which is suffused with a savage humour and rich, elaborate verbal textures.

'Poet and pervert' is a bald statement, but it grabs the attention and also draws a distance between the reader and Humbert, rather than making us complicit.

Looking at current US copy, I was rather taken aback by the description that appears on Amazon for the audiobook edition:

> When it was published in 1955, *Lolita* immediately became a cause célèbre because of the freedom and sophistication with which it handled the unusual erotic predilections of its protagonist. But Vladimir Nabokov's wise, ironic, elegant masterpiece owes its stature as one of the twentieth century's novels of record not to the controversy its material aroused but to its author's use of that material to tell a love story that is shocking in its beauty and tenderness.

Erotic predilections? Tenderness? Excuse me while I vomit.

A more successful piece of copy is the blurb on another UK edition from 2011, featuring a photograph of a young girl's freckled face on the front, clearly aiming it at a youngish reader. The back cover is adorned with review quotes (one of which memorably describes it as a Medusa's head with trick paper snakes), and the copy is interesting because it gets across the nature of the beast but it also gives Lolita agency – something a modern reader will respond to. I'm not quite as keen on the attempt at psychological justification of Humbert's actions, though:

Humbert Humbert, a European intellectual adrift in America, is a middle-aged college professor. Haunted by memories of a lost adolescent love, he falls outrageously (and illegally) in lust with his landlady's twelve-year-old daughter Dolores Haze. Obsessed, he'll do anything, will commit any crime, to possess his Lolita.

But once Lolita belongs to Humbert, once he has got what he wants, what next? And what of Lolita? How long is she willing to be possessed?

The parenthesised 'and illegally' in this copy points to something useful: when trying to describe controversial books, it's best to face the issue head on. The blurb copy on the inside front cover of the notorious 1960 edition of *Lady Chatterley's Lover* (the back cover features a biography of D. H. Lawrence), published after Penguin were prosecuted under the Obscene Publications Act and won their case, is a triumphant blast of defiance against prudery and the establishment of the day:

Lawrence wrote of *Lady Chatterley's Lover* 'I always labour the same thing, to make the sex relation valid and precious instead of shameful. And this novel is the furthest I've gone. To me it is beautiful and tender as the naked self…' This story of the love between a gamekeeper and the wife of a crippled intellectual is therefore one of 'phallic tenderness' and is never, in any sense of the word, pornographic. Unfortunately, the critics and censors who bitterly decried the book concentrated their attacks on the language and ignored the tenderness.

Lawrence knew that he would be attacked. 'It will bring me only abuse and hatred,' he said, and it did. It has taken over thirty years for it to be possible to publish the unmutilated version of the book in this country.

A palpable hit, I think, if you can ignore the dated reference to 'crippled'. I especially admire the use of the word 'unmutilated', as if 'uncensored' or 'unexpurgated' weren't strong enough.

One book that definitely could be described as pornographic, in this case in its violence, is Bret Easton Ellis's satire *American Psycho*. The copy on the back cover cleverly draws us in and alienates us at the same time, and makes the *why* of the novel as clear as the *what*. Plus the first review on the book comes from a woman, Fay Weldon; important on a book that could be interpreted as misogynistic:

> Patrick Bateman is twenty-six and works on Wall Street; he is handsome, sophisticated, charming and intelligent. He is also a psychopath. Taking us to a head-on collision with America's greatest dream – and its worst nightmare – *American Psycho* is a bleak, bitter, black comedy about a world we all recognize but do not wish to confront.

The blurbs for similarly controversial titles *Last Exit to Brooklyn* and *A Clockwork Orange* also make serious points about the novels' intentions ('a notorious masterpiece', 'a serious exploration of the morality of free will'). In his Introduction to *Last Exit to Brooklyn*, Irvine Welsh wisely advises against the word 'cult' to describe such books, calling it 'ultimately marginalising and insulting' to the works of great writers. But what about a work whose intentions are less clear; which is just plain nasty?

The Marquis de Sade's *The 120 Days of Sodom* is a horrible, horrible book. There's no getting around it. But it is of historical and literary interest, and so it made sense to publish it as a Penguin Classic, in a new translation in 2016. In a sensitive and perceptive Introduction, the translators describe it as 'perhaps the most challenging text ever written … As difficult as it may be, *The 120 Days* needs to be read actively, and thoughtfully.' They wisely discuss the historical context of the novel's composition, and ultimately argue for its place in the canon because it is the definition of a classic: 'a work that is impossible to ignore'.

When writing the copy, I tried to be honest, and talked about its 'raw brutality'. I didn't want to shy away from the unpleasantness. And that is what copy for a 'difficult' book should do. A blurb does not have to be a defence. It does not have to make the reader complicit. But it can make a case for a book's continuing existence. There is a reason it is being published, after all. We cannot wish away troubling, or even morally reprehensible, writers. Nor should we.* But we can take care over the language we use to frame and discuss them, and publish them with a little thought.

---

* 'Cancel culture' is in itself a problematic phrase. But if I were to dip a toe into the culture wars, I would come down on the 'think before you censor, or even censure, if it plays into the hands of a libertarian' side. Why make life easier for your enemies?

5.

WILD AND
WHIRLING WORDS

Blurbs Are Us

Beasts, Quests and Monsters

Story

> All great literature is one of two stories: a man goes on a journey or a stranger comes to town.
>
> TOLSTOY

Let me tell you a story.

Poor, unlucky and alone, our heroine is dismissed by the world as the lowest of the low. But eventually she triumphs over adversity and her fortunes change. At last, her exceptional nature is revealed, and her inner goodness is recognised.

It's *Cinderella*, of course – versions of which have been found all over the world from China to ancient Egypt. It's also *Jane Eyre*, *The Ugly Duckling*, *Charlie and the Chocolate Factory*, the Harry Potter books, *Slumdog Millionaire* and *Pygmalion* – and thus *My Fair Lady* and *Pretty Woman* ('Cinderfuckinrella' as Vivian's sassy pal Kit De Luca observes). In other words, the classic rags to riches tale – otherwise known as 'unrecognised virtue rewarded'. It is just one of what many consider to be the archetypal plots of storytelling.

Nora Ephron said that 'everything is copy', to which I would add, and copy is everything. The way we tell stories is intrinsic to who we are, and who we always have been. According to Christopher Booker, there are seven basic plots running through human history: overcoming the monster (think *Beowulf* or *Jaws*); rags to riches; the quest; voyage and return; comedy; tragedy;

and rebirth. The Irish playwright Denis Johnston identified eight: unrecognised virtue; fatal flaw; debt that must be paid; love triangle; spider and the fly; boy meets girl plus obstacles; gift that is taken; and irrepressible hero (incidentally, all of them can be found in the film *Casablanca*). The eighteenth-century Italian playwright Carlo Gozzi claimed there were thirty-six.* However, the Aarne–Thompson folklore index, first published in 1910, tops them all by listing 2,500 basic plots from around the world – *Cinderella* is 510A.

The only thing that's clear, then, is that nobody really knows how many there are. But basic plots are still an invaluable way to think about how copy works on us. We know that blurbs should have a beginning, middle and end: 'a formal pattern, as tight as a sonnet's'.† Even if a book has many complex strands, by focusing on one of them, we tell an overarching story: as William Goldman calls it, 'the spine'. Too many, and the threads become tangled. What's more, telling a story in different ways can change the tenor of a tale.

Take this, on one edition of *Wuthering Heights*:

As darkness falls, a man caught in a snowstorm is forced to shelter at the strange, grim house Wuthering Heights. It is a place he will never forget. There he will come to learn the story of Cathy: how she was forced to choose between her well-meaning husband and the dangerous man she had loved

----

* Although when the French writer Georges Polti updated Gozzi's work over a century later in *Les Trente-six Situations dramatiques*, he included 'a woman enamoured of a bull' as one of his sub-divisions, which suggests he may have been on shaky ground.

† Jeremy Lewis in *Kindred Spirits*.

BEASTS, QUESTS AND MONSTERS

since she was young. How her choice led to betrayal and terrible revenge – and continues to torment those in the present.

There are countless ways to interpret Emily Brontë's novel: boy meets girl plus obstacles, tragedy, love triangle, fatal flaw. This copy twists the tale a little, and tells it from the viewpoint of the narrator, Lockwood, using him as a way into the dark relationship of Cathy and Heathcliff. It is the classic 'voyage and return' plot, placing our hero into a strange new world from which he will not come back unscathed. It reads more like a gothic novel than a love story (which, of course, many would argue it is).

But what about this?

> It starts with the rats. Vomiting blood, they die in their hundreds, then in their thousands. When the rats are all gone, the citizens begin to fall sick. Like the rats, they too die in ever greater numbers. The authorities quarantine the town. Cut off, the terrified townspeople must face this horror alone … A monstrous evil has entered their lives, but they will never surrender to it.

If you haven't already guessed, it's Albert Camus's *The Plague*, told as an 'overcoming the monster' story on the cover of an edition aimed at younger readers.

For hours of creative fun – if you get your kicks from this kind of thing – you can also retell familiar stories as if they are something else entirely. Why not try *The Sound of Music* as a romantic love triangle from the Baroness's point of view:*

....

* For further pro-Baroness reading, I highly recommend Melinda Taub's 'I Regret to Inform You That My Wedding to Captain Von Trapp Has Been Cancelled', available on mcsweeneys.net.

Elsa dazzles everyone she meets at her glittering Vienna salons. The only thing missing from her life is a man who is her equal. When she meets a lonely widower, struggling to bring up his children alone, it seems that they can save each other. But then a young nanny – very young – comes into their lives and threatens to take away everything. Will Elsa fight for the man she loves? And can she win?

In a similar vein, this is a friend's retelling of *Jaws* as a heartwarming buddy movie:

One hot summer day, three hopelessly mismatched middle-aged misfits – brooding Brody, bespectacled Hooper and barely socialised Quint – set out on a fishing expedition. Before long they've got drunk, told lies and almost come to blows. In fact, it's not too long before they manage to sink their boat, catch and then lose the biggest fish of their lives. By the time they head for home, these warring old men have come to understand the meaning of friendship…

All stories are open to multiple interpretations, and this exercise shows how far you can take it. Creativity is just playing with words, after all. In a way, we're re-cutting the story, just as a film editor would do, or the marketing person who produces the movie trailer: picking out certain elements and foregrounding them. In the words of veteran Hollywood editor Dede Allen, 'Editing is not taking out, it's putting together. It's taking a story, which has been photographed from many different angles and, very often, in many different takes and making it play in the best possible way that it can.'

In *On Writing*, Stephen King prefers to talk about story rather than plot. In his words, 'Stories are found things, like fossils in the ground.' Once he has unearthed this nugget – a situation, a character such as *Misery*'s Annie Wilkes, who came to him in a dream – the story follows from there. He mistrusts what he calls 'Developing the Plot', something which he sees as akin to the 1920s potboiler novelist Edgar Wallace's notorious 'Plot Wheel': an actual device that spun round to reveal handy writing prompts such as 'a fortuitous arrival' or 'Heroine declares her love'.

King prefers to work from intuition, which indicates that story is perhaps something beyond our control altogether. This is what John Yorke's storytelling bible, *Into the Woods*, gets to the heart of. In Yorke's view, rather than distinct plots, 'Storytelling has a shape. It dominates the way all stories are told and can be traced back not just to the Renaissance, but to the very beginning of the recorded word.' This unifying structure governs everything from seemingly 'plotless' literary fiction to avant-garde arthouse movies to airport blockbusters. Each, in their own way, starts with 'Once upon a time': *something* happening to someone. This something is known as the inciting incident. In every story there is a set-up, an incident leading to a confrontation, a crisis and a resolution. This structure has been around since the ancient Greeks, but Yorke turns it into something deeper: a journey that echoes the primal fairy-tale journey into the woods, and leads to change.

As he says, all stories have the premise: 'what if…?' This idea is illustrated perfectly by the clever ads I saw recently for Apple TV's new line-up of original dramas. They are mini-blurbs in action. Each short advert features a clip from the show, overlaid with a sentence being typed out on screen. And every time, a little cursor goes back and changes something in the description. So 'A nanny is hired to watch a baby for a young couple' becomes 'A nanny is hired to watch a baby *doll* for a young couple', complete with footage of said creepy toy doll having its nappy changed. 'A lawyer defends a young man accused of murder' becomes 'A lawyer defends a young man, *his son*, accused of murder'. This is it: the 'what if?', the *something*.

Starting a piece of copy with the word 'when' is an obvious way of foregrounding the inciting incident, but, as I've argued in 'King of First Lines', it's a tired formulation that's best avoided. There are better ways of doing it, such as this blurb for *Hotel du Lac*:

> Into the rarefied atmosphere of the Hotel du Lac timidly walks Edith Hope, romantic novelist and holder of modest dreams. Edith has been exiled from home after embarrassing herself and her friends. She has refused to sacrifice her ideals and remains stubbornly single. But among the pampered women and minor nobility Edith finds Mr Neville, and her chance to escape from a life of humiliating loneliness is renewed…

Even Anita Brookner's greatest fans would not describe her novels as action-packed, yet here we are presented with a moving story of intriguing incident (and who could forget those veal-coloured walls?).

Look at effective copy on novels without structured plots, and the pattern is the same. The blurb on W. G. Sebald's ruminative exploration of memory, *Austerlitz*, reshapes and restructures the impressionistic events of the novel into something linear:

In 1939, five-year-old Jacques Austerlitz is sent to England on a Kindertransport and placed with foster parents. This childless couple promptly erase from the boy all knowledge of his identity … Later in life, after a career as an architectural historian, Austerlitz – having avoided all clues that might point to his origin – finds the past returning to haunt him and he is forced to explore what happened fifty years before.

Anything can be turned into a story. As Dolly Alderton says of Nora Ephron, 'She knew how to shape any narrative with suspense, tension, relief, surprise and finale.' And, likewise, however impressionistic, experimental or rule-breaking a novel may be, identifying its underlying shape – an incident, a resolution (or not) – connects with us. Something changes; someone is changed. For John Yorke, this is at the heart of who we are:

> The shape of all stories: the enduring pattern of how someone is found by being lost. All tales, then, are at some level a journey into the woods to find the missing part of us, to retrieve it and make ourselves whole. Storytelling is as simple – and complex – as that.

Into the woods we go – encountering monsters and, even worse, ourselves – over, and over, again.

Don't Mention Jesus
The Briefing Process

MIRANDA: I need ten or fifteen skirts from Calvin Klein...
ANDY: What kind of skirts?
MIRANDA: Please bore someone else with your... questions.

'Make it POP!' 'Jazz it up!' 'Can the ice look a bit warmer?' 'Is Christmas really this red?' 'The colours are great. Just change them.' 'Here's what I came up with. Can you make it look like this?' And, the ever helpful 'I'll know it when I see it, but this isn't it.' These are just some of the examples of vague, annoying or just plain bad creative briefs that a group of Irish artists and illustrators decided to turn into posters to make themselves feel better.

Anyone who creates things for a living will have to follow a brief at some point. And, as this indicates, copywriters have it quite easy compared to designers. A cover design is sometimes seen as a silver bullet that will make everything better for a problematic book. One publishing genius, who shall remain nameless, got so frustrated after a particularly tricky cover briefing meeting that they wrote some minutes in the form of haiku:

Playful A format
Eccentric, earthy, friendly
Art to 'do something'

Followed by

> 'Something's not working'
> 'Distressed photo still too camp?'
> Much silent nodding

As well as clearly being a missed opportunity for a book, these haiku give a good idea of how confounding the briefing process can be for designers. Sometimes the same goes for copy, which becomes a receptacle for all sorts of existential word worries. A title, strapline or blurb can often be seen as a sticking plaster over a book that no one is quite sure how to pitch clearly – or they want to pitch it as something it isn't. My particular favourites are: 'Like this, but obviously not this.' 'You know, different but pretty much the same.' 'Can we replace this line with something better?' (Does the 'we' mean you're going to help then?) 'Is there a better quote for this?' (Yes, there was an *amazing* one, but I hid it away in a drawer.)

Copywriters are adept at being adaptable. It's our *sine qua non*. Not being an expert in a subject, and approaching it from a layperson's perspective, can be an asset. We are used to picking out particular aspects of a text and trying on different voices; that's all part of the game. We will often write copy for books that don't yet exist, or are only partially written, but this can aid the process as you're forced to think laterally, and you don't get mired in detail. The point is that writing blurbs is *fun*.

But still, when I asked some of my fellow copywriters about challenging briefs (I shall take their names to the grave) I had the feeling I'd opened a floodgate: 'Sometimes, I am asked to write a blurb for a book, and the client sends me – as an "example" – a blurb for ANOTHER book that is NOTHING LIKE the book I'm working on, i.e. tonally entirely different, and it just doesn't work. But the client wants what the client wants…' 'I've worked on books where we've had no text, and I've had to try and find a hook to grab a reader from absolutely nothing. I've also had books where what's clearly the USP is something the editor/author doesn't want mentioned – like working on erotic fiction and having to pretend it wasn't being bought for the sex, but because it was a Classic Love Story For All Time. Sure, sure…' 'Trying to write an engaging blurb for super long, famous books in a very short paragraph, due to design constraints. Specifically, the Bible!'

For big-name commercial fiction, especially, the blurb is the focal point for all sorts of anxieties about the book's contents. Of an upcoming novel by a famous writer: 'There's a manuscript but I'm not allowed to read it, and apparently it isn't very funny but I have to make it sound like it is. And I have to think of a title.' Or there was the book that featured a lot of horse-riding – but 'don't mention horses anywhere!'

It's like the screenwriter Allan Burns, who was told, 'This script's got to be twenty-five per cent funnier.' A few weeks into rewrites, he told the studio, 'Well, I'm only eighteen per cent funnier so far, which means I've got to be thirty-one per cent funnier the rest of the way.' They didn't get the joke.

Contradictory messages around copy can sometimes feel as going-down-the-rabbit-hole as this mock advertisement for a 'BBC Director of Better' in the TV series *W1A*:

The successful candidate will be a passionate listener, will have experience of the future rather than the past, and will be capable of defining the big questions by establishing the answers first and working backwards from there, whilst remaining calm and where necessary in Salford.

In other words, 'I'd like the moon on a stick, please. But don't mention moons. Or sticks.'

I was once, many years ago, asked to write copy for a book narrated by a middle-aged man without mentioning the middle-aged man ('concentrate on the daughter instead as it's more appealing to the market'). I also had to describe a book featuring Jesus as a character – Jim Crace's superb novel *Quarantine* – without mentioning the 'J' word as it might be considered off-putting. I tried to turn this into an advantage, and built a sense of intrigue around the mysterious person who joins a group of travellers in the Judean desert ('There is also a faint figure in the distance, fasting for forty days, a Galilean who they say has the power to work miracles…') although I think it's fairly obvious what's going on. I note that the current Picador edition now *does* mention Jesus on the back cover, which seems much more straightforward to me.

The worst briefing horror story I've heard is from a publishing copywriter who not only once had a piece of copy torn up in front of them by an irate editor, but also had to write one blurb for a popular novel again, and again, and again: 'I wrote 21 different versions before the publisher was satisfied. She even rang me up when I was on paternity leave to demand I left the nursery I was in with my daughter and provide her with a new version (this was around version 14). Publishers can often lose perspective.'

I have a feeling I've got off pretty lightly.

Lizards, All of Us

The Science Part

What's going in in our brains when we read a blurb? Do certain words press certain psychological buttons? In other words: is there a science of persuasion? I've always wondered. The idea has been around since the *Mad Men* days of the 1950s, when rumours of 'subliminal advertising' in cinemas, flashing up slogans like 'Drink Coca-Cola', caused a moral panic – even though the stories proved to be a hoax.

This notion of marketers manipulating our unconscious reached its zenith in the 1970s, with the publication of *Subliminal Seduction* by Wilson Bryan Key, which promised to reveal 'the secret ways ad men arouse your desires to sell their products'. 'Are you being sexually aroused by this picture?' the strapline on the front cover asks us, above a photograph of a martini on ice (we could only be in the decade of dubious taste, couldn't we). The back cover blurb is slightly icky too, talking of 'media rape', and promising to reveal things like: 'The place in a TV commercial where you can view an obscene act.' It's paranoid, to say the least.

I'm generally resistant to this kind of thinking. It seems to me typical of a conspiracy theory-prone mind-set that's convinced someone, somewhere, is 'up to something'. In a 1977 article in the *Washington Post*, the author of *Subliminal Seduction*

LIZARDS, ALL OF US

even becomes certain that his publisher's art department had secretly hidden the image of a flasher in one of the ice cubes on his front cover. To which most designers would reply, 'If only I had the time.'

Paranoia aside, though, is there some evidence that certain techniques of persuasion are effective? Could my copywriter's hunches about which words work (and which don't) be confirmed by science? I tried to find out, and this is what I discovered.

WHAT LIES BENEATH

It pains me to say that the most successful political slogan of recent years has been 'Take Back Control'. The entire campaign run by those who wanted Britain to leave the EU was anti-rational, and that's why it worked. It ignored statistics and economic benefits and played straight to its audience's emotions: fear and nostalgia. It's a similar story with 'Make America Great Again'. Less of a dog-whistle, more of a klaxon.*

The more I read about the mind, the more it became clear that most experts agree we're not as clever as we think we are. Our brains are illogical, erratic, biased, lazy, narcissistic, contradictory and error-prone. Donald Trump, in other words. We misunderstand statistics. We misread situations. We are irrational decision-makers – even when making huge choices like voting in elections or buying a house. As the behavioural economist Richard Thaler puts it, 'All of us, whether we know

....

* These formulae also employ simple language and few syllables. The Flesch–Kinkaid 'readability test' was used in 2015 to calculate that the average Trump speech was aimed at the reading level of a nine-year-old.

it or not, take our emotions, eccentricities and idiosyncrasies to the cash register.'

If we're not paragons of reason, then something else inside the Russian doll set that is our brain is running things; something beyond our control. Storytellers might call it the unconscious. As Susan Cooper says of writing fantasy, 'We don't altogether know what we're doing. It's the hauntings in the unconscious mind of the fantasy writer, not understood or even recognized, that lead him or her to choose fantasy as a medium. It's really not a conscious choice. The unconscious is in charge.'

Psychologists might *not* call it the unconscious these days, but the inference is the same. According to Nobel Prize-winning psychologist Daniel Kahneman, our brains have two 'systems' of thinking. System 1 is fast and instinctive, whereas System 2 is slow and effortful. In Kahneman's words, 'System 1 runs the show. That's the one you want to move.'

Take the famous 'Linda' experiment, for example. Read this description of her:

> Linda is thirty-one years old, single, outspoken, and very bright. She majored in philosophy. As a student, she was deeply concerned with issues of discrimination and social justice, and also participated in antinuclear demonstrations.
>
> Which alternative is more probable?
> Linda is a bank teller.
> Linda is a bank teller and is active in the feminist movement.

Which would you pick? Eighty-five per cent of the brainy students at Stanford ranked 'feminist bank teller' over 'bank teller' whereas the logical answer is that, statistically, she is far more likely *just* to be a bank teller. Something in our brains puts two and two together and comes up with five. The naturalist Stephen Jay Gould described grappling with Linda thus: 'a little homunculus in my head continues to jump up and down, shouting at me – "but she can't just be a bank teller; read the description."'

Some people compare this emotional pull to riding an elephant, some to having an 'inner chimp'. For flamboyant advertising guru Clotaire Rapaille, it's all about the lizard (but not in a David Icke way). In *The Culture Code*, he argues that words, when first learned by a child, make a primal, emotional imprint on us, influencing every decision we make throughout our lives. As he says, 'The reptilian brain always wins. If you want to sell successfully you have to appeal to it.'

Like the bizarre love child of sixties gurus Andy Warhol and Timothy Leary, Rapaille asks his clients to lie down in darkened rooms in order to access their inner child, before responding to a series of questions. He turns their answers into codes: the deep, symbolic meaning of a word that varies from culture to culture.

He used this method to determine that the American code word for a jeep was HORSE. It meant freedom, nature, the plains. The vehicle needed to have an open top and round lights instead of square ones, like eyes. Chrysler followed this advice and turned their fortunes around. Rapaille had the same success in Europe by using collective wartime memories to determine that the code word for jeep in France was LIBERATOR.

Yes, it's hugely stereotypical, and possibly horse/jeep shit, but it reminds me that words very rarely mean just one thing – or indeed what we think they mean. Language slips out of our control, and is bound up with emotion. I will never forget my English teacher Miss Walker telling us that today the word 'boat' conjures up travel or holidays, but a thousand years ago in the era of Viking raids it would have meant something else entirely: danger, fear, flight, and probably death.

As Virginia Woolf put it, 'Words are the wildest, freest, the most irresponsible, the most unteachable of all things … Words do not live in dictionaries, they live in the mind.'

The significance of words affects us at the deepest level.

OUR BRAINS' FAVOURITE WORDS

Not only are words freighted with connotations, they influence our minds in different ways.

Why did US Republicans campaigning against inheritance tax in the US in the 1990s rename it 'the Death Tax' and win? Why do so many thriller blurbs use the language of fear: 'They want you, and they want you dead.' The answer is that we respond to negative words more powerfully. Neuroscientists have run thousands of experiments, seeing which parts of our brains 'light up', for example, when an individual is emotionally aroused. According to Kahneman, 'Emotionally loaded words quickly attract attention, and bad words (war, crime) attract attention faster than do happy words (peace, love).'

This preference for bad over good is just one of countless biases that our minds are prone to. We make so many tiny decisions every day (apparently processing around eleven million pieces of information at any time), that we need to take mental shortcuts. They're called 'heuristics', which I think is just a fancy way of saying 'things writers have always suspected'.

The reason a good piece of copy should always start with a bang, or why a journalist will pack as much as they can into the lead? It's the bias known as the Primacy Effect: what we hear or read first dominates what we remember. Our brains start modelling words as soon as we read them, even before the end of a sentence – so we should start with the things we really want our audience to take away.

We also respond primarily to vivid, specific, concrete detail that appeals to our senses – the neural networks associated with the sensations of touch, taste, smell and sound are activated when we see the right words. It's at the heart of horror or suspense writing. A good example is the copy on Susan Hill's *The Woman in Black*, which starts with the words 'Her ravaged face was a mask', and goes on to describe 'bleached salt marshes' and 'shuttered rooms'. It's 'image-making', as a psychologist would say.

When we read metaphors, even familiar ones, there is increased activity in our brains – and the fresher and newer the metaphor, the greater the action. In the opening of *Cook, Eat, Repeat*, Nigella Lawson notes how 'Simile and metaphor can often evoke the flavours of a dish … so much more directly,' recalling a memorable description she once read of the first taste of champagne as like 'an apple peeled with a steel knife'. Blurbs can use metaphors to be memorable too, such as the one on my ancient copy of *The London Nobody Knows*, which charmingly claims that it is 'as enticing as Portobello Road on a Saturday afternoon', or the copy on Nancy Mitford's *The Blessing*, which describes it as 'tailored as brilliantly as a New Look Dior suit'.

Humorous books do it too. How many car-related metaphors has the poor copywriter who created the blurbs for Jeremy Clarkson's books come up with? 'Full throttle', 'under the bonnet', 'he's put his foot down', 'seatbelts on'… 'this is writing with its foot to the floor, the brake lines cut and the speed limit smashed to smithereens. Sit back and enjoy the ride.'

These linguistic tricks, as corny as they may be, stick in our heads and please our minds at a basic level. Feel your neurons firing with joy!

Finally, there is the simplification bias. When we retell a story, or write a blurb, we instinctively streamline it and pick out the most memorable details, condensing and distilling like a *parfumier*. It's why any copywriter worth their salt knows the rather well-worn 'KISS' formulation ('keep it simple, stupid'). It is also why simplicity is (or should be) at the heart of all effective communication, especially when the words can be life-saving. When I asked health psychologist Dr Katie Newby about government slogans at the start of the Covid pandemic, her view was that 'Messaging needs to clearly state the behaviour required so STAY HOME was a good one. Their biggest clanger was with STAY ALERT. It means nothing.' It's the concrete versus the nebulous again. Our lizardy minds naturally try to turn the chaos and confusion of life into something clear and graspable. Which brings us to stories, our brains' favourite thing of all.

STORYTELLING MACHINES

> There is no fiction or nonfiction as we commonly understand the distinction; there is only narrative.
>
> E. L. DOCTOROW

What happens if we see the words 'bananas' and 'vomit' next to each other? We immediately start connecting them, working out cause and effect and imagining a sequence of events that ends with a pile of yellow mess. We feel disgust. According to psychologists, this is because our brains are 'associative machines', with one mental picture triggering another, and another: in other words, a narrative.

Of all our biases, humans are biased most towards making sense of the chaos of the world through story. This is known as 'the Narrative Paradigm'. We are storytelling, and story-making, creatures. To quote Will Storr in *The Science of Storytelling*: 'When posed with even the deepest questions about reality, human brains tend towards story.' We're narrative addicts. It explains everything from betting on who 'H' was in *Line of Duty* to creation myths and religion.* And, without even realising it, 'Storytellers engage a number of neural processes that evolved for a variety of reasons and are waiting to be played like instruments in an orchestra.'

One of the things the brain responds to most is *change*, which results in a surge of neural activity. What's going on, what's going to happen, our little grey cells ask? It's why so many books will entice us with a first line that contains something we don't expect ('It was a bright cold day in April, and the clocks were striking thirteen'), and why a good blurb often sets this up: 'A naïve young secretary forsakes Cleveland for San Francisco, tumbling headlong into a brave new world of laundromat Lotharios, cut throat debutantes and Jockey Shorts dance contests,' begins the copy on Armistead Maupin's *Tales of the City*. Mary Ann is entering an unfamiliar world. Or John Boyne's *The Heart's Invisible Furies*: 'Cast out from her West Cork village, sixteen years old and pregnant, Catherine Goggin makes her way to Dublin to start afresh.'

•••

* The marketing guru Sir John Hegarty even went as far as saying that Christianity is the greatest advertising campaign of all, with its recognisable logo and unforgettable story.

We are suckers for novelty, endlessly curious: according to Storr, 'Nine-week-old babies are drawn to unfamiliar images over ones they've seen before.' Humans are desperate to solve the mystery. What else is writing a blurb if it's not exciting these instincts by holding something back, with the promise of discovery if we open the book? Our brains are fascinated by other humans, and specifically by human unpredictability. This is why focusing on a lead character, with all their flaws, works well in a blurb, such as that for Candice Carty-Williams's *Queenie*:

> Queenie Jenkins can't cut a break. Well, apart from the one from her long term boyfriend, Tom. That's definitely just a break though. Definitely not a break up. Then there's her boss who doesn't seem to see her and her Caribbean family who don't seem to listen (if it's not Jesus or water rates, they're not interested). She's trying to fit in two worlds that don't really understand her. It's no wonder she's struggling...

Apparently, our curious, story-making imaginations are so keen to fill in the gaps that we do it all the time. According to *The Mind is Flat*, life is pretty much one big hallucination: 'The brain is ultimately a biological machine that creates, improvises, dreams and imagines ... Our flow of conscious thought, including our explanations of our own and each other's behaviour, are creations in the moment.' No hidden depths or inner self, in other words. We're making it *all* up as we go along, and we're not even aware that this is happening.

As the 'Father of Advertising' David Ogilvy said, 'The problem is that people don't think how they feel, they don't say what they think and they don't do what they say.' So perhaps copywriters have always known we are scatter-brained flibber-tigibbets, responding to things beyond our control.

I wonder if the science of words points to something else quite satisfying too, though, namely that the narrative devices – mystery, metaphor, vividness – used in books, blurbs, advertising and most forms of persuasive communication are not just flourishes; they are essential to how we function. As Martin Amis said, 'Style is not something grappled onto regular prose; it is intrinsic to perception.'

A Musical Interlude

At first sight musical theatre might not have a place in this book – although I think it should have a place everywhere. Just think of the positive life lessons the great musicals teach us: climb every mountain, the sun'll come out tomorrow, put on your Sunday clothes when you feel down and out, you'll never walk alone, pick a pocket or two…*

Fiddler on the Roof, however, is special. Based on *Tevye and His Daughters* by Sholem Aleichem, this celebrated musical teaches us – among many things – that happiness is impermanent and you should never let your parents fix you up with the butcher. It also has a lot to tell us about pitch (the marketing rather than musical kind) and the creative process. The story of its greatest song's genesis has become something of a Broadway legend. It goes like this.

Imagine we are in a rehearsal studio; you know, the kind with mirrors and a piano and people wearing black. The director/choreographer Jerome Robbins and the lyricist Sheldon Harnick have been struggling over the musical's opening number. Night after night, Jerry drives everyone crazy by saying, 'But what's this musical about?', and Sheldon replies, 'Well, it's about a milkman called Tevye, he's got five daughters, there's a

....

* They can also teach us about writing, such as Stephen Sondheim's advice on lyrics: 'Less is more, content dictates form and God is in the details.'

294

pogrom…' but each time Jerry says, 'No, that's not it. What's it *about*?' The same question, and the same answers, over and over again. This goes on for days, until, exasperated, Sheldon shouts, 'For God's sake, Jerry, it's about TRADITION.' At last. 'YES, that's it! That's the answer! Write about that!' orders Jerry. The minute he hears the word, he knows. Suddenly the story can be understood by people around the world, from London to Tokyo. The number is written, and a smash hit is born.

It's the perfect illustration of how to cut through the guff and get to the beating heart of something, whether it's a musical or a book. There's a similar anecdote in Nora Ephron's *I Feel Bad About My Neck*, where she recalls learning the craft of journalism. The teacher gave the students this list of facts, and asked them to turn it into the lead of a story: 'Kenneth L. Peters, the principal of Beverly Hills High School, announced today that the faculty of the high school will travel to Sacramento on Thursday for a colloquium in new teaching methods.' Each student proudly proffered their finely crafted sentences, and each one was thrown into the bin by the teacher, who then said, 'The lead to the story is, "There will be no school Thursday."'

Sometimes you need to forget incidental detail, and home in on what really matters. I find myself thinking about this a lot, and anyone who works with books probably does. I've lost count of the number of times I've sat in a meeting and wanted to grab an editor by the collar and shout, 'Yes, you've said it's beautifully written and the author is an expert in their field, but what is the *point* of this book?' Of course I don't, I just sit and nod sagely and say, 'Mmm, absolutely,' in the manner of a character in the BBC spoof *W1A*.*

---

* I try to follow screenwriter William Goldman's advice on meetings: 'There

For me, the lesson of *Fiddler* for anyone writing, pitching or trying to communicate is this: always ask yourself, what's really going on here? Why should anyone care? And how do we make them care? As Grayson Perry recently said, when people describe something as 'popular' or 'commercial' what they really mean is, it's relevant.

is one crucial rule that must be followed in all creative meetings: Never speak first. At least at the start, your job is to shut up … If *you* begin, they can counterpunch. Try never to give them the chance.'

Oceans Apart

Supersized American Copy

> We have really everything in common with America
> nowadays, except, of course, language.
>
> OSCAR WILDE

Like many bibliophiles, I enjoy nothing more than the feel,
and even the smell, of a foreign book. I like American ones
especially, with their soft covers, floppy pages that don't need
jamming open, and rough edges that don't give me paper cuts.
But the *copy*. It is always so unbelievably long. Is there some
kind of cultural blurb code? It is a question that has irked me
for some time.

I'm not really a subscriber to the idea that we're two countries divided by a common language, except for when fright-
ful terms such as 'furlough' elbow their way into the lexicon.
I suspect the whole US/UK cultural misunderstanding thing
is mostly baloney – or balderdash, depending on where you're
coming from. We just find each other exotic, that's all.

Richard Osman's cosy crime bestseller *The Thursday
Murder Club* couldn't be more English if it tried – in the
Acknowledgements he apologises to his US editors for 'making
you have to google Ryman's, Holland & Barrett, and Sainsbury's
Taste the Difference' – and yet it has gone down a storm in the
States. I like to imagine it's because American readers thrilled
over all this mysterious terminology, just as self-confessed

Anglophile Benjamin Dreyer describes relishing the words 'pong', 'ta' and 'tuppence' in his childhood reading, and I did when I first read the Sweet Valley High series and encountered 'bangs' (fringes), 'lavaliers' (pendants), beauty pageants and boys called Todd.

It's like people who say that Americans have no sense of irony. Guys – there are over 300 million of them. As Eddie Izzard put it, 'It's Middle America that has no sense of irony, and that's not even a geographical location, that's just a sensibility, and middle Britain has no sense of irony, and middle Scandinavia has no sense of irony and middle Prague has no sense of irony.'

Readers are readers, wherever they come from. Yet it's undeniable that, when we look at the same books in the US and the UK, there are marked differences in the ways they are presented to their audiences.

Most books are published with different cover designs for different international markets. Lisa Taddeo's intense study of female desire, *Three Women*, was a hit on both sides of the Atlantic, but the covers are worlds apart. The UK design is, as Taddeo puts it, 'absolutely gorgeous', using a contemporary typeface over a painting by the Dutch master De Heem, *A Garland of Fruit*. It manages to convey sensuality and fecundity without being overtly sexual – the designer at Bloomsbury, Greg Heinimann, was 'wary of my male gaze' – but it also screams this is a classy yet juicy read. It could be a work of fiction or non-fiction, and that's deliberate. The US cover, by comparison, is a more sober treatment: a simple, striking typographical design presenting the book as a serious work of analysis.

Front cover copy also often differs between markets. As I have noted in the chapter 'It's never safe to go back into the water', subtitles are usually longer on US books. For example, the original subtitle for *Eat Pray Love*, 'One Woman's Search for Everything Across Italy, India and Indonesia', was chopped down to 'One Woman's Search for Everything' for the UK edition. Sometimes a book's title will be altered too: P. G. Wodehouse's and Agatha Christie's novels are notorious for confounding readers with their diverging English-language titles. More recent tweaks include changing Tana French's thriller *The Wych Elm* to *The Witch Elm* for the US – a tiny alteration, but one that loses some of the novel's gothic allure – and Stuart Turton's *The Seven Deaths of Evelyn Hardcastle* to *The 7½ Deaths of Evelyn Hardcastle*. Apparently the extra fraction was to avoid a clash with another title featuring the word 'Seven' in the States, which is a shame as I rather loved the idea of a brash New York publisher bawling 'Make that number BIGGER!' – no stereotypes to be seen here, oh no.*

And now to the blurbs. The word 'blurb' brings us to our first potential diplomatic incident, as it *does* mean different things either side of the Atlantic: in the UK it is any kind of descriptive copy, whereas in the States it is generally an endorsement or review. (Which in effect makes this whole book a potential minefield of verbal misunderstandings.)

When we start to look at the copy on the back covers of books both here and in the US, the differences become stark.

....

* The UK blurb for this book contains one of my favourite examples of unintentional bathos. It opens by thrillingly describing an ingenious time-loop murder in a country house, but ends with the line 'And someone is desperate to stop him ever escaping Blackheath…' It made me giggle because I guess Blackheath is meant to be the name of the country house, but it just sounds like there are problems with Southeastern trains.

I asked an American editor for her view, and she was adamant that their copy is 'definitely longer, and also more hyperbolic. There are far more adjectives.' In fact, just more of everything. In the States, copy is supersized.

One of the biggest transatlantic publishing events of recent years was the publication of Harper Lee's *Go Set a Watchman*. The UK cover copy is minimal: a brief quotation from the text, one line telling us: 'From Harper Lee comes a landmark new novel set two decades after her beloved Pulitzer Prize-winning masterpiece, *To Kill a Mockingbird*', and six short review quotes. Here, as on so many well-designed covers, blank space is just as important as text. By comparison, the copy on the US paper-back (whose gently retro front cover design I actually prefer) is looooong, over 300 words including reviews and an author biography, with lengthy sentences that feel rather grand: 'perfectly captures a painful yet necessary transition out of the illusions of the past – a journey that can only be guided by one's own conscience'. It is, to use a great American coinage, highfalutin.

Even light-hearted books get the wordy treatment in the US. Nora Ephron's *I Feel Bad About My Neck* is one of the funniest books in existence, and the UK copy goes straight in for a show, don't tell, giving us the warm humour of Ephron's voice with light-hearted bullet points taken from her essay 'What I Wish I'd Known':

- Never marry a man you wouldn't want to be divorced from.
- If the shoe doesn't fit in the shoe store, it's never going to fit.
- When your children are teenagers, it's important to have a dog so that someone in the house is happy to see you.
- Anything you think is wrong with your body at the age of thirty-five you will be nostalgic for by the age of forty-five.

The US copy, however, goes for a far loftier approach. Yes, it gives us some funny details, but it is also at pains to list Ephron's accomplishments, and to bombard us with adjectival clusters:

> From Nora Ephron, the writer and filmmaker whose films *Sleepless in Seattle* and *When Harry Met Sally* defined romance for a generation, and whose latest, *Julie & Julia*, celebrated the pleasures of cooking and the thrill of self-reinvention: a disarming, intimate, and hilarious book on being a woman today ...
>
> Utterly courageous, uproariously funny, and unexpectedly moving in its truth telling ...

And on it goes, ad infinitum. Again and again, US copy is longer, fancier and more earnest in tone than its UK counterpart. The aim seems to be comprehensiveness, covering all bases rather than enticing the reader in through punchy sentences, intrigue or tension. The busy, cluttered back jackets exist as a vehicle for words, rather than a vehicle for design; to get across as much information as possible.

Everyone seems to have their pet theory for what one US editor called 'the odd verbosity of American book blurbs and quotations'. Several people I asked cited the pluralistic, diverse nature of their society, which means that the reams of review quotes we find on and inside books aim 'to make sure the reader knows that it's not just been reviewed in the *New York Times* or the *Post*, say, but also by the *Dallas Morning News*'. It's democratic, with copy aiming to speak to everyone: 'high and low brow, but also different audience segments, based on gender, race, sexuality. Americans are super tuned in to identity politics and it's very, very present in publishing.'

Another mentioned the predominance of book clubs, which have been around in the States for centuries, starting as women's 'reading circles', and now the number one driver of sales, with powerhouses like Oprah Winfrey heralding what Toni Morrison called 'a reading revolution'. Does all that lengthy paratextual material – quotes, copy, biography, as well as the reading group questions inside – aid the discussion?

And, of course, we can't dismiss what a New York-based journalist described to me as 'the hyperbolic nature of American culture and speech'. In *The Adventure of English* Melvyn Bragg suggests this is rooted in history, and geography: as US settlers pushed further westwards, so American English gained more words and expanded on a grand scale. 'Confidence bred ornate, baroque words', such as shebang, skedaddle, hunky-dory, splendiferous, lickety-split… 'A style of speech as big as the country. It was called Tall Talk.' In other words, hyperbole.

Copy everywhere in the US is wordier – they have made long-form journalism their own, after all. Their broadsheet headlines and articles can appear ponderous compared to ours – as one *Financial Times* reporter described it, 'self-reverential, long-winded, stuffy' – whereas UK journalism cuts to the chase. The flipside of these different print cultures, however, is that 'You can be sure that the quotes in an American newspaper story are genuine and the facts have been checked. Pick up many a British newspaper and you'd be foolish to count on either.'

This, to me, is one of the key differences in our literary culture. In some ways, I think Americans valorise their language more than we do. I mean it. The written word is at the heart of its national identity and founding myths: from the *Mayflower* colonisers who sought freedom to read their English-language Bible, to Noah Webster's celebrated dictionary of uniquely

Americanised spellings. According to Bragg, 'Correct spelling came to be seen as a standard of education and civilization throughout America, and it still is today. The Spelling Bee became part of the life of every town and village.'* In the land of go-getters, using the language properly is a path to success.

In comparison, we English treat our mother tongue with far less reverence, perhaps something to do with a stubborn anti-intellectual streak that runs from the conservative pragmatism of Edmund Burke to 'people have had enough of experts' today. As Leonard Woolf said in 1959, 'no people has ever despised and distrusted the intellect and intellectuals more than the British'.† (I would replace British with English here, however.)

While I'm indulging in some cultural stereotyping, it's interesting to look at the other extreme: French book covers and blurbs, or lack thereof. If American book covers are wordy bear hugs, there's more than a hint of a Gallic shrug about their continental cousins. One publishing sales manager I spoke to, who worked in both London and Paris for many years, described French book packaging as 'wilfully anti-commercial, an anti-design that hasn't evolved'. In her view, it reflects the seriousness of their literary culture. Bookselling is revered as a profession, Amazon is used infrequently and independent

* A further incarnation of the American Dream is that the Spelling Bee, which came out of white foundational myths, is now increasingly being won by South-Asian Americans – seven out of the eight winners of the 2019 national championship, to be precise.

† There is a good Brussels joke about this. How do you tell the difference between a British official and a French one? The Briton says: 'This idea works fine in theory but will it work in practice?' The Frenchman says: 'This idea works fine in practice but will it work in theory?'

bookshops receive state subsidy. In 2019 Britain had around 800 independent bookshops; in France it was 2,500.

French book design is understated, to say the least, with publishers such as Gallimard and Folio favouring plain white covers with as few words of sparse type as possible. Particularly severe are Les Éditions de Minuit, whose only decoration is a blue border and the symbol of a star and the letter 'M' on the back – *no* copy. A book may have won a major prize or garnered universal acclaim, but you would never know it from these jackets.

A case in point is Leïla Slimani's *Lullaby*, the dark tale of a murderous nanny. It is the genuine definition of an international bestseller: a smash in the US, the UK and in France, where it won the nation's most prestigious literary prize, the Prix Goncourt, and its author became a celebrity, courted by the media and politicians alike.

The classy design on the British edition, published by Faber, features the torso of a woman wearing what looks like a blue and white nursemaid's outfit. The copy tells us it is an international bestseller, the review quote tells us it is a thriller, and it even uses the first two sentences of the book as a macabre tagline: 'The baby is dead. It took only a few seconds.' On the back, there's the prize win in large letters, a paragraph of so-so copy and a generous slathering of six review quotes. It's all very selling.

The US equivalent uses the same image, but it has a different title. Rather than sticking with the English translation of the French title, *Chanson Douce*, they've gone for *The Perfect Nanny*. According to the American editor, 'I didn't want to call it *Lullaby*, because that sounds sleepily forgettable, and my goal is to reach a big commercial readership. We're getting this book into places like Walmart.' The front cover features a *New York*

Times bestseller sticker, and the back cover is typically busy, with a blurb that's similar to the UK one, but with more breathless hype:

> Building tension with every page, *The Perfect Nanny* is a compulsive, riveting, bravely observed exploration of power, class, race, domesticity, motherhood, and madness.

And now to the French edition, published by Folio. The current cover is, I'm afraid to say, pretty ugly – not even *jolie laide* – featuring nothing but the title, the author and a still from the recent film. On the back there is a quotation from the text, a short blurb and, in the tiniest lettering imaginable at the very bottom, 'Prix Goncourt 2016'. No review quotes. That's all we're getting. It is the complete opposite of the fulsome praise we see on so many US editions. Is it a missed opportunity, or a deliberate holding back? Does it respect the reader more, or less?

These extremes in packaging are telling. One wants to give us everything – too much perhaps; the other can barely bring itself to sell the book. Perhaps these are easy clichés in one sense, but they speak to me as a copywriter.* Not only do the blurbs we read on books carry with them their own history, and encapsulate our desires as readers – or the readers we want to be. They are also inescapably bound up with the literary cultures that created them.

• •

* I was delighted to learn from *The Bookseller's Tale* that the word 'cliché' comes, like so many English literary terms, from the early printing process: 'the sound a group of often-combined words makes as its metal letters drop into place on the compositor's tray'.

The Pun Wot Won It

I love a pun, as you may have guessed from the title of this book. Just hear me out! I realise they are the Marmite of the language world, described variously as the lowest form of humour* and the highest form of literature,† but at their best they tell us much about language, and ourselves. Like any form of wordplay or unnecessary flourish, they should be used sparingly – and they just need to be *good*. Kingsley Amis noted that 'Puns are good, bad, and indifferent, and only those who lack the wit to make them are unaware of the fact.'

I wonder if he had Dorothy Parker's gems 'It serves me right for putting all my eggs in one bastard' or 'I'd rather have a bottle in front of me than a frontal lobotomy' in mind when he meant a good pun? Or maybe Quentin Crisp's 'I became one of the stately homos of England'? These double meanings have a sting in the tail, born of experience. The best puns are disconcerting and come from dark places, such as the one I discovered on the blurb for *Look Who's Back*, the satirical German novel about a resurrected Hitler: 'HE'S BACK. AND HE'S FÜHRIOUS.'

....

* By Samuel Johnson and other curmudgeons.
† Alfred Hitchcock, surprisingly.

THE PUN WOT WON IT

Puns have been knocking around since the ancient world,* employed by everyone from Cicero and Shakespeare to the essayist Charles Lamb, who frequently engaged in pun-offs with his friends and described *double entendres* as 'a pistol let off at the ear; not a feather to tickle the intellect'. Lamb's words show why many have mixed feelings about puns. They are disruptive and attention-seeking, like a burp at a dinner party or a raspberry blown in polite discourse. It's why tabloids love them – please refer to the classic *Sun* headline celebrating Caledonian Thistle's shock victory over Celtic in the Scottish Cup: 'Super Caley Go Ballistic, Celtic Are Atrocious'. (My personal favourite, however, is 'You've Lost That Living Feeling' upon the death of one of the Righteous Brothers.) Even the *Telegraph* got in on the act in 2020, ridiculing a farcical temporary voting system outside the House of Commons with 'I wanna queue like Commons people queue', and the classy *New York Times* with its divine 'When an Eel Climbs a Ramp to Eat Squid from a Clamp, That's a Moray'.†

There's something competitive about punning: it's a showy form of wordplay. There is, I discovered, a monthly punning tournament in Brooklyn called Punderdome, and countless pun rundowns (pundowns?) in the media, often involving restaurants with truly excellent names such as Abra Kebabra and School of Wok. I think that's the point: they're the dad joke we know we're

* They are even, according to the philologist Dr Irving Finkel, responsible for the origins of writing in the Egyptians and Sumerians. The rebus principle, which enabled pictorial language to evolve a double meaning, is in effect a visual pun.

† The adult comic *Viz* loved homophones so much it dedicated an entire recurring strip to them, Finbarr Saunders and his Double Entendres.

307

going to groan at, but we can't help the corners of our mouths twitching as we 'get' the double meaning. Apparently, in that split second between reading and eye-rolling, both the visual and verbal sides of our brains are working together in harmony to help us on the way.

But puns can be more than a cheap thrill. Sigmund Freud was fascinated by the psychology of jokes, and saw puns as a kind of psychic release valve enabling us to cope with the taboo, or to puncture those who are more powerful or a threat to us – such as Clive James's flawless critique of the super-rich residents of Monaco as 'the haves and the have yachts'.

The reason some people don't like puns, according to John Pollack, who loves them so much he wrote a whole book on them called *The Pun Also Rises*, is that 'Puns are threatening because puns reveal the arbitrariness of meaning, and the layers of nuance that can be packed onto a single word … So people who dislike puns tend to be people who seek a level of control that doesn't exist. If you have an approach to the world that is rules-based, driven by hierarchy and threatened by irreverence, then you're not going to like puns.' This confirms everything I've long suspected about pun-phobes.

At their best, puns are a celebration of language's slipperiness, its lack of control, its multiple meanings and its pleasures. Alexander Pope said that puns speak 'twice as much by being split'.

Puns can be truly great when they come from unexpected sources. I was mad with joy when I read that Hilary Mantel's essay collection was to be titled *Mantel Pieces*, which also brought to mind Fay Weldon's inspired *Auto Da Fay* and Carrie Fisher's *Wishful Drinking*. Can any of them compete with Pam St Clement (aka Pat Butcher's) *The End of an Earring*, however?

At my workplace, we seem to allow ourselves roughly one pun title every five years. My recent favourites were *Please Can We Have Our Balls Back?*, a book about why the British are rubbish at sport, and *Pie Fidelity*, a book about why everyone thinks the British are rubbish at food. Perhaps calling a book about knitting *Purls of Wisdom* wasn't my finest hour, though.

To quote the doyenne of the double meaning Dorothy Parker again: 'There's a hell of a distance between wise-cracking and wit. Wit has truth in it; wise-cracking is simply calisthenics with words.' A bad pun expends energy for the sake of it; a good one does it to make us look to the heavens and titter, or to think twice.

$\mathcal{S}$ell Sell Sell

Which words sell? This question may sound venal, even vulgar to some, but money makes the world go round and all that. Writers, unless they're on a private income and doing it for fun, are trying to sell their books, and publishers – even if they're on a private income, which some still seem to be – are trying to help them sell their books. So knowing which words are more profitable than others, whether in books or on them, seems a prudent investment.

Is there a formula for a bestseller? Much advice for writers suggests there is. The internet is brimming with tools claiming to generate the perfect book title, the perfect plot and the perfect blurb. There are lists of 'power words' guaranteed to sell, some of which I find a little strange. For example, one of them lists 'piranha' as a 'fear' power word. What have these people been smoking?

A more reliable and scientific guide is, I discovered, a nifty computer algorithm that was invented to analyse hundreds of bestsellers and see what they have in common. It collected information on syntax, sentence length, punctuation, plots, nouns, verbs and adjectives, to uncover the patterns inherent to books that succeed – whether genre fiction or more literary works. Despite being pathologically scared of technology, I found the results instructive.

According to *The Bestseller Code*, the word 'do' appears twice as often in a hit book than in a flop (whereas 'very' is used infrequently). Characters in bestsellers are far more likely to 'need,' 'want,' 'miss' and 'love'. They also grab, ask, look, hold, like, reach, push, pull, start, work and arrive. All active, positive, physical verbs. In comparison, characters in commercial flops are passive: they accept, suppose, wish and yawn.

First lines, apparently, are a key indicator of success, such as those of two books from 1995. This is the first line of John Grisham's *The Rainmaker*:

> My decision to become a lawyer was irrevocably sealed when
> I realised my father hated the legal profession.

And this is the opening of Martin Amis's *The Information*:

> Cities at night, I feel, contain men who cry in their sleep and
> then say nothing.

Amis's novel, despite marketing, publicity and a headline-grabbing advance of £500,000, did not sell as well as anticipated, whereas Grisham's was a smash. But why? Amis's sentence is far more intriguing to my mind, but according to the algorithms Grisham's encompasses decision, conflict and family: all the ingredients of a bestseller. In contrast Amis's contains 'words of emptiness' – night, sleep, nothing – and its narrator, the 'I', is tucked away in a subordinate clause. Computer says no.

It is the same story with book titles. The study identifies place (*Cold Mountain*), roles (*The Alchemist*) and event (*One Day*) as sure-fire winners. A solid commercial blockbuster is more likely to have a two-word title, whereas a literary one is often longer (*The Curious Incident of the Dog in the Night-Time*). There's a joke on social media that you can generate your own 'quirky novel title' by adding [current mood] + [object to your right] of [grandmother's first name] + [last thing you ate]. Mine would be 'The Comfortable Cup of Trixie Stollen'. Ooh, that's quite good.

A member of the Romantic Novelists' Association once told me that the word 'secret' practically guarantees a hit. Names are also crowd-pleasers if you glance at a list of the bestselling novels of all time, from *Don Quixote* to *Bridget Jones's Diary*. Numbers seem to play a part too (*Catch-22*, *Around the World in Eighty Days*), which makes me wonder, does this make *The Secret Diary of Adrian Mole Aged 13¾* the perfect title? But here the jig is up. *Adrian Mole* works because Sue Townsend is a stone-cold comic genius, not just because it has a great title. All the formulae in the world won't make a difference if the book's a dud.

Apparently a New York publishing CEO once declared that calling a book *Lincoln's Doctor's Dog* would result in a mega-hit (the winning combination of beloved president, health and animals). But two books with this title were subsequently published, believe it or not, and bombed. There are similar publishing jokes about commissioning books called *Hitler's Cats*. We know that it wouldn't work, though, because it's too on the nose, too cynical. What people really want is something that is familiar, yet fresh at the same time. 'A classic with a twist,' as a Grattan's clothing catalogue from the 1980s might have said. A title that feels as though it has been there all along.

Think, for a moment, about what you most wanted as a young child (apart from food). I would wager that stories and toys are near the top of the list. This is why I think *Toy Story* is probably the cleverest film title ever created. It's simple to the point of ridiculousness, but it homes in what children really want like a heat-seeking missile, and it makes us remember what we desired as children too. In a similar vein *Money Heist*, the English translation of a series originally titled *House of Paper* in Spanish, has been one of Netflix's biggest worldwide hits. You don't really have to ask what it's about, surely? It's almost brazen. In a further stroke of genius, the gang of robbers in the show are all given the names of cities as aliases: it's impossible to forget them.

I think this audacity is intrinsic to language that sells. There is no coyness, or lack of confidence. My hunch is that a best-selling title is bold, simple, unequivocal, even shameless – think Michael Moore's million-copy-selling *Stupid White Men* – but without sounding like a Channel 5 'Eaten by an Escalator' documentary.

If we know which words in books and book titles sell, what about the blurbs? Is there a way of finding out what kind of language helps to shift copies? I've always yearned to get inside a potential reader's head to find out, and, in a sense, the rise of ebooks has (sort of) made this possible. People in publishing often used to talk about the prospect of the digital book much in the same aghast tones with which Dame Edith Evans says 'A haandbaaag?' in *The Importance of Being Earnest*. 'An electronic book?!' It would never catch on. A mere flash in the pan. Surely it could never replace the book!

How wrong we were, and yet, in a sense, how right too. Unlike the music and newspaper industries, which have suffered as a result of the digital revolution, publishing has managed to survive the transformation, with physical books and ebooks co-existing harmoniously for several years now – although ebooks sell far more in some genres such as crime. Their rise means that publishers are now able to quantify what works and what doesn't.

I thought I was obsessed with blurbs, but I realised this was a mere bagatelle compared to the relentless, laser-like focus on copy at a digital publisher when I spoke to Jenny Geras, managing director of Bookouture. As I discovered, data and research are used to make sure that everything – title, cover, blurb – hits the perfect sweet spot. Each word is studied, accounted for and changed if it isn't getting enough traction, even those crazy hyperbolic subtitles that we see on Amazon: 'A nail-biting mystery suspense thriller', 'An unputdownable psychological thriller with a breathtaking twist', ad infinitum. The words are pure genre cues: signifiers at their most direct.

There is also a formula for blurbs. Descriptions are broken up, bolded and spaced out to attract the eye and create impact. Just as the copy that would appear above the fold in a newspaper had to grab the reader's attention even before they opened it, the first line of copy only works if it has an immediate emotional hook that makes the reader care. And just as the Pet Shop Boys (almost) sang, you can *never* be boring. Research shows that the best-performing lines put the reader in the place of the hero, or the victim. They need drama or a sense of peril, a clear, focused plot – and relatable characters. 'Amazon reviewers will punish an unsympathetic main character such as a mistress. Their point of view would make a book less successful than a wife's,' Jenny notes. Any bad behaviour, an alienating world – for that read too rich and posh – is also a turn-off for audiences.

Above all, 'Big digital readers are prolific. They consume ebooks *voraciously*.' Every part of the book has to work hard: as soon as a reader finishes an ebook there's an immediate opportunity to get them to download another one, or BUY IT NOW.

I do understand that this might sound mercenary, somewhat lacking in romance. There's a lot of bougie literary pearl-clutching that goes on around such naked commercialism. But, just like Skegness, it's bracing. Publishers of popular digital fiction are doing what every other publisher is doing, which is trying to sell books. They are just more upfront about it. And there is something pure in their use of words. Copy has nowhere to hide; you can't make an average description look better with a pretty design. Certainly there is no interaction with or love of the book as a physical object – I'm never going to have a favourite ebook blurb – but there is more direct interaction with language.

So knowing what we do, could there be a secret formula for cover copy? Might it be possible to invent some kind of digital Great Blurb Generator™? Could my job one day be done by a piece of software? You might think so, but thankfully my attempts to create a successful blurb using some of the online 'create a book blurb' tools available were laughably bad. When I entered the ingredients of *Jane Eyre* into one of them, it titled my book *The Good Governess* (nice, I admit). The first line was quite promising too: 'The night of the wedding changes everything for Jane Eyre, an eighteen-year-old governess from Lowood.' But then it all went horribly wrong:

> She can't prove it – at least not without some mysterious rooms.
> Will her conscience allow her to do whatever is needed to stop the brooding people?

It's a similar story with the 'ImprovBot' built by Edinburgh University, which mined data from eight years of programme 'blurbs' for Festival Fringe shows to invent comically surreal summaries of new, non-existent productions. Which one of these nonsensical nightmares piques your interest? *The Waters of Leaves* ('the haunting story of a man who's seen a medical coming of age story')? Or maybe *Wedding Mission*, which 'explores how the secrets are spiralling out of the past'. They are almost too close to shows that could be real, and parody the language of blurbs rather brilliantly. But they also show (praise be, my job is saved) that there's no substitute for the real thing.

There may not be a magical Casaubon-like 'Key to all Copy', but there are tricks and tips scattered throughout this book, and a few gut instincts I was glad to have confirmed by the data. In the end it shows that the secrets of 'selling' words are also the secrets of good words. Successful books, and blurbs, use short, clean sentences. They avoid too many adjectives, adverbs and qualifiers such as 'very'. Their language is clear and concrete; active rather than passive. These are rules that can be found in any writing guides, from Orwell's advice to Strunk's *The Elements of Style*. My secret two-word formula for copy that sells, then? Write well.

Ventriloquism

> Hello! So, are you enjoying leafing through my pages and getting between my covers? (Saucy!) Yes, you've guessed it (you really are on the ball today, aren't you?), I'm a book. You know, those rectangular papery things invented thousands of years ago, that you turn to when you've run out of stuff to watch on Netflix, or the train's delayed and your phone's dead. Well, all I can say is thanks for picking me up. Just don't drop me in the bath, butter fingers!

And so on. Innocent Smoothies, according to most people, have a lot to answer for. The drinks company, founded in 1999, did some lovely things, including the 'Supergran' initiative, where each bottle sported a little knitted woolly hat in aid of charity. But they were also responsible for the rise of what is now known as 'wackaging' – products talking to us on their packaging in a friendly, quirky, casual, 'nice' tone of voice.

Innocent's chief copywriter publicly repented in a recent *Spectator* article, describing how the voice he had created 'became twee, cloying and creepy. I remember physically recoiling when, on the base of one Innocent carton, it said "Stop looking at my bottom". No, no, no! It wasn't supposed to be like this. And then, as if to torture me for what I'd started, the "Innocent" tone of voice spawned hundreds of excruciating imitators.'

It really did. One journalist noted how the tone of voice used on the Waitrose Cooks' Ingredients range ('Eminent and

Elegant Basil') is 'now starting to sound like Nicholas Witchell reporting on the queen'. The oat cream in my fridge has taken leave of its senses, telling me that 'By consuming the contents of this carton, you will be summoned when the fourth moon rises under the emerald sky and the rabbit runs through the 14th sector, to gather in a field of oats and watch the paranoia burn. For realz.' And the Virgin Trains 'talking toilets' were a good enough reason for them to lose their franchise. As the copywriter Nick Asbury notes, 'A lot of brands use tone of voice like air freshener, spraying it around to mask underlying smells.' They produce their own guidelines on how to address consumers, which often use words like 'compelling', 'inclusive', 'warm' and 'accessible' (but then who would want to talk to their customers in a cold, elitist voice?).

Some brands go further than tone, creating their own special vocabulary for their products. I am in permanent awe of whoever dreams up the names for Essie's nail polish: Spin the Bottle, Resort Fling and Romper Room are just some of the delights available. But they are amateurs compared to the masters of brand naming, Farrow & Ball, whose arch, almost camp paint colours (Elephant's Breath, Mouse's Back, Sulking Room Pink) were superbly spoofed by Marian Keyes in her novel *The Mystery of Mercy Close*: 'He'd done his walls with paint from Holy Basil. God, I yearned for their colours. I hadn't been able to afford them myself but I knew their colour chart like the back of my hand. His hall was done in Gangrene, his stairs in Agony and his living room – unless I was very much mistaken – in Dead Whale.' The language they use is part of who they are. It's ridiculous, but then so are tins of paint that cost fifty quid.

As well as tone of voice, some organisations now have to think about the *actual* voice they use too. In our age of Alexa and

Amazon Echo, a BBC brand director told me, media companies who will appear on these oral platforms need to consider not just phrasing and language, but 'our spoken voice'. Should it have a regional accent? Should it be formal or casual? Should it say 'Hi?' It's a linguistic minefield, especially when, as she put it, 'every word we utter is a potential lightning rod for the defunders'.

But how does a copywriter do 'voice' when they are writing in order to sell a book? It can't be as prescriptive as the examples I've given. Ideally, we should use a tone of voice, but it should be that of the author, not a guideline. What do I mean by voice? Take these passages of description from two recently published books:

1. 'There had been many years of his life when he was a tall, good-looking man, no gut, strolling about the campus at Harvard, and people did look at him then, for all those years, he would see students glance at him with deference, and also women, they looked at him.'
2. 'The Belvedere Golf Club. On the green were Thomas Holroyd, Andrew Bragg, Vincent Ives. Butcher, baker, candlestick-maker. Actually, the owner of a haulage company, a travel-agent-cum-hotelier and a telecom-equipment area manager. It was Vince's turn to tee off.'

The first is from *Olive, Again* by Elizabeth Strout, and the second is from *Big Sky* by Kate Atkinson. Both popular literary fiction, yet the voice of each is distinctive. The first, with its sub-clauses and 'ands', feels leisurely, almost calm, with a dry wit. The second I would describe as bouncy, eager, exuberant, with its short sentences and hyphens. It is funny too. If Strout's humour is dry, cool and understated, Atkinson's is sparkling and sarcastic. They're just *different*.

Whatever an author's tone of voice is, it enters your head as you are reading the book. It is a copywriter's job, wherever possible, to ape that voice you hear in your ear. When I asked Jini Reddy, blurb writer-turned journalist-turned author of *Wanderland*, about what she had learned from her experiences, she said, 'To be a mimic. The books I worked on as a copywriter were so varied that I learned to imitate the voice of the author, and adapt my tone and style accordingly.' Her life was made complete when, after trying to recreate Muriel Spark's crisp voice in a blurb, she received a note from the author thanking her for her 'pithy' copy.

This chimes with what another copywriter told me when I interviewed her for a job (I will remember her application letter always because it said that 'Apart from being Daniel Craig's dresser I can't think of a better job than writing blurbs.'). She described it as like being an actor, because you are constantly putting on different voices. Blurb writing is ventriloquism.

The copywriter David Abbott, who was responsible for such advertising classics as the Yellow Pages 'J. R. Hartley' TV ad and *Economist* posters ('I never read The Economist.' Management Trainee. Aged 42.), was renowned for the wit and easy charm of the tone he used in his work – the genuine article before everything went all 'Hi, I'm a loo'. Abbott described how 'Like many other copywriters, I read my copy out aloud as I write. It helps me check the rhythm of the line and ultimately the flow of the whole piece. I often adopt the appropriate accent or tone, though my general "reading-copy" voice is laughably mid-Atlantic (I read silently if there are other people in the room).'

I was delighted by this because I always read the blurbs I'm writing in my head as I go, but usually in the voice of somebody well known. So, for a thriller I will choose someone like Jeremy Clarkson – dramatic, emphatic – and for a literary classic a thespian like Judi Dench or Juliet Stevenson – measured, elegant, rhythmical. And if it's a Muriel Spark, then Maggie Smith in her best Jean Brodie Edinburgh accent, of course.

This is the essential difference between a writer and a copywriter. If you're a writer, it's all about finding your voice. If you're a copywriter, it's usually about expressing someone else's. One is an art; one is a craft (or if it's an art, it's the art of imitation). You just have to listen.

What Women Don't Want

Sexist Blurbs

Bubbly. Feisty. Bossy. Shrill. Strident. Wittering. Weeping. Nag. Hag. Witch. Shrew. Hysterical. Ditzy. Fragile. Childlike. Kooky. Whip-smart. Girly swot (yes, I'm looking at you, Alexander Boris de Pfeffel Johnson). I could go on. Behold, my ever-expanding list of words that are rarely or never used to describe men – it doesn't even include the obvious sluts, spinsters and bitches; they're a given. Even phrases like 'strong woman' niggle me: as Caitlin Moran says, are the men doing it? No, because it's automatically assumed they are powerful.

Language is gendered. But what about the language of books, and the way they are packaged and sold? Well, if an alien were to land on Earth and go to a bookshop or an Amazon books' page to see what the female of the species looks like, it might be forgiven for thinking that most women and girls were blurry, had no faces and spent a lot of time on beaches, or running off into the distance. Or that they mainly consist of ponytails, lips or shoes. Often just legs.

Book covers both reflect and feed sexist tropes, and have been the subject of contention for several years now, with authors such as Fay Weldon criticising the recent designs used on her jackets – many of which do indeed feature said headless women in a variety of dresses. In 2013, this disparity prompted the

Young Adult author Maureen Johnson to launch the Coverflip project on Twitter, where her fans were asked to redesign famous books by male authors as if they had been female: cue pastel colours, soft typefaces and, yes, blurred women.

It was even worse when I started out in publishing over twenty years ago, however. You couldn't move for pink. Books by female writers such as the comic genius Marian Keyes, who touches on everything from death to alcoholism, AIDS to eating disorders, were published with assorted rainbows, handbags, balloons, hearts, bras, stars and oh so many shoes adorning their covers. This was at the height of the 'chick lit' phenomenon, a much-derided and now thankfully unfashionable label for any piece of writing by a woman about relationships.

Things have definitely improved a little since then. Pink has been reclaimed by millennials for a start, and even feminists are allowed to wear it, according to activist and author Scarlett Curtis. Kate Atkinson – in my view one of the greatest formal experimenters of our time, who should have won every literary prize out there – has previously been published with covers featuring the ubiquitous pastel-hued girl/woman haring off somewhere, but now her newly designed jackets are bold, bright and neutral. I'm also pleased to report that Marian Keyes's covers have become increasingly subtle and sophisticated over the years, but of course these moves reflect changing fashions and tastes as much as a desire for equality.

Unfortunately it's true that publishers are, on the whole, pretty unimaginative; followers rather than leaders. We know what sells and we rarely stray from a formula, so 'female' covers are an easy shortcut to reach a specific readership. If it involves pastel colours, it's a beach read; if it involves a lot of black, someone's going to die. The downside of this, of course, is that wildly varying books by and about women get lumped together – and are viewed as more lightweight as a result.

The publication of Elena Ferrante's phenomenal Neapolitan Novels took this signalling to another, more interesting level. These novels are complex, dark, violent, yet their almost kitsch covers feature, you guessed it, faceless pastel-coloured women and girls staring into the distance, often on beaches. Many readers were horrified at the packaging, but Ferrante chose these images herself, with her publisher Europa Editions stating 'many people didn't understand the game we were playing, that of, let's say, dressing an extremely refined story with a touch of vulgarity'. By looking down on these 'unliterary' covers, are we looking down on the very idea of books that are clearly aimed at women? Can't a book jacket depict a woman doing something 'domestic', and still be literary?

Marian Keyes demolished the idea of women's fiction being a lesser pursuit in a speech at the Hay Festival, deriding the idea of the 'chick lit' label as a device 'to mock women and anything they love'. She goes on, 'It's a simple fact that one way of keeping women shut up is to call the things they love "fluff".'

In the *Atlantic* Helen Lewis, the author of *Difficult Women*, talks about the 'seriousness gap' between male and female writers. Centuries after women started writing and buying novels, the notion is that books by and about women are primarily concerned with the domestic, the intimate, the emotional and the personal, whereas men write about the universal, the intellectual. We still talk about 'women's fiction', but rarely 'men's fiction' – after all, books written by men are for everyone, aren't they? As Kate Mosse, the novelist and founder of the Women's Prize for Fiction, says, 'I think there's still a sense that men's writing is universal, and women's writing is for women.'

I thought, before I started writing this piece, that perhaps the few female Booker Prize-winning authors such as Anne Enright might have it a little easier, but lo, when you look at the Wikipedia entry for Enright's award-winning *The Gathering*, it describes her as an 'Irish women's fiction writer', while her main entry tells us that 'her writing explores themes such as family, love, identity and motherhood'. Is this strictly necessary?

The authors Jonathan Franzen and Jennifer Weiner have been duking it out over the issue of seriousness since 2010, with Weiner criticising the 'Franzenfrenzy' that greeted the publication of his novel *Freedom*. In her eyes, women writing about domestic situations were seen as limited in their appeal, but when Franzen 'writes a book about a family…we are told this is a book about America'.

The statistics back it up. In the UK, sixty per cent of novels published are by women, and seventy-five per cent of novels are bought by women, yet fewer than nine per cent of novels ever shortlisted for major literary prizes are by women.* Since 1969, thirty-two men and eighteen women have won the Booker Prize.

It's not just prizes; women get less review space too. In recent years the non-profit organisation VIDA have measured the space devoted to male and female authors in publications such as the *New York Times*, *Times Literary Supplement* and the *London Review of Books*, and discovered that both male reviewers and male authors dominate the literary pages. That's not all. In 2019 the Emilia Report (named after England's first published female poet, Emilia Bassano) analysed coverage of male and female writers

* There's also much (mostly anecdotal) evidence that men are more inclined towards non-fiction, preferring hard, masculine facts about financial crashes to feelings.

and found that women were twice as likely to have their ages referenced – or, in the case of Sally Rooney, her appearance, 'like a startled deer with sensuous lips', according to one Swiss critic.

Joanne Harris reported: 'In general, when you compare the coverage of my work to that of men writing in similar areas, the emphasis in my case has been on the domestic, and in theirs on the academic. Women are still viewed as a niche group, dealing solely with women's issues, whereas men (even in the same area) are thought of as dealing with important, universal themes.'

Before the reviewing even starts, there's evidence that the very beginning of the publishing process favours men. In 2015 the writer Catherine Nichols submitted a proposal to fifty agents, first under her own name, and then under that of a male pseudonym – his manuscript was requested seventeen times; hers just twice.

Nichols was one of the people behind the Reclaim Her Name project of 2020, which released twenty-five classic works by women, previously published under male pseudonyms, with the female author's name on the jacket for the first time. Although the project received criticism for historical inaccuracies, it remains a useful reminder of how women's words are still sidelined, over 150 years since Charlotte Brontë explained the decision to use male names: 'We did not like to declare ourselves women, because – without at the time suspecting that our mode of writing and thinking was not what is called "feminine" – we had a vague impression that authoresses are liable to be looked on with prejudice.'* J. K. Rowling notoriously

* I'd say it was more than a vague impression. When she was twenty Brontë received a letter from poet laureate Robert Southey saying 'literature cannot be the business of a woman's life & it ought not to be.'

chose a gender-neutral pseudonym, and I wondered whether by changing my name to 'L. E. Willder' I might double my readership of this book: research has shown a woman is far more likely to read a book by a man than vice versa.* According to Mary Ann Sieghart in *The Authority Gap*, readers of the top ten women authors in the UK (a list including writers such as Jane Austen and Margaret Atwood) are eighty-one per cent female. As Bernardine Evaristo says, 'I've known this for a very long time, that men just aren't interested in reading our literature.'

I think Rebecca Solnit nails it when she says 'a book without women is often said to be about humanity, but a book with women in the foreground is a woman's book'. The language used by publishers and people like me to describe books bears this out. I looked at books that fall broadly into the literary fiction category to judge the differences. At first glance I was pleasantly surprised by both the covers and the language. Things have definitely moved on, with far fewer 'gendered' covers than I had anticipated. Words like 'love', 'family' and 'marriage', which I had thought would occur far more in the descriptions of books by women, appear on books by both male and female authors. But there are still subtle differences, which support the idea of men speaking for everyone, but women just for women. Julian Barnes is described as 'one of Britain's greatest mappers of the human heart', *Stoner* as 'a story of universal value', authors

---

* In *Stet* Diana Athill describes the literary brainwashing that led men to be taken more seriously: 'to a large extent I had been shaped by my background to please men … you actually saw yourself as men saw you, so you knew what would happen if you became assertive and behaved in a way which men thought tiresome and ridiculous. Grotesquely, you would start to look tiresome and ridiculous in your own eyes.'

frequently as 'masters' of their craft or art, a gendered term if ever there was one.* More novels by and about women are described using words such as 'beautiful' and 'intimate'.

If you think this sounds pretty (for that read 'completely') unscientific, you are right. Fortunately I was delighted to discover that the science part had already been done for me. When a team of researchers analysed the description copy on Goodreads for some 275 novels shortlisted for the Booker Prize between 1969 and 2017, they discovered that not only did male characters figure more prominently in plots, they were more likely to be described as rich, powerful, wealthy or strong, while female characters were depicted as beautiful, lovely or romantic. The men got to be doctors, professors, novelists or directors, but the occupations most used to describe female characters were 'teacher' or 'whore'. Oh dear. It gets worse. Men were associated with verbs such as 'affirms', 'foresees' and 'encounters' while for women it was 'falls', 'loves', 'worships', 'fears'. The researchers did notice, however, that there has been a shift in recent years, with more female writers and more active female protagonists appearing.

In *Nabokov's Favourite Word is Mauve*, which looks at classic literature through data, Ben Blatt conducts his own version of the Bechdel Test: if a novel describes male actions three times as much as female actions, it doesn't pass. The answer, which will surprise no one, is that almost everything apart from *The*

....

* The feminist classic *The Madwoman in the Attic* dissects the patriarchal language of authorship thus: 'because he is an author, a "man of letters" is simultaneously, like his divine counterpart, a father, a master or ruler, and an owner … a progenitor, a procreator, an aesthetic patriarch whose pen is an instrument of generative power like his penis.' Amen to that.

Prime of Miss Jean Brodie fails. He also analyses the top five verbs used after 'he' or 'she' in classic literature. Men mutter, grin, shout, chuckle and kill. Women shiver, weep, murmur, scream and marry. The silly little things. Best of all, he discovers that the word 'interrupted' is far more likely to be used to describe a female character when the author is male. Just pipe down, women, okay?

So can blurbs be sexist? The answer is undoubtedly yes, as can writers, reviewers and the whole darn literary world. It made me think (or, I couldn't help but wonder, as a certain someone from the 'chick lit' genre once said) whether I'd been guilty of internalising gendered language in the past myself, describing a female character as beautiful, or by her looks, far too many times, or using the word 'master' to define a male writer. As I've discussed elsewhere, picking out details to grab attention is good, but this has made me think far more carefully about the adjectives and the descriptions I go for. Publishers, and copywriters, use broad brushstrokes, but I'm determined that mine are going to be more subtle, and less pink, in future.

Zadie Smith

Big Ideas and a Little Mouse

These are but wild and whirling words

HAMLET, ACT 1 SCENE 5

'Believe the hype.' These words, from a *Times* review, appeared on the side of a bus advertising Zadie Smith's debut novel *White Teeth* twenty years ago. A piece of hype about hype being used to hype something could seem like the perfect illustration of the nefariousness of marketing, to a cynic. I think it shows something else as well: that when a book is truly great, it can cut through the miasma of selling words swirling around it, and that these words become part of the story of a book itself too.

I remember, when *White Teeth* came out, how refreshing it was to read a book that felt both clever and joyful at the same time. It already seemed like a genuine, fully formed phenomenon, and the review coverage was astonishing, with the *Sunday Times* saying things like 'For once, here is a Big New Literary Find that hasn't been oversold,' and articles appearing about the reviews themselves in that incestuous, self-obsessed media way, as the *Guardian* remarked on the book's 'astonishing chorus of praise'. The words surrounding *White Teeth* had already become self-referencing, and a self-fulfilling prophecy.

This chorus of words was also reflected in the blurb for the original paperback edition of *White Teeth*, which is close to perfection and remains one of my favourite pieces of copy. It breaks the rules by doing rather a lot of telling as well as showing, but in a way that feels charming, confident and propulsive, rather than hackneyed:

> One of the most talked about debut novels of all time, *White Teeth* is a funny, generous, big-hearted novel, adored by critics and readers alike. Dealing – among many other things – with friendship, love, war, three cultures and three families over three generations, one brown mouse, and the tricky way the past has of coming back and biting you on the ankle, it is a life-affirming, riotous must-read of a book.

This blurb takes a huge, multi-faceted novel with numerous characters and plot strands, and boils it down to something that feels light, bouncy and carefree. I think it's the contrast between the big themes and the little mouse I like best: a good example of an hourglass-shaped blurb, as seen in the 'Triangle, Diamond or Hourglass?' chapter. It's stayed with me since it was written by a former colleague nearly two decades ago, which is about the best thing a piece of copy can do.* But perhaps the real reason it works is because everything it says is more or less *true*. It acknowledges the acclaim around the book and makes that part of the story that is being told. It feels authentic, just as the novel felt like an authentic voice of multicultural Britain at the time.

Of course, nothing is that simple, as a *Guardian* article written twenty years after publication remarked, with that past

••

* The author of this long-lasting blurb was creative copywriter Ben North, who died during the writing of this book, just before he would have turned fifty. He also wrote short stories and poetry, including *Thirty-Three Poems: Some of Which Are About Death*.

optimism now souring amid the rise of populism. The article also showed us the ambivalence of the blurb's little brown mouse: 'The past – as the book keeps on reminding us – is always also in the present, even if we don't quite comprehend what it is doing there. And as the blurb suggests, this can cause problems. There's misunderstanding and alienation, sadness and loss.'

Even at the time of publication, Zadie Smith clearly felt uneasy about her novel being hailed as signifying a happy post-racial age, and hinted that her work would be less crowd-pleasing in future: 'When I was little, we'd go on holiday to Devon, and there, if you're black and you go into a sweetshop, for instance, everyone turns and looks at you. So my instinct as a child was always to over-compensate by trying to behave three times as well as every other child in the shop, so they knew I wasn't going to take anything or hurt anyone. I think that instinct has spilled over into my writing in some ways, which is not something I like very much or want to continue.'

White Teeth is both a book of its time and a genuinely time-less classic. I'm happy to see that the original copy is still being used on the book and on Amazon, because that was part of how it was seen and talked about when it became successful.

This brings me to probably the most important thing I have learned from writing this book: that blurbs, just as much as covers, reviews or prizes, are an indelible part of a book's life. Whether I've been looking at so-bad-they're-great blurbs, reading Roberto Calasso describing blurbs as 'a letter to a stranger' or listening to podcasters reading out old blurbs, it has reminded me of this fact. Some of the blurbs I've written in the past were *terrible*. But, good or bad, there they were, and here they are, bound up with a book's physical history.

Like old photographs or letters, blurbs – usually written by someone anonymous, often silly, frequently dated, occasionally inspired – come back from the past to bite us on the ankle. People would have read these little stories, maybe glossed over them and dismissed them, or perhaps decided that this book was for them because it said something about who they were. I find that strangely consoling.

$\mathbb{A}$cknowledgements

It's a truism that everyone in publishing is nice, but I didn't realise quite how nice until I started writing this book. First, the team at Oneworld. Eternal gratitude to my editor Cecilia Stein, without whom *Blurb Your Enthusiasm* would not exist. Part word magician, part impresario, part life-coach, she somehow willed a casual email asking, 'Might you want to write a book?' into an Actual Book. Thank you, Chech, for giving me the confidence to find my voice, deftly shaping my ideas and serenely dealing with the odd *crise de nerfs*. Thank you also to Kate Bland, Lucy Cooper, Holly Knox, Laura McFarlane, Mark Rusher and Rida Vaquas for your enthusiasm, expertise and talents ranging from translation to photography. Ben Summers for designing a wonderful cover – and the mice! Tamsin Shelton for making the copy-editing process a joy. And Sarah Bennie, my empathetic and indefatigable publicist, for doing her best to transform me from a nervous wreck into a proper author.

Special thanks to three publishing friends who made this book better. Colin Brush, my copywriting comrade of many years, was unbelievably generous with his time and knowledge in the face of many annoying questions, and blurbed enthusiastically about my book to everyone. My fellow debut author Rebecca Lee encouraged me so much during the early stages of writing, sharing the benefit of her experience and helping things make sense. And without the wise words of Sarah Topping, children's copywriter extraordinaire and lovely human, at least two chapters would not be here. Kweeeeep!

The niceness continues with these people who gave help and advice: Sam Binnie, Elizabeth Buchan, Madeleine Collinge, Henry Eliot, Adam Freudenheim, Jenny Geras, Kate Gunning, Sophie Hannah, Eva Hodgkin, Martin Latham, Jane Lingham, Kalle Mattila, Julia Murday, Katie Newby, David Pearson, Krystyna Plater, Natalie Ramm, Jini Reddy, John Seaton, Becky Stocks and Alan Trotter. Thanks to Penguin for putting me on furlough, when I wrote my proposal! To my colleagues Ania, Emma, Ingrid, Julie, Liz, Micca, Sam and Shauna for being the loveliest bunch you could wish to see on a Monday morning. To Sue Miles, who gave me my first job as a copywriter. To Alice Berry, Queen of Puns, for my book title. And to Polly, for the flowers and friendship. As I wrote this book in lockdown and I'm still scared to go to the pub even now, I owe a lot of people a lot of drinks.

And, of course, to family, past and present. My Mum, the one and only MW, for her endless generosity, affection, naughtiness and pride – and for instilling in me such terror of not doing my homework that I handed my manuscript in on time. Becca for being the greatest, most supportive sister on earth. Nancy with the laughing face for lighting up all our lives. Derek for making every Willder gathering a party. Bob for helping us keep on keeping on. Granny and Aunty for their bookshelves and love. And to my father, George Marcel Willder: teacher, poetry writer and book lover. He did not live to see me and my sister grow up, but we wish he had, and we think of him always.

Finally, my husband Tim. I feel I should call him 'my rock', but that's far too dull a term for the funniest, cleverest and best person I know in the good old world, eliminator of Pooterisms and bringer of joy. Thank you for making my heart laugh.

Bibliography

Ackroyd, P. *Dickens* (London: Guild Publishing, 1990)

Allister, G. 'The power of subtitle differences', *Guardian* [online], https://www.theguardian.com/books/booksblog/2008/nov/07/book-subtitle

Amis, K. *The King's English* (London: HarperCollins, 1997)

Amis, M. 'Martin Amis on the Genius of Jane Austen (and What the Adaptations Get Wrong)', *Literary Hub* [online], https://lithub.com/martin-amis-on-the-genius-of-jane-austen-and-what-the-adaptations-get-wrong/

Appleyard, B. 'Why the future looks bright for science fiction', *Sunday Times* [online], https://www.thetimes.co.uk/article/why-the-future-looks-bright-for-science-fiction-hl88z69wb

Archer, J. and Jockers, M. *The Bestseller Code* (London: Allen Lane, 2016)

Armitstead, C. 'Do spoilers for books actually improve them?', *Guardian* [online], https://www.theguardian.com/books/booksblog/2014/mar/20/spoilers-books-improve-them-reviewers-karen-joy-fowler

Athill, D. *Stet: An Editor's Life* (London: Granta Books, 2000)

Baines, P. *Penguin By Design: A Cover Story 1935–2005* (London: Penguin Books, 2005)

Bell, T. 'A book by any other name: why does the US change so many titles?', *Guardian* [online], https://www.theguardian.com/books/booksblog/2018/sep/13/us-uk-book-titles-changed

Bellos, D. *The Novel of the Century: The Extraordinary Adventure of Les Misérables* (London: Particular Books, 2017)

Berger, J. *Ways of Seeing* (London: BBC and Penguin Books, 1972)

Bertram, L. and Leving, Y. *Lolita – The Story of a Cover Girl: Vladimir Nabokov's Novel in Art and Design* (Blue Ash: Print Books, 2013)

Billen, A. 'How I learnt what women really think – by reading their books', *The Times* [online], https://www.thetimes.co.uk/article/how-i-learnt-what-women-really-think-by-reading-their-books-grwfwnhkr

Bindel, J. and Cummins, D. 'Mills & Boon: 100 Years of Heaven or Hell?', *Guardian* [online], https://www.theguardian.com/lifeandstyle/2007/dec/05/women.fiction?CMP=Share_AndroidApp_Other

Blatt, B. *Nabokov's Favourite Word is Mauve: The Literary Quirks and Oddities of Our Most-Loved Authors* (London: Simon & Schuster UK Ltd, 2017)

Bramley, E. V. 'In the Instagram age, you actually can judge a book by its cover', *Observer* [online], https://www.theguardian.com/books/2021/apr/18/in-the-instagram-age-you-actually-can-judge-a-book-by-its-cover

Buchan, E. 'Opinion: The art of the blurb', *BookBrunch* [online], https://www.bookbrunch.co.uk/page/free-article/opinion-the-art-of-the-blurb/

Bussel, R. 'Book subtitles are getting ridiculously long. What is going on?', *Washington Post* [online], https://www.washingtonpost.com/entertainment/books/book-subtitles-are-getting-ridiculously-long-what-is-going-on/2019/06/04/3150bcc8-86c3-11e9-98c1-e945ae5db8fb_story.html

Cain, S. '"Sloppy": Baileys under fire for Reclaim Her Name books for Women's prize', *Guardian* [online], https://www.theguardian.com/books/2020/aug/15/baileys-reclaim-her-name-wrong-black-abolitionist-frances-rollin-whipper-martin-r-delany

Calasso, R. *The Art of the Publisher*, trans. Richard Dixon (London: Penguin Books, 2015)

Calvino, I. *Why Read the Classics?*, trans. M. McLaughlin (London: Jonathan Cape, 1999)

Cascella, D. 'the secret euphoria of reading: on cento lettere a uno sconosciuto by roberto calasso', *3:AM Magazine* [online], https://www.3ammagazine.com/3am/the-secret-euphoria-of-reading-on-cento-lettere-a-uno-sconosciuto-by-roberto-calasso/

Chater, N. *The Mind is Flat: The Illusion of Mental Depth and the Improvised Mind* (London: Allen Lane, 2018)

Cohen, R. *How to Write Like Tolstoy: A Journey into the Minds of Our Greatest Writers* (London: Oneworld Publications, 2016)

Conran, S. *Lace* (London: Sidgwick & Jackson, 1982)

Cooke, S. 'Advertisements in Victorian Books and Magazines', *The Victorian Web* [online], https://victorianweb.org/art/design/advertisements/cooke.html

Dainton, M. and Zelley, E. *Applying Communication Theory for Professional Life: A Practical Introduction* (London: SAGE Publications, Inc; 2nd edition, 2010)

Davis, L. *Collected Stories of Lydia Davis* (London: Hamish Hamilton, 2010)

Dexter, G. *Why Not Catch-21? The Stories Behind the Titles* (London: Frances Lincoln Limited, 2007)

Dillard, J. P. and Shen, L. *The SAGE Handbook of Persuasion: Developments in Theory and Practice* (London: SAGE Publications, Inc; 2nd edition, 2012)

Dreyer, B. *Dreyer's English: An Utterly Correct Guide to Clarity and Style* (London: Arrow, 2020)

Eliot, H. *The Penguin Classics Book* (London: Particular Books, 2018)

Ephron, N. *I Feel Bad About My Neck* (London: Doubleday, 2006)

Fadiman, A. *Ex Libris: Confessions of a Common Reader* (London: Allen Lane, 1999)

Farwell, E. 'Those Descriptions on the Inside of Book Covers Are Full of It', *Slate* [online], https://slate.com/culture/2021/06/book-jacket-copy-useless-luster-silence.html

Fassler, J. 'Why Stephen King Spends "Months and Even Years" Writing Opening Sentences', *The Atlantic* [online], https://www.theatlantic.com/entertainment/archive/2013/07/why-stephen-king-spends-months-and-even-years-writing-opening-sentences/278043/

Flood, A. 'Male and female writers' media coverage reveals "marked bias"', *Guardian* [online], https://www.theguardian.com/books/2019/mar/18/male-and-female-writers-media-coverage-reveals-marked-bias

Forna, N. 'As a Black Lord of the Rings fan, I felt left out of fantasy worlds. So I created my own', *Guardian* [online], https://www.theguardian.com/books/2021/feb/22/namina-forna-lord-of-the-rings-jrr-tolkien-fan-the-guilded-ones

Gertz, S. 'Victorian Advertisements in Charles Dickens' Serial Novels', *Fine Books* [online], https://www.finebooksmagazine.com/blog/victorian-advertisements-charles-dickens-serial-novels

Gilbert, S. M. and Gubar, S. *The Madwoman in the Attic: The Woman Writer and the Nineteenth-Century Literary Imagination* (London: Yale University Press, 1979)

Goldman, W. *Adventures in the Screen Trade: A Personal View of Hollywood* (London: Macdonald & Co Ltd, 1984)

Hare, S. *Penguin Portrait: Allen Lane and the Penguin Editors 1935–1970* (London: Penguin, 1995)

Hitchens, C. *Orwell's Victory* (London: Allen Lane, 2002)

Hollis, D. ' "Animal Farm" video game coming to mark the book's 75th anniversary', *NME* [online], https://www.nme.com/news/gaming-news/animal-farm-video-game-coming-to-mark-the-books-75th-anniversary-2731499

Hornby, N. *Ten Years in the Tub: A Decade Soaking in Great Books* (San Francisco: McSweeney's, 2014)

Hunt, T. *The English Civil War at First Hand* (London: Weidenfeld & Nicolson, 2002)

Kahneman, D. *Thinking, Fast and Slow* (London: Allen Lane, 2011)

Kelly, R. 'Robert Harris' Guide to Writing a Bestseller', *Esquire* [online], https://www.esquire.com/uk/culture/a10706/robert-harris-guide-to-writing-bestseller-book/

Kelly, S. *The Book of Lost Books: An Incomplete History of All the Great Books You Will Never Read* (London: Viking, 2005)

King, S. *On Writing: A Memoir of the Craft* (London: Hodder & Stoughton, 2000)

Knowles, T. 'Coronavirus: Shoppers judge books by back covers', *The Times* [online], https://www.thetimes.co.uk/article/coronavirus-shoppers-judge-books-by-back-covers-txn9tmjbm

Kwakkel, E. 'Medieval Spam: The Oldest Advertisements for Books', *Medievalbooks* [online], https://medievalbooks.nl/2014/12/05/medieval-spam-the-oldest-advertisements-for-books/

—'The oldest surviving printed advertisement in English (London, 1477)', *Medievalbooks* [online], https://medievalbooks.nl/2019/01/24/

the-oldest-surviving-printed-advertisement-in-english-london-1477/

Latham, M. *The Bookseller's Tale* (London: Particular Books, 2020)

Leith, S. *Write to the Point: How to be Clear, Correct and Persuasive on the Page* (London: Profile Books, 2018)

Levinovitz, A. 'I Greet You in the Middle of a Great Career: A Brief History of Blurbs', *The Millions* [online], https://themillions.com/2012/02/i-greet-you-in-the-middle-of-a-great-career-a-brief-history-of-blurbs.html

Lewis, J. *Kindred Spirits: Adrift in Literary London* (London: Faber & Faber Ltd, 2008)

Lewis, H. 'The Hazards of Writing While Female', *The Atlantic* [online], https://www.theatlantic.com/international/archive/2019/08/sally-rooney-and-hazards-writing-while-female/596218/

Mangan, L. *Bookworm: A Memoir of Childhood Reading* (London: Square Peg, 2018)

Manguel, A. *A History of Reading* (London: HarperCollins, 1996)

Mazin, C. 'How to Write a Movie Transcript', *Scriptnotes* [online], https://johnaugust.com/2019/scriptnotes-ep-403-how-to-write-a-movie-transcript

McCrum, R. 'Publishers be bold: Why It's Time to Ditch the Subtitle', *Guardian* [online], https://www.theguardian.com/books/booksblog/2009/sep/21/william-golding-subtitles

McHugh, J. 'How women invented book clubs, changing reading and their lives', *Independent* [online], https://www.independent.co.uk/life-style/women-book-clubs-reading-america-b1823819.html

McLuhan, M. and Fiore, Q. *The Medium is the Massage: An Inventory of Effects* (London: Bantam Books, 1967)

Miller, A. *My Year of Reading Dangerously: How Fifty Great Books Saved My Life* (London: Fourth Estate, 2014)

Mullan, J. *The Artful Dickens: The Tricks and Ploys of the Great Novelist* (London: Bloomsbury, 2020)

Norris, M. *Between You & Me: Confessions of a Comma Queen* (New York: W.W. Norton, 2015)

Orwell, G. *A Life in Letters* (London: Harvill Secker; 1st Edition, 2010)

Perloff, R. M. *The Dynamics of Persuasion: Communication and Attitudes in the 21st Century* (Oxford: Routledge, 2003)

Philpott, M. L. 'Why, Exactly, Do We Have Subtitles on Books?', *Literary Hub* [online], https://lithub.com/why-exactly-do-we-have-subtitles-on-books/

Pinker, S. *The Sense of Style: The Thinking Person's Guide to Writing in the 21st Century* (London: Allen Lane, 2014)

—*The Stuff of Thought: Language as a Window into Human Nature* (London: Allen Lane, 2007)

Pollard, C. *Fierce Bad Rabbits: The Tales Behind Children's Picture Books* (London: Fig Tree, 2019)

Rapaille, C. *The Culture Code* (New York: Broadway Books, 2006)

Rentzenbrink, C. *Dear Reader: The Comfort and Joy of Books* (London: Picador, 2020)

Schlaff, M. 'Publishers' Advertisements in the Nineteenth Century' [online], https://sites.google.com/a/umich.edu/from-tablet-to-tablet/final-projects/macaila-schlaff-13

Schuchard, R. 'T. S. Eliot as Publisher: Book Reports, Blurbs, Poets' [online], https://tseliot.com/editorials/eliot-as-publisher

Sieghart, M. A. 'Why do so few men read books by women?', *Guardian* [online], https://www.theguardian.com/books/2021/jul/09/why-do-so-few-men-read-books-by-women

Spufford, F. *The Child That Books Built* (London: Faber & Faber, 2002)

Storr, W. *The Science of Storytelling* (London: William Collins, 2019)

Sullivan, M. C. *Jane Austen Cover to Cover: 200 Years of Classic Covers* (Philadelphia: Quirk Books, 2014)

Sutherland, J. *How to Read a Novel: A User's Guide* (London: Profile Books Ltd, 2006)

Tandon, S. 'An IBM team identified deep gender bias from 50 years of Booker Prize shortlists', *Quartz India* [online], https://qz.com/india/1333644/ibm-identifies-gender-bias-in-booker-prize-novel-shortlists/

Taylor, D. J. *Orwell: The Life* (London: Chatto & Windus, 2003)

—'Dazzling insight', *TLS* [online], https://www.the-tls.co.uk/articles/dazzling-insight/

Thompson, D. *Hit Makers: How Things Become Popular* (London: Allen Lane, 2017)

Tomalin, C. *Charles Dickens: A Life* (London: Viking, 2011)

Truss, L. *Eats, Shoots & Leaves: The Zero Tolerance Approach to Punctuation* (London: Profile Books Ltd, 2003)

Usher, S. 'I hate everybody including you', *Letters of Note* [online], https://news.lettersofnote.com/p/i-hate-everybody-including-you?s=09

Yagoda, B. 'The Subtitle That Changed America', *New York Times* [online], https://www.nytimes.com/2005/02/20/books/review/the-subtitle-that-changed-america.html

Yorke, J. *Into the Woods: How Stories Work and Why We Tell Them* (London: Penguin Books, 2013)

RESOURCES

Backlisted (https://www.backlisted.fm/)

Penguin Cover Design (https://penguincoverdesign.com/)

The Art of Penguin Science Fiction (https://www.penguinsciencefiction.org/)

The Biblio File (https://thebibliofile.ca/)

Pulp Librarian (https://twitter.com/PulpLibrarian)

$\mathbb{A}$ppendix

In the spirit of bold postmodern literary experimentation – well, just for fun really – I asked six different copywriters (and one non-human online blurb generator) to write a blurb for *Blurb Your Enthusiasm*. They were all given the same brief, but as you can see, the results are very different. More proof, if any were needed, that there is no such thing as the 'best' blurb. But I think we can all agree one written by a person is better. And, for once, the copywriters get credited here.

A KNOWING BLURB

This is a book about the covers of books.

**About the words publishers use to
sell their wares to readers.**

**That jumble of lies, half-truths, exaggerations
and occasionally honest statements to
twist a credulous reader's arm.**

It's about titles and tag lines, good blurbs and bad ones, a love of words and a (mild) dislike of grammar police, author feuds and publishing peccadilloes, spoilers and spam, literary lore and bonkbusters, tropes and tricks, sexism and the silly things the book industry gets up to when it thinks no one is looking.

In short, this is the funniest, most entertaining book about how publishing really works from an insider with 25 years' experience of writing blurbs – and no time off for good behaviour.

BY COLIN BRUSH

A PLAYFUL BLURB

'What so wild as words are?'
– Robert Browning

~~In this literary tour de force~~
~~This unputdownable, searing and endlessly readable~~
~~When~~

It takes blood, sweat and tears to write a book, but it takes a considerable amount of time and effort to craft the blurb on the back too.

Blurbs – just as much as jackets, reviews or prizes – are an indelible part of a book's life. From Dickens to Dahl, writing tips to publishing secrets and the art and craft of cover persuasion, this is the outside story of the little story a reader first encounters; the history, the creative process and how blurbs affect us all.

BY SARAH TOPPING

AN EXUBERANT BLURB

A blurb about blurbs? Now we're talking. In fact, you've probably read more works by this author than any other (even if you've never heard of her). Because if anyone can expose the dark arts of publishing, it's Louise Willder – copywriter and expert book blurber for over twenty-five years.

Here she takes us on a brilliantly entertaining journey into how words work – from medieval spam to Twitterature via so-bad-they're-great bonkbusters. Discover what made Charles Dickens a master of marketing, which author demanded his critics be eaten by bears, and why the world's best *Animal Farm* blurb is for a video game.

Plus there are writing tips galore! Does including the word 'secret' in a book title guarantee a hit? How did Coleen Rooney become queen of the ellipsis? What can all writers learn from *Fiddler on the Roof*? And why – when it comes to the science of persuasion – are our brains more Donald Trump than we might care to believe?

But don't just listen to me; turn to page 69! (more on that later). Here is a witty, beguiling love letter to the power of words.

BY NATALIE RAMM

A META BLURB

How can a guide to the paragraph on the back of books be exciting, gossipy, revealing, and funny?

How is it so thrilling that it keeps you reading late into the night?

Seriously, I'm asking – *how*?

As Darwin did with pigeons, as Hawking did with [check which field], Louise Willder takes a subject rendered invisible by its dullness and turns it into a seat-of-the-pants, edge-of-the-page thrilling romantic horrifying child-pleasing internationally available read and actually makes you want to know about it. Repeatedly.

In this adjective-filled, adverbly written work of writing, Willder needlessly destroys the careers of her copywriting contemporaries by skewering their tricks, revealing their secrets, and making their job look shamefully simple, while reminding you how those little blurbs open doors into uncountable new worlds. A haunting tour de force of genre-defying wit and love, *Blurb Your Enthusiasm* will take you gently by the hand of Reading and hold your head under the water of Literary Appeal until you finally, finally appreciate the Art of Blurbs.

In other words: You'll never look at the back of a book the same way again.

BY SAM BINNIE

A CONVIVIAL BLURB

You walk into a bookshop.

A breathtaking array of books awaits you.

But how on earth are you going to decide what to read?

Welcome to the blurb – the craft of writing cover copy that seduces us to read... pretty much anything. Here publishing copywriter extraordinaire (five thousand blurbs and counting) and blurb connoisseur Louise Willder guides us through the most intriguing aspects of books and how to sell them, from dissecting puff pieces to trying the page 69 test, and from the joy of puns to the curious and often unhinged blurbs of the past. She dangles gossipy titbits on the eccentric world of publishing and asks the burning questions – What are the worst words to use in a blurb? Which words sell the most books? Is it okay to swear on a book cover? And are spoilers really that bad?*

Blurb your Enthusiasm is a wise and hilarious response to the eternal conundrum of whether you really can judge a book by its cover.

* Spoiler: apparently not!

BY MADELEINE COLLINGE

A WRY BLURB

**You've already read dozens of books written by
Louise Willder (at least a little bit) – she just
doesn't normally get her name on the front.**

But she's been the blurber for more than 5,000 books, luring
readers with her siren song of 100-or-so words (a bit like these)
on the cover (and only occasionally the words 'unputdownable'
and 'tour de force'). It's a delicate, under-appreciated literary
art: compression and ventriloquism, introduction and come-on.
And it's made her the perfect guide to literary persuasion.

Blurb Your Enthusiasm is the result, a book for the hopelessly bookish. If you've ever wondered about all the ways books
entice us to read them, here it is, the art, business, and history
of it all: titles, quotes and straplines, blurbs, cover designs and
opening lines, from classics to bonkbusters, with questionable
publisher decisions and grumpy authors along the way.

It's an unputdownable tour de force.

BY ALAN NEVENS

A COMPUTER-GENERATED BLURB

**What would you do if you knew there were boring
blurbs with shocking habits near the ones you love?**

The night of the book sale changes everything for Louise, a
49-year-old copywriter from the publishing world.

One moment, she is discussing books with her passionate
friend; the next, watching with horror as boring blurbs attack
them.

She knows these blurbs came from the bookshop but she
can't prove it – at least not without some brilliant words.

The strong, curious woman knows that her creative life is over. She acquires some brilliant words and is reborn as the hero who will save the world from boring blurbs.

However, Louise finds herself troubled by her creative ideals and becomes overwhelmed with moral questions. Will her conscience allow her to do whatever is needed to stop the boring blurbs?

BY A DERANGED PIECE OF SOFTWARE